THE MAKING OF PENNSYLVANIA

SECOND EDITION

MAP SHOWING PENNSYLVANIA BOUNDARY DISPUTES

THE MAKING OF PENNSYLVANIA

AN ANALYSIS OF THE ELEMENTS OF THE
POPULATION AND THE FORMATIVE
INFLUENCES THAT CREATED
ONE OF THE GREATEST
OF THE AMERICAN
STATES

BY

SYDNEY GEORGE FISHER

AUTHOR OF "PENNSYLVANIA: COLONY AND COMMONWEALTH"

IRA J. FRIEDMAN, Inc.
Port Washington, L.I., N.Y.

THE MAKING OF PENNSYLVANIA

First published 1896
Reissued 1969 by Ira J. Friedman, Inc.

Library of Congress Catalog Card No: 69-18292
Manufactured in the United States of America

KEYSTONE STATE HISTORICAL PUBLICATIONS SERIES NO. 2

PREFACE TO THE SECOND EDITION

THE exhaustion of the first edition of this work within such a short time, and the numerous and sometimes lively criticisms which have been brought to my attention, seem to show that Pennsylvanians are, after all, more interested in their history than was generally supposed. They are, at least, not entirely indifferent.

A new chapter has been added called "Results," dealing in a general way with some of the consequences which have flowed from the miscellaneous character of the population and the tendency of some of the elements to form little colonies of their own. I have also taken this opportunity to go over the whole work and make any corrections or changes which the various criticisms I have received have suggested.

Since the first edition was published, another volume, entitled "Pennsylvania: Colony and Commonwealth," has been printed, and is now ready to be given to the public.

PHILADELPHIA, November, 1896.

PREFACE

MOST of the English Colonies in America were founded by people of pure Anglo-Saxon stock, and each colony had usually a religion of its own, with comparatively little intermixture of other faiths. Virginia and the New England colonies were particularly pure in their people and religion, and the history of each of them is the simple story of a people of one language, nation, and religion, thoroughly homogeneous, and always acting as a unit. But Pennsylvania was altogether different, and no other colony had such a mixture of languages, nationalities, and religions. Dutch, Swedes, English, Germans, Scotch-Irish, Welsh; Quakers, Presbyterians, Episcopalians, Lutherans, Reformed, Mennonites, Tunkers, and Moravians, all had a share in creating it.

Many of these divisions led a more or less distinct life of their own in colonial times, some of them wishing to found a colony for themselves within the province; and they all acted and reacted on each other, changed sides in politics, and produced movements and counter-currents which make the history of the State extremely varied and interesting, and at the same time rather difficult to trace.

The present volume deals with each of these divisions in detail, describes their motives and characteristics, and shows, with more or less completeness, the part each played in making the State. It is an analysis of our original population, and without this analysis it is impossible to have an intelligent understanding of our history. We must break up our people into their original elements before we can know who and what they were, and how they worked together. This analysis once mastered, much that is obscure in the politics and history of the State becomes very plain.

Most of the sects that founded our commonwealth were conspicuous for their freedom from the Middle Age dogmas, and their extreme advancement in the line of the Reformation; and the Quakers were the most advanced of them all. The people of the other colonies belonged usually to more conservative forms of religion, were less liberal in their opinions, and, in some instances, as in New England, indulged in the conservatism of religious persecution. The effect of this liberalism on the growth of Pennsylvania, in the system of laws, the early development of science, medicine, the mechanic arts, and manufacturing, is fully treated in a separate chapter.

It has also been found necessary to describe with some detail three important controversies, carried on for many years, which are part of the making of the State, because they threatened to affect very seriously our boundaries and size. The Connecticut claim, as it was called, was a claim by the Colony of Connecticut to the whole northern half of Pennsylvania. The dispute lasted nearly fifty years, and at times assumed the proportions of actual warfare and bloodshed. Connecticut was at first, and indeed for a long time, successful in asserting her title. She settled a portion of the disputed territory, and thus added to our population another incongruous element, which lived separate from the rest of the commonwealth and still maintains its own traditions and pride of history.

The controversies with Maryland and Virginia about our southern and western boundaries added no new element to our population, but they were quite serious. The dispute with Maryland lasted over seventy years, and several times resulted in bloodshed. If the Lords Baltimore had been successful in maintaining their claim, the Maryland line would have passed just north of Philadelphia, and that city would have no longer belonged to Pennsylvania. If the Virginia claim had been successful, the western boundary of our State would have been east of Pittsburg.

If the Connecticut, Maryland, and Virginia controversies had all gone against us, we should have been reduced to an insignificant strip of land containing neither Philadelphia nor Pittsburg. The successful resistance to these attacks, which aimed to strip us of the positions and land that have made us the second State of the Union, is certainly as much a part of our making as the characteristics of our original population.

In order to reveal the Pennsylvanians as they lived and moved in provincial days, it has been necessary to handle with some detail and considerable frankness the numerous religious opinions which for nearly a hundred years were seething and conflicting, especially among the Germans. To have omitted these details, or to have ignored their sharp differences and peculiarities, would have been to conceal the true life of the people.

Religious opinion had a strange intensity in those

Preface

times. I do not mean that men are now less religious. On the contrary, I think, in the best sense of the word, they are more so, and that there is more pure faith in God and love for man than there ever was, except among the Christians of the first century. But in the seventeenth and eighteenth centuries men were just coming through the Reformation, were just learning to think for themselves, and they were full of controversial religion and religious aggressiveness. Religion then controlled a man's political opinions and his whole conduct in unreligious matters in a way which no one now living has seen.

It is impossible to describe this condition of affairs in Pennsylvania without discussing numerous phases of thought which were very dear and holy to good men long since dead, and are still dear to the living. I am compelled to be fair; to be critical, and yet not blindly critical. But I cannot, of course, see and feel in every faith as its followers see and feel. I am writing history, not advocacy, and to give the condition of all the divisions necessarily involves a certain coldness and impartiality to each, which, without this explanation, might appear to arise from religious indifference or scepticism.

An exhaustive citation of authorities would be unsuited to the scope and intention of the book; but I have thought it well to call attention to some of the more important, so far as they seemed likely to be of interest or use to the general reader. In some of the chapters the principal authorities are mentioned in the text, and in others a foot-note at the end contains them.

PHILADELPHIA, April, 1896.

THE MAKING OF PENNSYLVANIA

SECOND EDITION

CONTENTS

Contents

THE

MAKING OF PENNSYLVANIA

CHAPTER I.

THE DUTCH, THE SWEDES, AND THE DUKE OF YORK.

IT is the custom to consider the history of Pennsylvania as beginning with the early settlements on Delaware Bay, for the reason that some of these ancient people extended their habitations for a few miles within the present limits of our State, and also because any title the Dutch had to the land on the river included part of our present territory.

The early settlers were first of all the Dutch, who, beginning in the year 1623, occupied the shores of the Delaware for fifteen years. After them came the Swedes, who held the country for seventeen years. The Dutch reconquered the country and held it for nine years, when the English took it and, under the Duke of York, held it until the arrival of Penn and the Quakers in 1682.

The Dutch were the first Europeans who attempted to occupy Pennsylvania. Any right they may have had to it, as well as their right to New York, was acquired by the discoveries of Henry Hudson, who was an Englishman in their employ. Hudson belonged to a family of explorers. They were all interested in the Muscovy Company, an organization founded in 1555 and devoted to discovering a path for commerce to China by going around either the northern extremity of Europe or the northern extremity of America. Hudson made several voyages for this purpose under the direction of the English nation before he entered the service of the Dutch.

Very little is known about him. He appears to have had a house in London, and rather a large family. He was one of those Englishmen, as numerous three hundred years ago as now, who are willing to sacrifice everything and endure everything for the sake of sailing unknown seas and exploring unknown lands. He was a rough, intelligent, daring navigator. Many of the observations of latitude which he took are almost as accurate as those of modern times, and he penetrated far towards the pole. He was by no means overscrupulous in dealing with inferior races. When he landed at Portland, Maine, he had no hesitation in driving the Indians from their village and robbing them of their property. "We took the spoyle of them," his log-book says in its sturdy English, "as they would have done of us."

The way in which he happened to discover the Delaware was somewhat curious. The Dutch had employed him to try once more to discover the route to China by going to the northeast around the northern end of Europe. He attempted it, but was driven back by the ice. If he had followed his instructions, he would have returned home; for he had no authority to attempt anything except to find the northeast passage. But just before he left Holland, he had received a letter from Captain John Smith, of Virginia, also a great explorer, telling him that there was a passage through the land a little way north of Virginia, which probably led to the Pacific Ocean.

Smith had evidently been told by the Indians of Delaware Bay, and, not having explored it, supposed it might be the passage long sought by every one. Hudson decided to disregard his instructions from Holland and follow out the suggestion of Smith. He bore away for the coast of America, and made the land somewhere near Portland, Maine, where he robbed the Indians. He explored the coast of New England, getting as far south as Cape Cod. Then he stood out to sea, and went far southward to Virginia, so as to begin his work from the starting-point Smith had mentioned. He made the mouth of Chesapeake Bay, and speaks of it in his log-book as the place of the English settlements. He saw Cape Charles at the mouth of the bay, and described it very accurately, calling it Dry Cape. He then began to work carefully northward along the shore, looking into every inlet and bay, passing by Chincoteague, and describing the general appearance of the coast as we know it to-day. It is rather remarkable that he escaped the dangerous shoals. His vessel was a small one, called the Halve-Maan, or Half-Moon, of about eighty tons' burden, with from fifteen to twenty Dutch and English sailors. She was probably about the size of one of our ordinary two-masted coasting schooners, but square-rigged, low in the bows and high-turreted astern.

His arrival at Cape Henlopen and Delaware Bay is announced in his log-book by the statement that the land suddenly turned to the west and northwest. He could see Cape May on the opposite side of the bay, and he took its latitude, varying only three minutes from the most accurate observations of modern times. He had not proceeded far, however, when he became entangled in those shoals which still extend up and down the very middle of the bay. Indeed, he got aground before he was fairly within the bay, and apparently upon that shoal which is now known to extend southward from Cape Henlopen and is called the Hen and Chickens.

Large vessels now usually pass outside of this shoal. But Hudson, without the local knowledge of the modern coaster, attempted to go inside of it, and was caught on it at some point close to the cape. This is evident from an entry which the mate, Robert Juet, made in the log-book. "On a sudden," he says, "we came into three fathoms; then we bore up, and had but 10 feet water, and joined to the point." But the tide was rising, and they were soon off; and the mate says, "As soon as we were over, we had 5, 6, 7, 8, 9, 10, 12 and 13 fathoms;" which shows that they had passed into the deep water, now marked on the sailing charts as directly north of the shoal and in front of the cape. They turned into the bay and passed close to the spot where the Breakwater now is, and where the fleets of merchant vessels seek shelter from storms.

But soon they were again in trouble. "The bay," Juet says, "we found shoal, and had sight of beaches and dry sand." Probably they encountered shoals near what are now known as the Shears, close to the cape, and also perhaps Brown's shoal and the Brandywine, which lie near the main channel. The navigation of these waters is now regulated by an elaborate system of buoys and colored range lights. But Hudson and his mate, surrounded by what seemed to be endless sand and forests, were utterly bewildered; and they described their difficulties in language so natural and sailor-like, that we feel as if we must have known those two burly Englishmen, now nearly three hundred years in their graves.

If Hudson had remained another day in the bay and exercised a little more patience he might have found the main channel and worked his way up it. But he and Juet were thoroughly disgusted. It was the 28th of August, 1609. "A hot day," Juet says; and those who have summered at Cape May can readily believe him. They entered the bay at noon and remained in it scarcely six hours. About five in the afternoon they sailed out, and at seven in the evening were safely anchored in the ocean far from the troublesome shoals. Judging by the currents and the bars and sand, they concluded that a great river poured into the bay. If it was the northwest passage it was too shallow to become a very convenient highway for commerce. The much-perplexed Juet entered in the log-book,—" He that will thoroughly discover this great bay must have a small pinnace that will draw but four or five foot water to sound before him."

So they sailed away again up the coast of New Jersey, sounding and observing until the land again trended to the west and northwest, and they entered the harbor of New York. There were no shoals, and they sailed far up the river until satisfied that it was not the course to China.

Hudson never really reached the Delaware River, and was only a few miles within the capes of the bay. But he had done enough to give his employers a vague claim to all the adjacent country. Six hours of tacking and hauling and sailors' oaths and ten lines of Juet's handwriting in the log-book were enough to give the Dutch an empire of thousands of square miles of territory which may fairly be said to have included a large part of Pennsylvania.

The year after Hudson discovered the Delaware he started again for China by the northwest. He entered and explored Hudson's Bay, which still bears his name. But his crew, Juet among them, mutinied, turned him and his son adrift in a boat, and his adventurous career was closed. Juet soon died of famine, and his body followed that of his master into the sea.

The Delaware was named from Lord Delaware, who visited the mouth of the bay a year after Hudson, and eight years later made another voyage to the same place, where he met his death. Like Hudson, he was troubled by the sand bars, and reported the bay unnavigable.

Other visitors have given other names. The old maps are very curious. Each of the three nations, Dutch, Swede, and English, that contended for the possession had their own charts and renamed all important points. The Indians called it Pontaxat and Mariskiton. The Swedes called it New Swedeland stream. On some maps it appears as Arasapha; on others as New Port, May, and Godyn's Bay. The Dutch called it Nassau, Prince Hindrick, and sometimes Charles River. But they usually spoke of it as the Zuydt, or South River, as they called the Hudson the North.

The first person who conquered the shoals and really explored the river was a Dutchman, Captain Hendrick-

son. In the year 1616 he penetrated as far as the
Schuylkill, just below the present site of Philadelphia.
He had a small yacht, the "Onrust," or "Restless,"
only forty-five feet long, which had been built at New
York after the loss of his larger ship. In using this
boat he may have been influenced by Juet's warning
that it would require a vessel of light draft to explore
thoroughly that great bay.

The first settlement of the Dutch on South River was
about the year 1623, shortly after the founding of Massachusetts. The expedition was conducted by Cornelius
Mey, who gave his last name to one of the capes of the
Delaware and his first name to the other. His last
name, with the spelling altered, has stayed where he
placed it. But Cape Cornelius is now known as Cape
Henlopen. William Penn attempted to rename it after
that man in whom he unwisely placed confidence, James
II., but fortunately without effect.

The Dutch settlement was called Fort Nassau, and
was at Gloucester Point, on the Jersey side of the river,
almost opposite the present site of Philadelphia, and now
famous for its shad parties. It was under the control of
the Dutch West India Company, a powerful organization of Holland traders who managed for their nation
the colonization in America.

They gave the land to patroons, who held it on a
feudal tenure, as in New York. But it does not appear
that any of these grants extended to Pennsylvania. Of
the two that were made one was of the land round Cape
Henlopen and the other of land around Cape May. In
fact, the Dutch preferred to stay down the bay. They
found Fort Nassau too high up and in 1650 abandoned it

for Fort Casimir, which, under English rule, became New Castle, now in the State of Delaware. They were traders rather than settlers. Their principal object was the collection of furs, and their actual occupation barely reached Pennsylvania.

One of their establishments, called Zwanendal, or Valley of the Swans, was, in all probability, near the present site of Lewes at Cape Henlopen. It was soon destroyed. They had set up the arms of Holland painted on a piece of tin. An Indian took it down to make a tobacco-pipe, and for this insult to a great nation was killed. His tribe made short work of the Dutchmen.

The undisturbed possession of the Dutch lasted only fifteen years, or until 1638, when the Swedes appeared. Before the Swedes came the Dutch had penetrated into Pennsylvania to the extent of purchasing from the Indians the valley of the Schuylkill, where they built a fort called Beversrede. The trade in beaver-skins at this point they described as enormous and much more valuable than the whale fishery which they had established at Cape Henlopen.

It was also about this time that a company of twelve or thirteen adventurers from Connecticut, under the lead of a certain George Holmes, attempted to establish themselves on the Delaware and drive out the Dutch. They had the temerity to attack Fort Nassau, but were easily made prisoners and sent to New York. Some years afterwards, or about 1640, other attempts were made by Connecticut and two settlements effected, one at Salem, New Jersey, and the other on the Schuylkill in Pennsylvania. They claimed the land as English territory and part of Virginia. They bought out the Indian title, and to account for their ease in purchasing it related a likely story. A Pequot Indian from New England was in the country and told the Pennsylvania Indians that these Connecticut men were persons of such honest and exemplary lives that, although they had killed many of his tribe and driven him from his home, yet they ought to be given whatever they wanted.

This was the beginning of that spirit of enterprise on the part of the people of Connecticut which had for its object the acquisition of the territory of Pennsylvania. All through the time of the Swedes and Dutch we read of meetings being held in New England, especially at New Haven, church meetings as well as political meetings, for the purpose of sending expeditions to the Delaware. Scarcely a year passed without negotiations and letters and demands for the land. In 1665 they had so far perfected their plans that they thought their Delaware plantations might become larger than the home colony in Connecticut. In that event they had arranged that the governor should be part of the time in Connecticut and part of the time on the Delaware, and if the new plantation should grow still larger that he should reside altogether on the Delaware.

They expected much relief in tax rates as well as profit from the enterprise; and the old documents are very amusing in the way in which they mingle these economic considerations with religious zeal. Connecticut, we are assured, wanted the Delaware for "the forwarding of the Gospel and the good of posterity therein that they may live under the wings of Christ." * .Their

---

* Hazard's Annals, 174.

admiration for the beauty and fertility of our State never abated until they had claimed and partly settled the northern half of it, which brought on a long contention lasting until after the Revolution. Their early attempts on the Delaware were, however, easily disposed of by the Dutch and Swedes.

Sweden was not much given to colonization, and it is not likely that her people would have appeared on the Delaware had it not been for peculiar circumstances. She had for some years been living under the guidance of Gustavus Adolphus, her greatest ruler. He had led her to take the unaccustomed part of conqueror, and, inspired by his genius and enthusiasm, she had waged war with no little success against Russia, Poland, and Austria. Gustavus was an ardent Protestant; and he had joined his forces to those of Germany in the thirty years' war against the Catholic reaction, when his career was cut short by death. Conquests and success had given to both him and his people new ideas which extended out beyond the rocks and fiords of their native land. When, therefore, William Usselinex, a renegade Hollander, suggested the formation of a Swedish West India Company for colonization, Gustavus eagerly accepted his plans and afterwards spoke of the enterprise as the brightest jewel of his kingdom.

He never lived to carry out the plans which the experience of Usselinex in the Dutch West India Company had prepared for him. But, after his death, under the reign of Christina, her Prime Minister, Oxenstjerna, sent the first settlers to the Delaware. They arrived in two vessels, the Key of Kalmar and the Griffen, all under command of Peter Minuit, another renegade Dutchman, conspicuous in the early history of New York. They settled near the present site of Wilmington, Delaware, calling the place Christina, after their queen, who became remarkable in the annals of royalty for having resigned a throne of which she professed to have become tired.

The Swedes, once established, proved themselves better colonists than the Dutch. They bought from the Indians some land above Cape May on the Jersey side of the river. But their principal purchase was on the other bank, and has been described as extending from Cape Henlopen to what was afterwards known as the Falls of the Delaware, opposite the present site of Trenton, where the river becomes shoal and rapid. A careful investigation, however, shows this purchase to have been of much smaller extent. It began at Bombay Hook, some distance above Henlopen, and ended at the Schuylkill. Their intention was to take the land not actually occupied by the Dutch; and so they bought the land which lay between the two Dutch settlements on the west bank, the one at Henlopen and the other on the Schuylkill. They confined themselves almost exclusively to this tract, declaring that it belonged to them, and calling it New Sweden.

They of course had not even the shadow of a title to it. It has been said that Oxenstjerna professed to have secured from Charles I. a document surrendering to Sweden any rights the English might have to the lands on the Delaware. But such a document has never been found. The Swedes were flushed with the recent conquests and glory of their nation, and were inclined to bear themselves like Romans and take what they wanted. The Dutch protested; declared that the land was theirs by discovery, possession, and, in addition to that, had been sealed to them by the blood of their slain. They called on the Swedes to prove their right; and the Swedes haughtily replied by telling the Dutch to go and live within the borders of New Jersey, where they would be unmolested and allowed to worship God as they pleased.*

In 1650 the Dutch, finding Fort Nassau was too high up the river, abandoned it, and established another on the present site of New Castle, calling it Fort Casimir. This was in the midst of the Swedes' tract, and the intention evidently was to cut in half their settlements. Four years afterwards the Swedes captured this fort on Trinity Sunday, and called it, in honor of that day, Trefalldigheet. Afterwards, when the Dutch retook it, they called it New Amstel, and under the subsequent English rule it became New Castle.

The Swedes had pretty much complete control of the west shore. They spread up into Pennsylvania, founding the town of Upland, afterwards called Chester by William Penn. Their most northern settlements reached to the present limits of Philadelphia. At Tinicum, now a few miles below the city, Printz, their governor, built a fort of hemlock logs, a commodious mansion house, and

---

* The Dutch had no more right to the country than the Swedes. The English claimed it by right of the discoveries of John and Sebastian Cabot, who had visited several points on the North American Continent before Hudson reached the Delaware. In 1889 the question came before the Superior Court of the city of New York in a case involving the rights of certain owners of land on the Bowery, and was decided in favor of the English title, in a very learned opinion by Judge Truax. Mortimer *vs.* N. Y. Elevated R. R., 6 N. Y. Supplement, 898.

planted an orchard. He also built a pleasure house, whatever that may have been. Tinicum was a curious sort of island formed in the bank of the river by Darby Creek separating into two branches and making a half circle as it flowed into the Delaware. The fort was called New Gottenburg, and the private establishment was long known as Printz's Hall.

Printz was a jolly good fellow; and is described by De Vries, one of the Dutch patroons, as weighing four hundred pounds and taking three drinks at every meal. It may be added, in mitigation of this statement, that Printz was at that time at Fort Elsingborg, lower down the Delaware, where he had fired at De Vries' ship until she surrendered.

Seriously considered, Printz was a man of education and ability. He had been deprived of his rank of lieutenant-colonel for surrendering the German town of Chemnitz, but was afterwards restored, and lived to be a general. His government on the Delaware was vigorous. He kept both the Dutch and the New Englanders at bay, and managed to live like a gentleman. He added to his amusements a small yacht, which, after he had gone, lay for many years rotting on the shore, a sort of landmark and object of interest to the people. He was certainly the first yachtsman of the Delaware, and probably the first American yachtsman. Tinicum still retains the sporting tendencies which he established. Its little inn has long been the resort of duck and rail shooters; and two of the principal yacht clubs of the city have erected on it their houses and wharves close to the site of Printz's fort and mansion.

Fort Elsingborg, from which Printz had fired on De

Vries' ship, was the only stronghold the Swedes attempted to occupy on the Jersey side. It was situated
on a point of land which still bears its name near the
present town of Salem. There was considerable style
kept up in all these little forts, whether held by Dutch
or Swedes. Vessels of the enemy were regularly fired
upon and brought to anchor. The smallest sloop was
expected to lower her ensign or show some mark of
respect in passing a fort. If she failed in this duty, and
a shot had to be fired to improve her manners, she might
expect to be asked to pay for the powder and ball that
had been used. Distinguished persons were suitably
entertained, and if poverty or circumstances prevented
such entertainment ample apologies were made. Beekman, one of the Dutch governors, writes in the year 1663
to Stuyvesant, his superior at New York, saying that
Lord Baltimore from Maryland was about to visit
Altona, as Fort Christina, near Wilmington, was then
called, but that there was not a single draught of French
wine with which to treat that nobleman. "Send some,"
says the worthy Beekman, "and charge it to me."

It is a matter of some surprise how these little wooden
forts or block-houses were able to control the navigation
of the river. The waters were wide both in river and
bay, and the forts were usually at the widest places, and
in some instances with the main channel on the opposite
side. Any one who now stands on the site of one of
these ancient strongholds and looks out over the wide
expanse naturally concludes that a ship which kept close
to the further shore and paid no attention to the fort
would have been perfectly safe. But the cannon that
were used may have been of better range and accuracy

than has been generally supposed, or the moral effect of a shot or two and the consciousness that pursuit in open boats was possible may have been enough to bring a prudent captain to anchor.

The Swedes were more within the boundaries of Pennsylvania than the Dutch had been. But their principal places of abode were within the State of Delaware. Their numbers increased and they drove the Dutch almost entirely out of the fur trade. The first year of their arrival they exported thirty thousand skins, a number which is significant of the immense supply of beaver as well as of the value of the trade to the Dutch.

The importance of the trade became widely known and aroused the keen commercial sense of the Puritan colony in Massachusetts. Always thorough in their methods, whether of trade, religion, or literature, they resolved to strike at the source of the fur supply, which was supposed to be in the neighborhood of a great lake called Lyconia, to which the Delaware would lead them. They sent an expedition up the river, hoping to cut off the beaver from both Dutch and Swedes. But the little forts and their watchful garrisons stopped the Yankee vessel, and she returned to Boston.

The key to the beaver traffic on the Delaware was apparently the possession of the Schuylkill. The reason of this seems to have been that the Indians found it more convenient to meet the white man on the west bank of that stream. The places where they met appear to have been at the highland now occupied by Gray's Ferry Bridge and Bartram's Garden. This was the first natural landing place after passing the low ground and marshes near the river's mouth. Probably the woods were of a large growth free from underbrush, and afforded a convenient meeting place. Probably, also, the trails converged to that point. For nearly two hundred years afterwards Gray's Ferry was the natural highway from Philadelphia to the west and south.

Both Swedes and Dutch struggled for the control of this spot. The Dutch built forts and houses and the Swedes tore them down. The Swedes also tried to forestall the Dutch by establishing stations some miles in the interior to collect the furs at lower prices before they reached the river. The Dutch are said to have retaliated by furnishing the Indians with guns and ammunition, in the hope that they would be used for the benefit of Holland.

The Swedes were more than traders—they were thrifty and industrious cultivators of the soil, and had flourishing farms along the river. They brought with them their cattle, which grazed the meadows and marshes and roamed through the woods. These herds were very numerous when the Quakers arrived, and probably most of the common cattle of Eastern Pennsylvania are descended from them. The woods at that time were quite free from underbrush and afforded a short nutritious kind of grass. It was easy to ride on horseback almost anywhere among the trees. But the second growth, which came after cutting or burning the primeval forest, brought on the underbrush and destroyed the woodland pasturage.

The Swedes never attempted to clear the land of trees. They took the country as they found it; occupied the meadows and open lands along the river, diked them, cut the grass, ploughed and sowed, and made no attempt

The Dutch and the Swedes

to penetrate the interior. But as soon as the Englishman came he attacked the forests with his axe; and that simple instrument with a rifle is the natural coat-of-arms in America for all of British blood. In nothing is the difference in nationality so distinctly shown. The Dutchman builds trading-posts and lies in his ship off shore to collect the furs. The gentle Swede settles on the soft, rich meadow lands, and his cattle wax fat and his barns are full of hay. The Frenchman enters the forest, sympathizes with its inhabitants, and turns half savage to please them. All alike bow before the wilderness and accept it as a fact. But the Englishman destroys it. There is even something significant in the way his old charters gave the land straight across America from sea to sea. He grasped at the continent from the beginning, and but for him the oak and the pine would have triumphed and the prairies still be in possession of the Indian and the buffalo.

Nevertheless, the Swede seems to have lived a very happy and prosperous life on his meadows and marshes. He was surrounded by an abundance of game and fish and the products of his own thrifty agriculture, of which we can now scarcely conceive. The old accounts of game and birds along the Delaware read like fairy tales. The first settlers saw the meadows covered with huge flocks of white cranes which rose in clouds when a boat approached the shore. The finest varieties of fish could be almost taken with the hand. Ducks and wild geese covered the water, and outrageous stories were told of the number that could be killed at a single shot. The wild swans, now driven far to the south and soon likely to become extinct, were abundant, floating on the water

23

The Making of Pennsylvania

like drifted snow. On shore the Indians brought in fat bucks every day, which they sold for a few pipes of tobacco or a measure or two of powder. Turkeys, grouse, and varieties of song-birds which will never be seen again were in the woods and fields. Wild pigeons often filled the air like bees, and there was a famous roosting-place for them in the southern part of Philadelphia, which is said to have given the Indian name, Moyamensing, to that part of the city.

The Delaware Indians always claimed Pennsylvania as their special hunting-ground, and they had every reason to love it. The river and the country near Philadelphia seem to have been particularly favorable to wild animal life. All through the colonial period and for many years after the Revolution the game of Pennsylvania afforded an important and abundant supply of food and contributed not a little to the prosperity of the province. It might still be a source of profit as well as of pleasure if means had been taken to preserve it. Even as late as the beginning of the Civil War there were still within twenty miles of Philadelphia great quantities of small game, which have now totally disappeared, and even the varieties of birds which are not considered game have been largely exterminated.

The Swedes planted peaches and fruit-trees of all kinds, had flourishing gardens, and grew rich selling the products when the Quakers arrived. They made wine, beer, or brandy out of sassafras, persimmons, corn, and apparently anything that could be made to ferment ; and they imported Madeira. Acrelius, their historian, gives a long list of their drinks, and tells us that they always indulged in four meals a day.

The Dutch and the Swedes

Their rule, however, lasted only seventeen years. The Dutch, seeing them become of more and more importance, obtained assistance from Holland, overset their authority, and were again in the year 1655 in possession of the Delaware. Before they conquered the Swedes they appear to have bought from the Indians the present site of Philadelphia, and to have set up on it, according to their custom, the arms of Holland, which were promptly removed by the Swedes.

This second control by the Dutch lasted nine years. It was a rather barren conquest; for the Swedes continued to occupy the land, and there were comparatively few Dutch settlers. The whole population, Dutch and Swede, living at this time along the river and bay is said to have been only about three hundred and sixty-eight souls.

Under the Swedes the form of government, so far as it is known, appears to have been a very simple one. Pretty much everything was in the hands of the governor. Under the Dutch it was more elaborate. The West India Company had become indebted to the city of Amsterdam in a considerable sum for the expenses of the conquest and other matters, and the city was accordingly given an interest and control in the colony. Officers with strange titles ruled the shores of our river, which now seems as if it could never have been anything but English. There was the schout, who was a combination of sheriff and prosecuting attorney. There were schepens, who were inferior judges, something like our magistrates. Finally, there were the vice-director and his council, who regulated everybody and told them what to do with their goats and pigs.

The Making of Pennsylvania

When the Dutch were ousted by the English in 1664, both the Dutch and the Swedish dominion were ended forever, and those nations no longer figure in the history of our State. The Dutch have left behind them a few names, like Henlopen, Schuylkill, and Boomties Hoeck, now called Bombay Hook. Schuylkill meant Hidden creek, a name given because the mouth of the stream could not easily be seen from the river. The Indian name for it was Manaiung, now applied, in the form Manayunk, to a suburb near the Wissahickon. The Swedes, although excellent pioneers and settlers, left very few names of places. Some of the descendants of both nations are still with us. The Swedes are said to have been quite numerous for a long time after the English conquest. Sixty years after the arrival of Penn and the Quakers, there are said to have been nearly a thousand persons on the river speaking the Swedish language.

This English conquest of the Dutch in 1664 included also the conquest of the same nation in New York, which with New Jersey and a large part of New England was immediately given to the Duke of York, brother of Charles II., by a deed which afterwards figured in our history. It was claimed that the deed included Pennsylvania and Delaware. But how it could have reached so far is difficult to understand. After granting large and vaguely described tracts of land in eastern New England, the deed goes on to say, "All the land from the west side of the Connecticut River to the east side of Delaware Bay." By both common sense and law, as ordinarily understood, this could not possibly have given the duke a jurisdiction west of the Delaware. The way in which the grant was made to cross the river is best described in the language of those who maintained it. William Penn relied partially on this deed for his title to what is now the State of Delaware. In his lawsuit with Lord Baltimore about the Maryland boundary, his counsel frankly admitted that their claim through this deed was not a strong one. " But," they said, " it was a very large and extensive grant of several very large tracts and territories in America, and passed, as we say, all lands appertaining to those extensive tracts."

The better opinion is that it "passed, as we say," nothing whatever west of the Delaware. Neither Penn nor the duke placed much, if any, reliance on it for their title to either Delaware or Pennsylvania. When Penn, after obtaining his charter for Pennsylvania, decided to buy Delaware as an additional piece of territory, he bought it, it is true, from the duke, but not until the duke had obtained a special grant of it from the Crown, which shows very conclusively that both parties considered the old deed of 1664 worthless so far as concerned any land west of the Delaware.

When Penn got his charter for Pennsylvania, he took a release from the duke of any rights he might have in that territory. But this was evidently a measure of abundant precaution to guard against any claims of the duke by reason of his occupancy. It can hardly be called a recognition of the validity of the old deed of 1664 as to land within the present limits of Pennsylvania.

Any occupancy the duke had had of Pennsylvania was very slight. The Swedes, Dutch, and English, over whom he ruled, were nearly all within the present limits of Delaware. New Castle, the head-quarters of his colony, was a Delaware town. Some of the settlers were scattered north of Delaware along the river as far up as the present site of Philadelphia. But they were comparatively few.

In 1673 the Dutch reconquered both New York and Pennsylvania, and held them for a few months. But the treaty of peace sent them back again to the English, the great colonizers and the race of destiny for America.

But little need be said of the remainder of this English occupation under the Duke of York. The principal public event was the trial of the Long Finn, a Scandinavian, professing to be of noble descent, who went about the country attempting to stir up the people to rebellion. He was sentenced to be whipped, branded in the face with the letter R, and sold as a servant in the Barbadoes. New Amstel, called by the Dutch Fort Casimir, was renamed New Castle, and became the head-quarters of the country. While under the duke, the people on the river and bay were considered as an appendix to New York, and were called the Delaware colony and sometimes the New Castle colony.

There were a few Swedes settled within what is now the southern part of Philadelphia. They farmed the rich meadow lands, some of which, until recently, were used for market gardens, and lie in what is called the Neck. In the year 1675 they established a church at a place they called Wiccaco, now near the corner of Christian and Front Streets. The building now long known as the Old Swedes' Church is still standing, and is one of the familiar antiquities of the city. The Swedes built churches of this kind wherever they had an important settlement. The one at Wilmington can be seen from the railroad passing through the town, and, like the others, is of a quaint and interesting type of architecture.

Under the rule of the Duke of York many English emigrants came to the river, increasing the population to two or three thousand at the time of the arrival of Penn. There is a curious story told of one of the ships called the Shield, which was bringing some people to Burlington in the year 1678. In beating up the river against the wind, she sailed on one of her tacks close up to the present site of Philadelphia near Walnut or Chestnut Street, where the bank was steep and high and the water deep close to the shore. In turning to go about on the other tack, her rigging touched the branches of an overhanging tree, and the people on board remarked that it was a good place to build a city. It seems hardly possible that the trees should have overhung so far as to touch the rigging of a ship. But the remark may have been made by those people and at that very spot. It was the natural place for a great city, and the best location that could be found on the river.

Those familiar with the shores of the Delaware know that there are comparatively few spots within a hundred miles of the capes where high land of any great extent comes down to the water's edge with depth sufficient for large ships. The banks are usually marshes or low meadows. The land at Philadelphia was not only high, comparatively level, and of sufficient extent, with unusual depth of water in front of it, but its position in the angle between the Delaware and the Schuylkill was by no means unimportant for military purposes. Penn always had an eye for such things, and, though a Quaker, could never forget the soldier days of his youth.

The Making of Pennsylvania

Ages before Philadelphia became the metropolis of America it had been the metropolis of the Indians. They came to that high land between the rivers to light their council-fires and settle their treaties and politics with the six nations of New York. A glance at the map shows its convenience for them. The Delaware and its bay were natural highways for a long distance north and south. The Chesapeake and its tributaries were near at hand. They could come down the Susquehanna to the mouth of the Swatara below Harrisburg, and follow up that stream, whose head-waters would bring them close to the Schuylkill. Trails branched out into the woods in all directions from the site of Philadelphia, and Germantown Avenue follows the line of one of them. It was in recognition of this immemorial meeting place that Penn was supposed to have reserved a small plot of land on the east side of Second Street near Walnut to which the Indians could continue to resort and build their council-fires. But this story of Penn's sentiment for the red men, though at one time widely circulated and generally believed, seems to be without foundation.

As finally made up under the duke the settlements on the Delaware consisted, first of all, of the people at Cape Henlopen, the name of whose abode was changed from Swansdale to Whorekill and afterwards to the modern Lewes. Whorekill was probably a corruption of Hoorn Kill, from the town of Hoorn in Holland. Next in passing up the bay was St. Jones, not far from Dover, and then came Wilmington, New Castle, and Upland, the last a small place within the modern limits of Pennsylvania. There were courts of law in all these little hamlets. The life of the people turned principally towards the bay and the river, and the attempts to penetrate inland were few. New Castle was the seat of government, and the important point in the opinion of the outside world. Penn fixed upon it as the place from which to calculate the boundaries of Pennsylvania, and it appears to have been the one point of which the exact location was well known in England.

The duke had a set of laws prepared for the government of all his domains, New York as well as the settlements on the Delaware. They were very elaborate, and show considerable ingenuity in the draughtsman. Everything was provided for,—branding of cattle, fees of constable, viewers of pipe-staves, killing of wolves, and cutting of underbrush. They were made up from the laws of the other English colonies, with improvements. They are sometimes quoted in a way likely to mislead. They were not passed by the people of the country, and are not typical of the state of thought and feeling either in Pennsylvania or in Delaware. They are merely the work of some theorizer in England, and should never be relied on to show the condition of the people who lived under them. They were not enforced on the Delaware until 1675, only seven years before the arrival of Penn. Previous to that the English had allowed the people to be governed by the mixture of Swedish and Dutch laws which had long prevailed. The intention of the English was to gradually change these Dutch laws and substitute the laws of the duke. When the duke's laws were adopted they were declared not to apply in matters relating to courts, county rates, and militia, which were left as before.

The Making of Pennsylvania

So far as Pennsylvania was concerned, there was little for the duke's laws to act upon, save rocks and trees. They are utterly inconsistent with the real laws of Pennsylvania enacted by Penn and the Quakers. They made the town the unit of division, after the manner of the New England system, from which they were largely copied. Penn made the county the unit of division. Afterwards the township and borough were added, and the Pennsylvania system became a combination of town and county government unknown in other communities. The duke's laws provided, among other things, for nine offences to be punished with death, among which were heresy, perjury, kidnapping, and smiting of parents. The Quaker laws established religious liberty, and made only murder punishable with death. The duke's laws also provided for an elaborate system of recruiting and disciplining the militia. The Quakers refused to have a militia, and none was adopted until shortly before the Revolution.

The Swedes, the Dutch, and the English under the duke made no important settlement, so far as Pennsylvania was concerned, and did nothing which materially affected after events. Their peculiar laws and customs soon became completely obsolete; they and their descendants were absorbed in the rest of the population; and there is no institution in Pennsylvania that can be traced to their influence. They were not in the line of the real beginning and progress of our Commonwealth. That Commonwealth was created by the Quakers, and to them must be given our more serious attention.*

---

* Hazard's Annals; Proud's Pennsylvania; Acrelius' New Sweden; The Duke of Yorke's Book of Laws; Sprinchorn's New Sweden.

CHAPTER II.

In histories of Pennsylvania the religious traits of her founders have usually been omitted entirely or disposed of in short notes in an appendix. Instead of that we should follow the order which actually occurred in which those traits formed the beginning and the foundation. The men who founded Pennsylvania, like those who founded most of the other colonies, were intensely religious; they came here because of religion; and they lived in a time when religious doctrines were the great and absorbing questions and were discussed with an intensity we can hardly realize. For several centuries before Pennsylvania was founded the people of Europe had been fighting, burning, and imprisoning each other about religion.

The sects of that time were distinct from one another. There was but little of that general resemblance which we now see. They were kept separate by persecution and their fierce contentions. Most of them could be recognized at once by their dress and manner. They gave to each colony they founded in America a marked individuality, which is now to a great extent lost. The citizens of our different States no longer reveal their origin at a glance. Their distinguishing characteristics become evident only on close observation. The man from Massachusetts associates easily with the Virginian, and we might have to look more than once before we could tell one from the other. But in colonial times we could have distinguished them in an instant, and in very early colonial times they would not have been congenial to each other. The solemn Puritan would have been shocked and the fox-hunting Virginian would have been bored.

The Pennsylvania Quaker was of still another type. Formal and stiff like the Puritan, he had, however, none of the Puritan sternness and severity. He believed in religious liberty, while the Puritan denied it. Bound down by rules of conduct as strict and narrow as any that the Puritan invented, he was, nevertheless, most liberal in his opinions and far ahead of the Puritan in philanthropy and all the most advanced ideas of the modern world. The Puritan was opposed to high living and the pleasures of the table, but was devoted to learning and literature. The Quaker, on the other hand, despised learning, poetry, music, and the fine arts as vicious amusements; but he seems to have had no rule or custom which prohibited very good living and a very liberal hospitality. During the early days of the Revolution, when the members of the Continental Congress were in Philadelphia, they were entertained in Quaker families in a way that astonished them, especially those from New England.

In order to see how the movement of the Reformation finally resulted in the Quakers and the Pennsylvania Dutch, we must rid our minds of the notion, which is so prevalent, that the Reformation was the work of one or two men, and that it occurred within a short space of time. It was really a reactionary drift or tendency, not

34

an organized movement, and it is impossible to assign dates to it. No one knows exactly when it began, nor has it yet ceased its action. Nothing could be more absurd than to suppose that Luther was its author. He was simply a leader among the Germans, as Calvin was among the French and Swiss, and, being a picturesque, vehement character, he has attracted to himself more attention than the others. About the year 1400, almost a hundred years before Luther was born, John Huss had preached the need of a reformation in Bohemia, and gathered quite a following; and half a century before that Wycliffe had preached it in England. The period of the Roman Empire is gone, and the Middle Age is gone; but we are hardly yet out of the period of the Reformation. We are still acted upon by its influences, and they will, in all probability, be with us for many years to come.

The Reformation, regarded as a period of evolution, may be looked at from many points of view. We may consider its development of morals, its development of the arts and conveniences of life, or its development of free government and republicanism; but the thread which we must briefly follow down to the Quakers is a purely religious one, namely, the development and decline of dogmatism.

It is hardly necessary to give the well-known details of the growth of dogmas in the Christian Church during the Middle Ages. From the fourth century the development went steadily on, and the ecclesiastics, with increasing power and increasing ingenuity, wove mesh by mesh a net-work over the human mind. In the fourth century the Bishop of Rome began to claim chief authority and show signs of developing into what is now the Pope. But infallibility was not claimed for him until the eleventh century, and not finally asserted until within our own time in the middle of the nineteenth. Mariolatry, or the worship of the Virgin, began about the year 400 and steadily increased. Image worship, which for many hundred years had been regarded as a heresy, began to be allowed in the seventh century, and after that developed to great excesses. Up to the twelfth century there were only two sacraments. After that there were seven. And so the dogmas increased, and miracles multiplied, and relics of saints appeared from every quarter, and all these things must be accepted and believed, until about the twelfth century there was a climax or congestion. The founding of the Inquisition in 1248 marks the time when the system had reached its height, for the Inquisition was absolutely necessary to hold the mass together and prevent reaction.

But the mass had become so great that it soon began to crumble of its own weight. The revival of the ancient learning of Greece and Rome and the invention of the printing-press assisted the inevitable day, and, as the people of Europe one by one began to realize their condition, the reaction was terrible. Men whose minds had for generations been in submission to authority, men who had for generations been accustomed to but the one idea of dogma, dogma, infallible dogma, and who had never dared to think for themselves, were shaken loose from their hold. They were free, and went about seeking rest. There was great wandering, disagreement, and searching of heart; and that was the Reformation.

The first point to observe in this reaction, the point

which concerns us in the history of Pennsylvania, is that men revolted against dogma by slow degrees. Wycliffe, the first great leader of the Reformation, could rid himself of only one dogma. He rejected transubstantiation and kept pretty much all the rest. John Huss, the next great leader, attacked at first only the fraudulent miracles of the ecclesiastics. Luther, who appeared a hundred years after Huss, was equally conservative. His famous ninety-five propositions were aimed only at the sale of indulgences, which at that time was carried to great excess.

Leaving the leaders, and taking up the various sects as they appear one after the other, we find the same slow movement. But there is this fact to be observed: the small and badly organized sects were always more progressive than the larger and stronger ones. Three or four hundred years ago there was a large number of these small sects, playing an important part in history, and now forgotten. Familists, Seekers, Ranters, Pietists, Antinomians, Anti-Scripturists, Enthusiasts, Soul Sleepers, Levellers, Adamites, Traskites, and Anabaptists are some of the names which were very familiar to the men of those days and now have to be looked for in dictionaries.

The great and strongly organized divisions of Christendom were comparatively conservative. The Church of England reformed itself from within, without changing its historic character; others which became prominent in the Reformation—the Lutherans, the Presbyterians, and the Independents—gave up some dogmas, but clung to others with great determination. They advanced carefully, and only a few steps, into liberty. Composed largely of the middle and upper classes, they shrank from the unsettling effects of radicalism, the disturbance to law and order and the rights of property. It was discovered early in the Reformation that property rights were closely entangled with the old religious thought. Luther saw this very clearly, and after the horrors of the peasants' war in Germany he became more conservative than ever.

But the numerous small sects were composed of men of the lower classes, who had nothing to lose by a change, and were unprejudiced by education. Many of them disposed of the whole dogmatic system with one stroke of their minds and relied entirely on their own thought and feeling; and reliance on individual conscience and judgment was the test of advancement in the Reformation. Some of these advanced within a year to a position which the great conservative denominations have only lately reached. They were the explorers and scouts, and, like all such adventurers, were far in front of the main army, and too few to be much respected by the enemy.

The main principles of pretty much all of them included the abrogation of the Old Testament, a denial of the necessity of forms, ceremonies, sacraments, and church government, and a reliance on contemplation and individual feeling and experience as the final authority in religion. These ideas nourished and supported for many years the Familists, Antinomians, Anabaptists, and others; and when these weak and badly-organized sects disappeared, the same ideas went to make up the stronger and more intelligent and practical Quakers.

Many of the early Baptists, both in England and Germany, were very much like the Quakers. They were opposed to a hireling ministry; they held that the church should be composed of equals; that the ordinances of the Old Testament were abolished; that the pagan names for months and days were unchristian, and they allowed women to preach. In fact, all these small and radical sects which we have mentioned, Familists, Antinomians, Seekers, Anabaptists, and others, were finally in England swallowed up in two large ones, the Baptists and the Quakers. In Germany they were absorbed by the Mennonites, Tunkers, and other people, many of whom came to Pennsylvania.

The Familistic and Antinomian sects could not last long. They were rather vague in their principles and almost entirely without organization. They maintained an uncertain existence for some years, until the feeling and motives which had caused their growth were satisfied in sects which were of a better class in life, retained just enough conservatism to steady them, and were able to have a more practical and enduring form of government.

The Baptists paid a little compliment to the past by accepting a few of the old dogmas in a modified form, and some of them were believers in predestination and election. They preceded the Quakers by only a few years. The other great divisions of the Reformation, the Congregationalists, Presbyterians, Lutherans, and others, all took their rise at a comparatively early period. But the Quakers showed no sign of any distinctive organization until about a hundred years afterwards; and the year 1650 is a convenient time from which to date their beginning.

They went far beyond the Baptists: rejected baptism altogether, and denied the necessity of any sacraments. The Reformation movement gradually led up step by step to the Quakers, who represented the extremest ideas of aversion to dogma; and they might be described as the high-water mark of the reaction. It would have been difficult to go farther. In fact, like many other radicals, the Quakers went so far that, as we shall see later on, they were compelled to take a few backward steps.

CHAPTER III.

THE doctrines of the Quakers were very peculiar and interesting. But we should make a great mistake if we described their doctrines and allowed that to stand as a picture of the people. The same might be said of other religions. It would be unfair to judge of the Roman Catholics of to-day by supposing that they still believed the literal statement of the doctrine of persecution which their Church adopted six hundred years ago. If we should read Jonathan Edwards' descriptions of the doctrines of Calvinism without having ever seen a Calvinist, we might suppose him to be a very different person from what he really is. If in the same way we should read of Quaker doctrine, we might expect to find the people an abstract essence of spirituality without enough of human nature left to stir the dust. Fortunately for the world, men do not always live up close to their creeds.

Excellent books have been written about the Quakers. Clarkson's Portraiture and Janney's History of them are both very complete in their way. But they describe the theoretical Quaker. The actual one was somewhat different, and was a product of the doctrines mollified, sometimes in a very unexpected way, by human passions.

This mollifying was very apparent in the Pennsylvania Quakers. In most countries they were a very retired sect. In England they were made up chiefly from the rural population. They were opposed to war, official oaths, and politics, and had no difficulty in living up to these notions. But in Pennsylvania they were the governing body, responsible for the political management of the country. Instead of avoiding politics, as too exciting for religious contemplation, they were compelled to take a very active part in them. They attempted to conduct their government without oaths, but were not entirely successful. They also attempted to conduct it without war or force, and in that they utterly failed. Their ablest men, like Logan and Dickinson, openly favored defensive war, and Dickinson carried a musket as a common soldier and was also a colonel in the Revolution.

Hundreds of others, when the temptation was strong upon them, enlisted in the army. Still larger numbers invented excuses to their consciences for indirectly supporting, by votes of supplies, or otherwise, the warlike measures which became absolutely necessary. When struck or insulted, they could not help retaliating, although they might afterwards write a letter to the meeting saying that they were sorry, or that they had intended only to lay their hands gently on their adversary. When they became magistrates, or sheriffs, or officials, they arrested and punished wrong-doers, although such action necessarily involved the use of force and violence. For two hundred years the world has been full of humorous stories to show how the Quaker remained human in spite of his doctrines. The Quaker who tossed a pirate overboard, saying, " Friend, thee has no business here," and the other one who cut the rope by which the intruder was climbing aboard, saying, " Friend, thee may have that," are fair samples of many others. A large part of the history of Pennsylvania is made up of attempts to coax or drive the Quakers into war, and their partial success.

The possession of power, the consciousness of having conducted a wonderfully successful colony, and the growth of wealth gave to them, in the height of their ascendency, about the time of the Revolution, a strong tincture of worldly honor and pride which their doctrines seemed to scorn. Judging by what we can read of them at this time, many of them were not without a certain amount of haughtiness and arrogance. They were by no means slow or retiring; on the contrary, they played a very active, earnest, and prominent part in all affairs of life, political, commercial, and social.

All these characteristics have of course now disappeared, and it is difficult to realize that they ever existed. The real Quaker, as he lived and moved in Pennsylvania, appears from time to time with more or less distinctness as we read the history of the State. But still it is necessary to have a clear idea of his theories, of what he might have been if he had lived his doctrines logically.

The fundamental principle of the Quakers was what they called the universal light, or the inward light. It was a feeling, they said, given to every man born into the world, and was sufficient to guide him to all religious truth and save his soul. It was not to be confounded with conscience, which was an original faculty of human nature, and existed in perfection in Adam and Eve before the fall. The inner light had been given by the Founder of Christianity, and, instead of being identical with conscience, its purpose was to enlighten conscience. It came to every individual on earth, heathen as well as Christian. The only limitation was that the heathen had the light but slightly, not so thoroughly as those races and nations called Christian.

The Quaker method of cultivating the inward light was by silence and meditation. They believed that by sitting still and fixing their thoughts on God they brought themselves into relation with Him. This stillness constitutes a large part of their worship. They sit silent in their meeting-houses ; not a word, or prayer, or sermon is heard until the spirit moves some one to speak; and it is not at all uncommon for these meetings to be held in perfect silence from beginning to end.

The belief that silent contemplation can develop relationship with God is very old, and is usually known in history by the name quietism. It has always formed a conspicuous part of the religions of India and China, and has prevailed to a greater or less extent among Christians. Extreme quietism, the quietism cultivated in the East, consists in a complete resignation of oneself into passiveness, into a state of mental inactivity without thought, reflection, hope, or wish; a state in which all external objects and ambitions are lost to sight, and the person withdraws into his inmost self. By this means, it is said, the soul is gradually brought into the divine presence until an actual union is effected, and man becomes absorbed in the infinite. It is easy to see that meditation of this kind, if continually practised, will gradually weaken the intellect, and quietism may become mental sleep and religion a mere dream.

Quaker Traits

Although many sects of Christianity have had more or less mysticism or quietism, there have probably never been any Christians who indulged in extreme quietism. The most pronounced Christian mystics have never maintained that we should give up all mental activity. But it is important to notice that as men advance in quietism they lose all hold on dogmas and sacraments. There undoubtedly have been Christian mystics who professed and tried to hold orthodox dogmas; but they regarded the dogmas as experiences to be realized rather than propositions to be believed. Quietism demands abstraction from all externals, and when the quietist state of mind is once attained dogmas and sacraments become useless.

The movement of thought which produced the Quakers in England about the year 1650 sent a wave of quietism all over Europe. It showed itself in the Church of Rome in 1675, when Molinos, the Quietist, led the movement with such success that the Pope became a convert, and the spread of it had to be stopped by the inquisition.

Molinos was a Spanish priest, who, after gaining some distinction in his own country, came to Rome to advance his ideas. He taught that men should seek God first by meditation, in which the doubts that troubled the soul were struggled with and subdued one by one. The second stage was contemplation, in which the soul ceased to struggle, no longer reasoned or reflected, but contemplated God in silence and repose. By this inaction the soul annihilated itself, returned to its beginning, which is the divine essence, and lost itself in God. This method, which he called the interior way, was, he said, the true growth of the soul by which it rose far beyond the need of all sacraments and ceremonies. He taught the people to go straight to God without the aid of priests, confessionals, beads, or images.

The formal statement of his doctrine can be found in his book; but his personal and practical application of it must have been much more effective. All who came in contact with him were trained in the art of contemplation and quietude, and were delighted with it. Their numbers and zeal prove his skill as a spiritual director. Like the Quakers, he believed in serenity, was opposed to all excitements, festivals, anniversaries, or anything that interfered with tranquillity, and he also resembled them in holding that by the interior way human nature could become perfect. Like the Quakers, he attempted to vitalize religion by returning to the first principles of consciousness. He attempted to develop the pure spirit by pure meditation.

The shattered condition of the Roman Church in the times of the Reformation is nowhere more clearly shown than in his success. His book, "The Spiritual Guide," was translated into several languages, and within six years passed through twenty editions. He was on the point of being made a cardinal, and it was heresy to differ from him. In Naples alone he was reported to have had twenty thousand converts. Multitudes flocked to him, or sought his advice by letter. It looked as if the Roman Church was about to turn Quaker.

His system kept spreading and increasing in power for nearly twenty years, and none but the Jesuits saw the danger of it. The idea, it is true, was not a new one. St. Bonaventura, St. Theresa, John of the Cross, and many others had not only written books on quietism, which had been approved by authority, but they had openly practised the doctrine, and had been commended for it. They practised it, however, in obedience to the ordinary rules of the Church, and they continued to profess their belief in the ordinary dogmas. The Church was willing to allow them an enthusiasm or a singularity, provided they would form themselves into an order and yield implicit obedience.

But Molinos and his followers were altogether outside of any rule or obedience. They held that every man's religion was contained within himself, and that quietism was the universal path to God. They carried their belief to its logical conclusion, and made no pretence of holding dogmas utterly inconsistent with it. They were not establishing an order with a discipline applicable only to those who should join it, but they were establishing a system to embrace all mankind. If their efforts had continued a few years longer the Church of the Middle Ages would have disappeared from the face of the earth, and Molinos would have been a greater man than either Luther or Calvin.

But the Jesuits, whose order had been founded for the express purpose of counteracting the effects of the Reformation, were untiring in their labors, and finally turned the tide. When it became evident that the people everywhere were becoming indifferent to masses, relics, rosaries, confessionals, and the other means by which the Church maintained her dominion, the Jesuits had an unanswerable argument. The inquisition was turned upon the heresy. Two hundred of the leaders, including Molinos, were instantly imprisoned, and such a reign of terror created that quietism was never heard of again in the Roman Church.*

Thus the Quaker movement came to naught in Italy and Spain. But it flourished abundantly in England, had considerable success in Germany, and spread to a slight extent in France, where there are still a few Quakers. It hardly suited the French temperament, or indeed the temperament of any people that had Latin blood in their veins. But it was natural enough to the German, and most natural of all to the serious-minded Englishman.

The Quaker, having made up his mind that every man could be saved and the religious life developed by sitting still and listening for the voice of God in the soul, had, necessarily, no use for any of the ordinary doctrines of his age. His extreme development of the principle of private judgment excluded them all. Other sects had played with that principle, or only half accepted it. But the Quaker took it to heart. The feeling that man must look within himself to discover his relations to the Deity, the feeling which inspired the heresies of the Antinomians and the Familists, and the philosophy of Descartes, reached its utmost religious expansion in the Quakers.

Most of the sects had retained two sacraments, baptism and the communion. But the Quaker felt that he had passed beyond the need of such aids and he rejected them altogether. The doctrine of exclusive salvation, which still lingered among Protestants, was swept out of existence in the Quaker's mind without the least hesi-

---

* Bigelow's Molinos the Quietist.

tation. He believed in the universal light which had come not only to every Christian heart, but to the heart of every heathen, and all would be saved who followed it. Belief in the universal light necessarily excluded predestination and election, and accordingly the Quakers were entirely outside the pale of Calvinism and became advocates of free will.

They succeeded in ridding themselves of every one of the ancient dogmas except, perhaps, the inspiration of Scripture. The Trinity they explained in a way of their own, which would not have been accepted by any other church of that age, Protestant or Catholic. They held that, although the three persons were mentioned in the Scriptures and declared to be one, yet the complicated doctrine of the Trinity as stated in the Athanasian creed was never heard of until three hundred years after Christ. They preferred, they said, the statement of Scripture to the statement of the schoolmen. They accepted the simple account in the New Testament, that the Father, Son, and Holy Ghost were one. But they rejected the scholastic doctrine that the three were each separate and distinct persons and substances, and yet also one. It was useless, they said, to inquire whether each one of the three, considered by itself, was a separate substance, or a separate manifestation, or a separate operation. Such idle metaphysics tended not to righteousness and were unknown to the primitive Christians.

On the doctrine of the atonement they were somewhat at sea. There were in reality two schools among them, and this is the point where they gradually took some backward steps. The first school were inclined to carry the doctrine of the inner light very far, and hold that the appearance of Christ on the earth was solely to confer his spirit, that is, the inner light, on all men; that it was his spirit that would save mankind, and not the shedding of his blood, or any mere act or event in his life; that he came to save men by giving them a spiritual principle which would change their hearts; that the idea of it being necessary, in order to save mankind, that Christ should be sacrificed and tortured, was a mere material and vulgar notion unworthy of belief and inconsistent with any sense of justice on the part of God.

This first school had their counterpart among some of the Germans and were very liberal. The other school were inclined to accept the doctrine of the atonement as usually stated, and held that the sacrifice and death were in themselves means of salvation, and no mere manifestations and proofs of the gift of the inward light.

During the first hundred and fifty years of Quakerism, the first, or liberal, school were quite numerous. The first occasion when the two parties had a direct and open dispute was in Pennsylvania in 1691. At that time George Keith, a prominent preacher among the Quakers, maintained that the sect was wrong in worshipping only the light and spirit of Christ within; they must worship also the man who was crucified at Jerusalem and was now in heaven as Mediator. The Quakers replied that they accepted not the man Christ in heaven as a mediator. The only Christ they worshipped was the spiritual Christ in each heart. His sufferings and death as man were simply incidents of his earthly life, and not fit subjects for worship. In other words, Keith attempted to give Quakerism a body and get rid of some of the vague spirituality. As he expressively put it, " the candle should have a candle-stick."

He gathered quite a number of followers in Pennsylvania and New Jersey. They separated from the sect and set up meeting-houses of their own, calling themselves Christian Friends, and were called by others Keithian Quakers. But their leader soon deserted them and joined the Church of England, after which they were gradually dispersed : some returned to the sect, but the majority were divided among the Baptists and the Church of England.

For more than a hundred years after this event there was no schism or open controversy. But, meanwhile, the party which Keith had represented was growing in numbers, slowly in America, more rapidly in England. By the year 1827 the large majority of Quakers had adopted the opinions which Keith and a small minority had been disowned for holding in 1691.

The change was gradual, and might have gone on for many years without attracting much notice. But the majority, or Orthodox Quakers, as they called themselves, insisted on a complete triumph, and in 1827 forced a separation, which seems likely to be permanent. The Hicksites, as the minority were called, were driven out of the sect for maintaining the very opinions which, in 1691, the Keithian Quakers were driven out for not maintaining.

Since the Hicksite separation there has been another split among the Quakers, which has created the Wilburites, who have taken ground midway between the Hicksites and the Orthodox. The Wilburites hold that Hicks went too far in his rationalistic treatment of the Bible, in regarding the story of the fall and the personality of the devil as mere allegories. They also hold that he exaggerated the doctrine of Christ within. On the other hand, they believe that the Orthodox have exaggerated the doctrine of the atonement and made too much of Christ's mere death and suffering, to the exclusion of his spirit. They of course claim to be the original Quakers.

The substance of the faith of the early Quakers was that they liked to believe that Christ was divine without being obliged to state his divinity in the form of a metaphysical subtlety. They liked to believe that he came to save the world, but in a spiritual sense, and not by means of death and physical suffering. This general spiritual idea of his divinity has now spread to every division of Christendom, and is the most sincere form of belief on the subject held in modern times. Millions of men and women who announce themselves as Trinitarians mean only that they believe in a general way in the divinity of Christ. Few of them care for the doctrine of the Trinity as taught in the Middle Ages, and few of them could even state it.

The inspiration and authority of the Scriptures were accepted by the Quakers, and this was the only point where they were at one with the great sects of the Reformation. But they added to this belief a new doctrine, which again took them far away from all other Protestants. They held that by means of the inner light new revelations could at any time be made to individuals, and as a matter of fact were often made; that these revelations of the spirit were equal in authority with the Scriptures, were from the same source, and would therefore never contradict the Holy Writings. The Scriptures, they said, were merely the utterances of the spirit, not the spirit itself. This belief in the doctrine of immediate and continued revelations, since the time of the Scriptures, somewhat resembled the Roman Catholic belief in the continuance of miracles since the time of the apostles, and was, perhaps, one reason why the Quakers were constantly charged with having a tendency towards papacy.

The doctrine of immediate revelations was the heresy for which Mrs. Hutchinson, the Antinomian, was banished by the General Court of Massachusetts. The Quakers absorbed pretty much all the Antinomians. They also held that heresy so dear to the Familists, as well as to the Antinomians, that the Old Testament was entirely abrogated and the New Dispensation alone in force.

We can, perhaps, realize more fully what a complete reversal of religious thought the Quaker movement represents when we consider that they were perfectionists. They believed that by contemplation and quietude a man could in this life reach a state in which he was free from sin. In this they contradicted not only all the other sects of the Reformation, but the whole tone of ecclesiastical thought for more than a thousand years. No doctrine of the Church had been more generally taught and believed than that which held that every human being remained miserable and wicked to the end of his days, and that perfection was possible only to God. When we find a great religious movement spreading over all Europe and holding out the possibility of human perfection, it is easy to see that the Middle Ages are past.

Having freed themselves from so much dogma, and especially from the dogma of exclusive salvation, the minds of the Quakers were back again in the normal human state, and they became strong believers in liberty of conscience. It was not a matter of expediency with them, but a principle about which there could not be the slightest doubt, and which they scarcely ever violated.

It is impossible to withhold admiration from them. They have the honor of being one of the few divisions of Christendom against which the charges of inhuman cruelty and selfish love of power cannot be brought.

Among the Quakers first appeared those ideas of philanthropy which may now be called the prevailing religion of the modern world. Long before Beccaria thought of writing his book on the misery of prisons, the Quakers had carried into effect in Pennsylvania the reforms which he is supposed to have originated. They introduced the idea that a prison should be a reformatory as well as a place of punishment—an abode of discipline and cleanliness, instead of a source of dirt, pestilence, and disorder.

As early as 1727 they began to agitate for the abolition of slavery, and many years before that date they had had the subject under discussion. Their fundamental principle, that all religious development must arise from a natural and direct relation between the individual soul and God, has had an enormous influence on modern thought, has stimulated morality, enlarged liberty, checked bigotry and despotism, and affected indirectly every other church and sect.

Fox is often spoken of as the founder of the Quaker sect, but that is hardly a correct description of him. He found the movement already in existence, and was himself aroused and inspired by it. Quakerism originated in natural causes far beyond the influence of any one man. But Fox undoubtedly organized the movement and forged it into shape. He was not a man of learning and intelligence, like his successors William Penn and Robert Barclay. But he was deep-hearted, full of religious fervor, and carried away and out of himself by the feeling of the times—qualities, perhaps, better suited to his purpose than mere logical or intellectual power.

He caught up the ideas around him, expressed them in vigorous speech, and made them respected by his heroic suffering. He was eminently fitted for the task. Tall of stature, with a piercing eye, commanding presence, and perfect courage, wild, fanatical, and superstitious, he fulfilled the idea of a prophet. He went up and down England preaching everywhere, and even visited America. He was continually getting into prison, and, his sufferings becoming as conspicuous as his earnestness, he was soon the rallying-point for the Quakers, and formed them into a sect. He slept so often in the woods, in barns, or in the cell of a prison, that he wore a suit of leather clothes, and Carlyle has quaintly remarked that it was an important day in the history of the world when George Fox decided to make himself a pair of leather breeches.

The outlandish doings of the Quakers, the bottle-breaking, and the giving warning of doom in the streets, were confined to the early days of the movement. They suffered severely for these irregularities, which gave the government an excuse for arresting them. But they were driven to irregularities by the laws which prevented their holding regular meetings. As the sect organized it grew more regular in behavior; it spread to the more orderly middle classes, and became the sedate, sober body which we know in our own time. Thus we find the Quakers who came to Pennsylvania were a very different set of people from those who thirty years before went to Massachusetts and Rhode Island. They were less extravagant in their behavior, and possessed more wealth and better education.

The method of enforcing the Quaker faith, as finally established, consisted of a severe discipline in morals and manners, and most of it was reasoned out on the principles of quietism. They prohibited every act of life, every amusement, and every occupation which interfered with tranquillity of mind, which tended to disturb the repose and meditation which were necessary to the development of the inward light. Not only cards and games of chance were forbidden, but all games of skill, all kinds of hunting and field sports, which, they said, aroused too much excitement in the mind. Balls and the theatre were equally dangerous. A man came home from such entertainments with his imagination heated and unfit for quietude. Novels and all works of fiction and poetry had the same effect and were condemned. They were particularly opposed to music. They not only banished it from their religious meetings, but refused to have their children taught it.

So far did the Quakers carry the idea of quietism that even the raising of the voice beyond ordinary limits was discouraged as tending to disturb the mind. For the same reason they tried to adopt plain clothes, and have them of the same fashion from year to year and from century to century. The sermons—or, rather, the testimonies in their meetings, for they hated the word sermon—showed no variety or range of knowledge, and were delivered in a peculiar monotonous tone. Complacency and serenity, evenness and monotony, were the great regulations of their lives. They opposed all kinds of speculation, and all hazardous or daring enterprises.

Two of their principles have always attracted great attention,—their objection to taking an oath and their objection to taking part in war. There was nothing new in these ideas. Plato, Epictetus, and other spiritually-minded philosophers had been opposed to oaths, for the same reason as the Quakers. They held them to be useless ceremonies, because men were bound to tell the truth at all times and under all circumstances, and the Quakers added to this argument several passages of Scripture.

The objection to war had been a very common opinion among the primitive Christians, as well as among some of the old sects. Ambrose, Origen, Chrysostom, Cyril, and many other saints and fathers had declared that to fight, or go to battle, or join an army was contrary to the express commands of Christ. The idea became a very definite principle with the Quakers, but they utterly failed in living up to it.

Part of their discipline was the duty of each member to watch the others and report their failings. Having no dogmas or ceremonies to occupy their attention, their whole energy was given to the correction of manners, and the most minute details of manners. Every family was carefully guarded and inquired into. A Quaker who married one of another faith was immediately dismissed from the society, and the reason given for this severe rule, which greatly depleted their numbers, was, that it was impossible to discipline the family of a mixed marriage. Failure to live up to Quaker habits and manners was supposed to be always followed by dismissal. The Quakers carried to a great extreme that idea so prevalent in the Reformation, that a church should consist only of the pure and perfect.

Their form of government began with the meeting or congregation, which consisted of the people of a neighborhood. From this delegates were sent to the monthly meeting, which was composed of the representatives from the congregations of a certain district, usually part of a county. From the monthly meeting delegates went to the quarterly meeting, which included a still larger district, and from these quarterly meetings delegates went to the yearly meeting, which represented the whole country. This system, which reminds us somewhat of the Presbyterian form of government, seems to have had for its object the minute investigation of the morals of the whole Quaker community. By an arrangement of written questions and answers between these different representative bodies, the condition of the people was passed in review every year.

A remarkable part of these Quaker assemblies was that they had no presiding officer, and that a question was never put to vote. The clerk, or secretary, watched the discussion and framed a resolution which seemed to him to be the sense of the meeting. If he failed to judge aright, the debate went on and the resolution was reframed by the clerk, and this process was kept up until debate ceased and the sense of the meeting had been ascertained.

Quaker Traits

One characteristic of the Quakers, which distinguished them in a marked degree from nearly all the other sects of the Reformation, was their indifference to politics. They avoided political discussions, as too exciting and disturbing, and the subject was generally a forbidden one in Quaker families.

Their objection was also grounded on their dislike of war and of oaths. They saw that governments were founded on force, and could be maintained only by armies, and that it was impossible to hold office in the governments of that time without taking an oath. They, therefore, except in Pennsylvania, their own colony, took no part in public life, and had no desire to do so. They lived quietly by themselves, and made it a rule to mix as little as possible with what they called the world. Since the time of the primitive Christians there never had been such apostles of gentleness. They were a striking contrast to the Puritans, every one of whom was a restless politician, whose religion included a theory of civil government which he felt it his duty to enforce.

That the result of the Quaker belief and discipline was remarkable purity of morals and innocence of life it is impossible to deny, and so evident has this been to all the world that the most cynical critics have seldom questioned it. But in their efforts to attain this result they lost sight of many qualities which are not only consistent with an upright life, but necessary to its perfection.

One of their foundation principles was that religious experience and growth were guided by the inward light, and in no way dependent on intellectual ability or knowledge. Fox, an unlettered man, was at great pains to show this, and it might have been expected from him.

The Making of Pennsylvania

But Barclay, a very learned and accomplished man, and the greatest theologian the Quakers have produced, was at equal pains to show it, and has taken up several pages of his book in proving the uselessness of Latin, Greek, mathematics, and natural philosophy. This was also very different from the Puritans, who made their religion an affair of the most hard-headed reasoning, who were always hungry for knowledge and never tired of argument.

It was strange that the Quakers, after having freed themselves almost entirely from dogma, should get into a state of mind that despised high learning. Their belief has been aptly described as a distorted rationalism. Not that they encouraged absolute ignorance and illiteracy, for they always had schools, and made a point that every child should be taught, and they were particularly careful in giving instruction to the poor. But their idea of education stopped at these schools. Reading, writing, and arithmetic were enough. For the higher walks of education, for scholarship, and extended knowledge they not only had no desire, but they distinctly disapproved of them.

In modern times they have greatly changed in this respect, and the Philadelphia Quakers have made most successful efforts in the direction of higher education, as their colleges, Bryn Mawr, Haverford, and Swarthmore, abundantly prove. They have interested themselves in the education of women, and also in women's rights, which is the natural outgrowth of the liberty always allowed by them to women in preaching and in the conduct of church affairs. But in 1789 John Dickinson had great difficulty in getting them to accept money to establish a high-class boarding-school, for most of them at that time doubted the value of anything beyond mere rudiments.

The contemplative, peaceful Quaker was in many respects no match for the argumentative, fighting Puritan. And yet there were circumstances in which the Quaker would have the advantage. There are two kinds of strength,—the strength of an astute mind and an aggressive spirit, and the strength of a martyr's nature, gentleness, perseverance, and resignation. When, thirty years before the settlement of Pennsylvania, the Quakers attempted to introduce their religion into Massachusetts, their method was triumphant in the face of both Puritan argument and Puritan cruelty.

It is easy to see a great deal in the regulations of the Quakers that seems narrow, belittling, or impolitic. The rule which dismisses every member who marries out of meeting seems suicidal, and has undoubtedly depleted their numbers. Many of their other customs seem also calculated to drive away able, spirited men and retain only the dull and commonplace. Yet it is astonishing how many remarkable men have been Quakers, and it is also curious to observe that most of them became remarkable by disregarding some of the most important regulations of the sect.

John Bright, who so long held such an eminent position in English politics, was, however, unusually consistent for so distinguished a Quaker. But most of the others have seemed to grow great by breaking the rules. William Penn was a man of this sort. He had not been bred a Quaker, and he indulged in politics, handsome dress, and appointed military governors over his colony, to an extent that might have brought dismissal to a man of less ascendency of character.

It is rather curious that the most eminent Quakers should have excelled in the fields of politics, war, art, and poetry, which were all under the ban of their doctrine. They have produced abler men in these lines than in philanthropy, which was their special province. Their contemplativeness and spirituality may be the cause of the poets. As for war, it was said, in Philadelphia during the Revolution, that the young Quakers who enlisted learned the manual of arms quicker than any others. It is certainly rather remarkable that Pennsylvania, a Quaker colony, should have produced so many distinguished generals and sent such a large proportion of troops to every war. One of the best painters of his time, Benjamin West, two of our best poets, Whittier and Bayard Taylor, and two of the ablest generals of the Revolution, Greene and Mifflin, were Quakers.

Whittier was born and bred in Massachusetts, of a Quaker family which was converted from Puritanism towards the close of the seventeenth century, when the Quakers invaded Boston. Benjamin West was a Pennsylvanian. He had a natural genius for art, which, unless it came by direct inspiration from heaven, must have been by reaction from extreme Quaker doctrine, for there was nothing in his surroundings to develop it. He could not even get brushes. But so strong were his instincts that, when a boy, as the story goes, he manufactured brushes out of the tail of the family cat, and made paint from the red and yellow earths given him by the Indians.

Pennsylvania in colonial days was an impossible place

for such a man. He went to study in Italy, and finally settled in England, where he became one of the founders of the Royal Academy, and was afterwards its president, succeeding Sir Joshua Reynolds. His pictures were mostly of the classical and historical type. Many of them, such as the Death of Wolfe, the Prodigal Son, Hector and Andromache, are still copied, and his place in art is a permanent one.

General Greene, of the Revolution, drove the British from the South, and in ability was second only to Washington. Unlike West and Whittier, he dropped his sect entirely when he joined the army. Mifflin was a Pennsylvanian born and bred, and a very distinguished soldier. He commanded the best-disciplined brigade in the Continental army, was governor of the State, and had a long and successful career in politics.

There were also two other very prominent Quakers in colonial Pennsylvania, James Logan and John Dickinson. Logan was a rare instance of a Scotch-Irishman turned Quaker. He had a strong character, combined with scholarly and cultivated tastes. In his early life, being deeply tinged with religious thought, he acquired an undue contempt for money and material things. But afterwards, becoming more balanced, he devoted himself to the commercial ventures in which Philadelphia gave so many opportunities, and acquired a fortune.

He was a lover of books, and founded the Loganian Library, which became part of the Philadelphia Library founded by Franklin. Like many of his fellow-colonists, he dabbled in scientific pursuits, and encouraged such pursuits in others. His quiet tastes and delicacy of feeling were undoubtedly of Quaker origin.

But the Scotch-Irishman in him would not down. He believed in war, and advocated it openly and boldly in the teeth of the protests of his sect, and yet was never cut off from meeting. He was secretary of the province, and represented the interests of the proprietors pretty much all his life. It was a stormy career for him. He was continually attacked by the popular party, and at one time had to endure an impeachment trial. He was always supremely indifferent to attacks and abuse, a trait which by some was attributed to strength of mind, and by others, to haughty arrogance. He was surly and morose at times in his old age, which was also a characteristic of Dickinson. Not a few of the Quakers, in the height of their power, were affected with some of the severe qualities which come of pride and success.

Dickinson was a lawyer, the author of the famous Farmer's Letters which had so much influence in the early part of the movement for independence. Like Logan, he believed in war, was colonel of a regiment, and fought at the battle of the Brandywine. He had a long career in Pennsylvania politics, as well as in national politics, and he largely controlled the destinies of the continent up to the Declaration of Independence. But he belonged to the conservative party, believed the Declaration to be premature, and his reputation has suffered.

All these men—Penn, Bright, West, Whittier, Greene, Mifflin, Logan, and Dickinson—were excellent citizens, of exemplary lives and valuable influence. They seem to have combined what was best in their faith with what was best in the world, and to have escaped what was narrow in both.

Bayard Taylor was also partly of Quaker origin, and

has left some interesting accounts of his struggles with the limitations of the sect in his Pennsylvania home. His ancestors were both Quaker and German, and, though his family had been dismissed from the society for the unpardonable offence of marrying out of meeting, his mother had had a great fondness for the Quaker belief, and taught it to her children.

Taylor grew up under Quaker influences, not only in his own home, but among his neighbors at Kennett Square. He always retained an affection for these associations, and even in mature years his letters were often written in the thee and thou language. But he reacted strongly from the narrowness of his surroundings. The story is told of his boyhood, that, having listened for a long time to interminable doctrine on the evils of oaths, both judicial and profane, he went out into a field, and, having delivered himself of all the swearing he could remember or invent, came back with his mind relieved. He sought delight in endless travel. His best poems were oriental, and the scenes he loved best were in the East, probably because its light, and passion, and color were the furthest remove he could find from the negations at Kennett Square. A large part of his Home Pastorals is an expression of the struggle between affection for his old home and revolt from its repression.

" Right and left are the homes of the slow, conservative farmers,
Loyal people and true, but, now that the battles are over,
Zealous for temperance, peace, and the right of suffrage for women,
Orderly, moral, are they—at least in the sense of suppression;
Given to preaching of rules, inflexible outlines of duty;
Seeing the sternness of life, but, alas! overlooking its graces.

*   *   *   *   *   *   *   *

The Making of Pennsylvania

Nay, but let me be just, nor speak with the alien language
Born of my blood; for, cradled among them, I know them and love them.
Was it my fault if a strain of the distant and dead generations
Rose in my being renewed, and made me other than these are?"

West and Whittier always remained Quakers, and apparently suffered little or no sense of repression. But if the Quakers had anything to do with making Taylor a poet, it must have been by process of reaction. The process was quite effective, however, for it is impossible to read his life and works without seeing that his whole nature was thoroughly poetic. His prose was poetry, and his travels attained their large popularity principally because they were written from the point of view of a poet.

The Quakers have played a great part in the world, and the decline and drying up of their sect in the present century is much to be deplored. Various causes have been given for it. In Pennsylvania the decay was hastened by certain political changes which drove them from power at the time of the Revolution.

But the general decline among them in all countries has usually been attributed to some of their peculiar rules of discipline, and also to the increase of wealth, which has, perhaps, been the strongest cause of all. They have been so thrifty, and such careful men of business, that most of them made fortunes. Now, it is impossible for a Quaker to obey the discipline of his meeting and at the same time spend a large income, unless he gives it all away in charity. He is allowed nothing else to spend it on. The consequence has been, that as Quaker families grew rich the sons and daughters were continually tempted to expand, at first in the direction of innocent little articles of clothes or innocent little amusements. But one thing led to another until, with increasing wealth and increasing knowledge of the world, the family suddenly found itself outside of meeting and gradually joined the Episcopalians.

The Quakers held their own in Pennsylvania for some years after the Revolution. But in the last sixty years they seem to have been disappearing. Whole districts of Philadelphia which were once entirely populated by them now contain scarcely any. Instead of being the strongest sect in Philadelphia and the adjoining counties, they are now in many respects the weakest.

Their disappearance from public life and influence after the Revolution changed the character of the city, and not for the better. It is only within the last twenty years that it has begun to recover from the effects of the retirement of the people who created its early reputation. It is now rapidly coming under new influences, and its future will be built on lines somewhat different from those of its past.

It will be a long time, however, before all the results of the Quaker dominion disappear. Their numbers may be fewer, but their influence is still potent, and many of their ideas have been unconsciously adopted by the people of other religions, among whom they have been living so closely for two hundred years. It is not easy to tell their exact condition and numbers. So many of them have given up the distinctive dress, and they are so retiring in their habits, that their existence is not very clearly marked. If we count only those who are plain Quakers of the old type, their numbers would be few. But if we add those who are part Episcopalian and part

Quaker, and those who may be called liberal Quakers, the Quaker influence still remains rather large in some respects.

It is sometimes said that the Quakers as a sect will soon be extinct, but this assertion is not supported by any definite facts or statistics. In the West they are said to be increasing, and apparently because they are willing to adopt more modern methods of worship. It is difficult to discover their numbers, and some of the estimates are mere guesses. Some authorities give the number of them in England, about the year 1700, at one hundred thousand. Other authorities put it at fifty or sixty thousand. At that time the population of Great Britain was about five or six million. Since then they have diminished rapidly, and in 1800 are said to have numbered only twenty thousand, and now only fifteen thousand.

In America they have had better success, and, counting all the divisions—Orthodox, Hicksites, and Wilburites— are now estimated at about one hundred and fifty thousand. This is probably too high. But if it is anywhere near the truth, it shows that in this country they have about held their own for the last hundred years, without either much gain or much loss. If the number one hundred and fifty thousand is correct, it would show a slight gain.

But when we consider the enormous growth of America in population, and the great increase in the numbers of other sects, it is easy to see that the Quakers have lost relatively and have made no real progress. In a country which has often doubled its population in thirty years, and where sects often double their numbers, to stand still is to lose. It will, however, be a long time before they are extinct, or anywhere near that condition, and it is safe to say that the man has not yet been born who will live to see the last of them.*

---

* Janney's History of the Quakers; Clarkson's Portraiture; Gurney's Observations; Barclay's Apology; Works of Penn; Marsh's Life of Fox; Turner's Quakers.

CHAPTER IV.

THE GERMANS.

THE Quakers were obliged to share Pennsylvania with a large number of Germans, who constituted that important body of the population still known as the Pennsylvania Dutch. This was the first appearance of Germans on the American continent. The struggle for the possession of the New World, which began soon after the first voyage of Columbus, had been confined to the Spanish, Portuguese, French, Dutch, Swedes, and English. The Germans, distracted by their own political divisions, took no part in the contest, and seemed to have no desire for colonization. They finally appeared in Pennsylvania half a century after most of the English colonies had been established, but they came as immigrants under the protection of the English nation, at first by the encouragement and persuasion of the Quakers, and afterwards by the encouragement of the British government.

The German element has been variously estimated as composing from one-third to one-half the population of Pennsylvania, and has unquestionably had a great influence on the development of our State. Whether that influence has been beneficial or injurious to our progress and highest interests is a question still debated among Pennsylvanians, and not likely to be settled in a way that will satisfy every one.

Some are of the opinion that where the Germans have

freely mixed and intermarried with the other elements of the population an excellent stock of people has been produced, but that unfortunately this intermixture has been of comparatively small extent. The great majority of the Germans have lived together in masses, with little or no intermarriage with other elements, and this isolation, combined with their slowness, their opposition to the public school system, and their retaining their language and customs, has checked the advancement of the State, which should be the first, instead of the second, in the Union. Others, however, have seen, in their thrift, steadiness, and love of liberty, the source not only of all that is great in the State, but of a large part of the greatness of the nation.

They are usually described as consisting of two main divisions, the sects and the church people. The sects arrived first, some of them as soon as the Quakers, and were made up of the Mennonites, Tunkers, Schwenkfelders, and others. The church people who came in a little later belonged to the two regular churches of Germany, the Reformed and the Lutheran.

The religious belief of the sects was the result of the same general causes which had produced the Quakers. The most prominent of them, and the first to arrive in the colony, were the Mennonites, or Mennists, a sect whose origin has been disputed. According to their own account they were the descendants of the Waldenses, those ancient heretics who had existed from time immemorial, who denied infant baptism and were guilty of many more supposed errors which afterwards cropped out in the Reformation. Others, however, have described the Mennonites as the descendants of the Anabaptists, who committed such violence and excess in the beginning of the sixteenth century.

The Mennonites undoubtedly held beliefs which were common to both the Waldenses and the Anabaptists. As they had none of the Anabaptist love of riot and disorder, it was said that they were the Anabaptists quieted and reformed. Very likely many people who had been among the old Anabaptists finally found themselves with the Mennonites, and probably some who were Waldenses, or whose ancestors had been Waldenses, were also with them. But the general cause of their existence was the same which created the Quakers, namely, the reaction against dogma, and probably most of them were recruited from the Roman Catholics and the Lutherans.

Their leader, Menno Simons, by whose name they were called, had been a Roman priest, and he first organized them about the year 1540. They resembled the Quakers in almost every respect, except that they had less quietism. They believed in the inward light, and that since the coming of Christ it had reached every man in the world, heathen as well as Christian. They were opposed to war and to oaths, and would take no part in government. They were opposed to a hireling ministry, premeditated sermons, and high education, and also to infant baptism. Ideas of this sort were floating about Europe all through the period of the Reformation, and every now and then some strong, earnest man was inspired by them and built up a sect. Thus Menno Simons made the Mennonites, and a hundred years afterwards George Fox, from the same ideas, made the Quakers.

The Germans

The Mennonites held very much the same opinions as the early Quakers on the doctrine of the Trinity, but they went not so far as the Quakers in abolishing sacraments. They retained baptism, applying it only to adults, and they retained the sacrament of the communion. They added another sacrament of their own, which consisted in washing each other's feet, and this they held was commanded by the Scriptures even more positively than the communion.

They were not quite so far advanced in the Reformation movement as the Quakers, for the reason that they were a hundred years older. But the two sects were so nearly alike that they always fraternized, preached in each other's meetings, and the Mennonites were often called German Quakers. In one respect they seem to have been somewhat in advance of the Quakers. They were the first people in Pennsylvania and the first people in America to suggest the abolition of negro slavery. In 1688 some of them who were living in Germantown sent a petition to that effect to the Quakers, who afterwards adopted the idea and became famous for the advocacy of it. The petition is full of quaint and curious expressions, especially one paragraph.

" If once these slaves (wch they say are so wicked and stubborn men) should joint themselves, fight for their freedom and handel their masters & mastrisses, as they did handel them before; will these masters and mastrisses tacke the sword at hand & warr against these poor slaves, licke we are able to believe, some will not refuse to doe ? Or have these negers not as much right to fight for their freedom, as you have to keep them slaves?"

The signers of this petition, who certainly deserve remembrance, were Gerret Hendricks, Derick Op de Graff,

The Making of Pennsylvania

Francis Daniel Pastorius, Abraham Op den Graef, all Germans or Hollanders. They are often spoken of as Quakers. Whittier treats them as such in his Pennsylvania Pilgrim, and possibly they were as much Quaker as Mennonite. Many of the German Mennonites, especially those who adopted English ways, became Quakers, and several prominent Quaker families in Philadelphia and other parts of the State are of German descent.

Throughout the greater part of the seventeenth century, before Pennsylvania was founded, the Mennonites and other German sects were fiercely persecuted by both Protestant and Catholic. In Germany they were hunted down by the Catholics, Lutherans, and Reformed, and in Switzerland by the Calvinists. They were constantly on the move from place to place, hiding in the mountains or the depths of the cities, or escaping to Holland, England, or America. Having refused to become the church militant, as was aptly said of them, they became the church migratory.

Long before William Penn received his charter, Gustavus Adolphus of Sweden is said to have invited the Mennonites to seek an asylum on the Delaware. His call seems to have been but little heeded, except by a small company of about twenty-five, who settled at Whorekill, on Delaware Bay, in 1662, where they were scattered and destroyed by the English two years afterwards, when the country was taken from the Dutch. The leader of the colony and his wife escaped, and after many years' wanderings in the wilderness came to Germantown, where they were cared for and given a home for the rest of their lives.

The important Mennonite immigation began to arrive

about the same time as the Quakers in 1682 or 1683, and was directly encouraged by William Penn. They went out to the beginning of the high land between the Delaware and the Schuylkill, about six miles north of Philadelphia, and founded Germantown, now a suburb of the city.

The most prominent man among them, and their leader, was Francis Daniel Pastorius, a school-master, who taught at Germantown, and also among the Quakers in Philadelphia. Like others of his nation, he had a prodigious capacity for absorbing all sorts of knowledge, was master of seven or eight languages, and well read in science and philosophy. At the age of twenty-two he is said to have disputed in public in several of these languages on science and law. He familiarized himself with questions of international importance, studied jurisprudence at Strasburg, Basle, and Jena, and was for a time a law lecturer at Frankfort.

But the absorption of all this knowledge was not enough for his German enthusiasm. He sought other scenes and amusements, and in company with a friend wandered for two years all over Europe, "feasting and dancing," as he tells us. Perhaps in the course of these journeyings he may have been seen, as we sometimes now see young Germans, roaming through Switzerland, staff in hand, knapsack on back, and pipe in mouth.

He was an enthusiast, ready for anything, and, as might have been expected, he was soon caught in one of the innumerable religious movements of his country. While lecturing on law at Frankfort he came under the mystic teachings of Spener, the leader of the pietists. The young and beautiful Eleanora Von Merlau was also of that faith, and added the mysticism of womanhood to the mysticism of religion. Such influences have sub-dued stronger men than the feasting, dancing young German, and the rest of his life was more serious. He came to America out of enthusiasm and sympathy for his fellow-countrymen, well content to begin life in a log-hut, to teach the children, and fill his garden with bees and flowers. This aspect of his character has been beau-tifully described by Whittier.

> " So, with his mystic neighbors settling down,
> The homespun frock beside the scholar's gown,
> Pastorius to the manners of the town

> "Added the freedom of the woods, and sought
> The bookless wisdom by experience taught,
> And learned to love his new-found home, while not

> " Forgetful of the old ; the seasons went
> Their rounds ; and somewhat to his spirit lent
> Of their own calm and measureless content."

Eleanora Von Merlau, her husband, Johann Wilhelm Petersen, and several other learned people, interested in the pietist movement in Germany, intended to settle in Pennsylvania. They formed a company called the Frank-fort Company, and bought from William Penn twenty-five thousand acres of land, which included the present site of Germantown. They sent out Pastorius, as their attorney and agent, with a selected company of weavers and farmers, intending soon to follow him. They never came, however, which was a great disappointment to him, and after managing the affairs of the company for seventeen years, he gave it up in disgust. It fell into bad hands, and was soon involved in troublesome litigation.

Pastorius continued to live his quiet life in Germantown, and was probably a very pleasant and genial sort
of man, although some of his pupils have given him
the reputation of being somewhat addicted to the rod.
Many pretty and homely traditions are connected with
his life. When he first arrived in Philadelphia, and before
he established himself in Germantown, he lived for a
time, like many of the Quakers, in a sort of half hut,
half cave, on the steep bank of the Delaware, probably
near the present Chestnut Street Wharf. Over the door
of this abode he placed a motto, " Parva domus, sed
amica bonis, procul este profani," which gave Penn much
amusement when he first visited the colony.

In Germantown, however, he built himself a substantial stone house. He wrote punning Latin verses,
one or two books of little importance that were published,
and an unpublished manuscript of a thousand pages, full
of philosophy and fancy, bees and flowers, and composed
in the seven languages of which he was the master.
He was a bailiff of Germantown, and represented it for
two years in the Assembly. He had the good sense to
recommend his children to study English, a piece of
advice which his countrymen were not in the habit of
giving. Whittier has pictured him in his garden musing
over the rejection of the petition for the abolition of
slavery.

> " He ceased, and, bound in spirit with the bound,
>   With folded arms and eyes that sought the ground,
>   Walked musingly his little garden round.

> " About him, beaded with the falling dew,
>   Rare plants of power and herbs of healing grew,
>   Such as Van Helmont and Agrippa knew.

The Making of Pennsylvania

" For, by the lore of Gorlitz' gentle sage,
   With the mild mystics of his dreamy age,
   He read the herbal signs of nature's page.

" As once he heard in sweet Von Merlau's bowers,
   Fair as herself, in boyhood's happy hours,
   The pious Spener read his creed in flowers."

Some of the Germans who came with the Mennonites were called Pietists. Pietism was the name for a school of religious thought established by Spener, which prevailed more or less among the Lutherans, the Reformed, and pretty much all the religious divisions of Germany. It is difficult to describe, because it assumed so many forms. In the main it was part of the reaction against dogma. Its adherents were opposed to all rigid systems of theology, and devoted themselves to moral perfection. At times it was mystic. In some of its forms it corresponded to what is known among us as evangelical Christianity, and it also seems to have contained something of the idea, carried to an extreme by the English Methodists, that religion must consist exclusively of an individual experience of each soul.

The Pietists are sometimes described as an offshoot from the Lutherans, and in this sense they may be said to have been composed of those who carried pietism to an extreme and separated from the regular Lutheran body, leaving in it a party who were moderate Pietists. Apparently, only a few who were distinctly known as Pietists came to Pennsylvania, but pietism in some form or other prevailed among most of the sects and church people.

The Tunkers, who were somewhat pietistic, came in large numbers, and are said to have been recruited very largely from the Reformed Church of Germany. They were somewhat like the Mennonites, but were peculiar in dress and manners. The word Tunker means a dipper, a baptizer by immersion. In Pennsylvania it has become corrupted into Dunker, Dunkard, and also into Tumpler, or Dumpler, referring to the motions of the baptized in the water. Like the Mennonites, they have the communion and the additional sacrament of washing each other's feet. They were very mystical, and have never made a statement of their doctrine, saying that the New Testament was enough. Many of them made a point of wearing long beards, coarse clothes, and walking with a solemn pace. Like the other German sects, they refused to take oaths or bear arms.

They first appeared in Germany at Schwartzenau, in 1708, and were driven by persecution to Crefeld and Holland. Between the years 1719 and 1729 the whole sect came over to America, most of them settling in Pennsylvania. Some of their leaders, like the leaders of the Mennonites, were men of education and intelligence. They grew and prospered as a religious body, and in 1850 are said to have numbered, in the United States, over two hundred thousand, with a thousand ministers.

Some of them separated and became the German Seventh-Day Baptists. This schism was accomplished by Conrad Beissel, a Pietist, who came to Pennsylvania in 1720. He preached to the Tunkers, and seems to have thought that they would be improved by a celibate and monastic life, and by observing the last, instead of the first, day of the week as the Sabbath. He adopted the life of a hermit, and in 1732 suddenly disappeared. He was soon found, however, still living as a hermit on the banks of Cocalico Creek, in Lancaster County, where he had a small farm and composed hymns. The Tunkers began to resort to him, and in a little while he had a monastic community of about three hundred strange, mystical, German souls, and afterwards one or two branch societies were established in other parts of Pennsylvania.

His settlement soon became known as the Monastery of Ephrata, and some of its curious buildings are still standing. There was a house for the brothers, a house for the sisters, a flour mill, paper mill, fulling mill, flax and oil press, a printing establishment, and a book bindery. Altogether they published about forty books, among them the Mennonite Martyr Book, some school books, and other volumes of a religious kind. Their books have been much admired for the excellence of the paper and printing, and they are valued by collectors. The sisters employed themselves in the ornamental writing of texts, and in copying hundreds of volumes of music, to which the monastery was deeply devoted. They had a school which is said to have achieved some reputation and attracted pupils from Philadelphia and Baltimore. The large room of this school and other parts of the monastery were used as a hospital for some of the Continental soldiers after the battle of the Brandy-wine.

In modern times attempts have been made to ignore the extraordinary eccentricities of these people, as well as of the other German sects, and modernize them. But the farther we go back to the contemporary accounts of them the more we discover of their strange habits. Gordon, who wrote previous to 1829, and had ample opportunity for obtaining his information from original sources, is a very safe authority.

The Germans

"They lived on vegetables solely, and slept on wooden benches, with blocks of wood for pillows, and attended worship four times in the twenty-four hours. This life macerated their bodies, and rendered their complexions pale and bloodless. Their dress consisted of a shirt, trowsers, and waistcoat, with a long white gown and cowl, of woollen in winter and linen in summer. The dress of the women differed from that of the men in petticoats only; with the cowls of their gowns they covered their faces when going into public. When walking they all used a solemn, steady pace, keeping straight forward, with their eyes fixed to the ground, not turning to give an answer when asked a question. On their occasional visits to their friends at Germantown, forty or fifty, thus strangely accoutred, with sandals on their feet, were seen following each other in Indian file. . . .

"Their sensual affections, driven from their natural channel, were poured forth on this mystic union with the Redeemer. By the unmarried of both sexes he was considered as an object of more than spiritual love : he was the bride of one, and the bridegroom of the other; in their songs and hymns, as in those of the Moravians, he was sometimes addressed in the strong and frequently not most delicate language of passion." (Gordon's Penna. 575, 576.)

We have also the authority of Endress, who was himself a German, and studied the Ephrata people from personal observation.

"Some of their writers of spiritual songs possessed well-regulated minds and a portion of poetic spirit. The mysticism of these created an imaginary world, instead of that which they had abandoned, where they permitted their affections to roam unchecked. The figure or image dearest to passion was enthroned in their hearts; that was their God, their Lord, their Redeemer. But the effusions of others were a jargon of inconsistent connections : turtle doves and lambs in conjugal union; cultivated fields, on which were sown pearls, and wine, and music; burning hearts united in keeping silence and singing at the same time songs of joy." (Hazard's Register, vol. v., 334.)

The society at Ephrata does not seem to have begun to decay until after the Revolution, and even far down into the present century schools and an academy were still in existence. A Sunday-school is said to have been established at Ephrata in 1740, nearly half a century before anything of the sort was begun in England.

In colonial times they were regarded as a curious community of Protestant monks and nuns. Travellers often made the long journey from Philadelphia to see them, and from one of these visitors we have an interesting description:

> "The performers sat with their heads inclined, their countenances solemn and dejected, their faces pale and emaciated from their manner of living, their clothing exceeding white and quite picturesque, and their music such as thrilled to the very soul. I almost began to think myself in the world of spirits, and that the objects before me were ethereal."

The desire for hermit life was by no means uncommon among those brooding, introspective Germans who came to Pennsylvania. Many of them retired to caves or solitary huts in the woods, and occasionally one is still to be found in remote parts of the State. In colonial times, and even in the early part of the present century, there seem to have been always a few of them in the neighborhood of Philadelphia. In the old records they are sometimes spoken of as Ridge Hermits, probably because many of them were settled at a place called the Ridge, near Germantown.

There was a whole sect devoted to this hermit life, and called the "Society of the Woman of the Wilderness," which arrived as early as 1694. They were probably the least numerous religious body that came from Germany, and they were apparently an order of Pietists. They settled among the dark, romantic ravines of the Wissahickon, now within the limits of Fairmount Park. After a time most of them returned to the world. But

The Germans

Kelpius, Seelig, Mathias, and a few others persevered to the end, and Whittier, in his Pennsylvania Pilgrim, has a short verse for Kelpius :

> "Or painful Kelpius from his hermit den,
> By Wissahickon, maddest of good men,
> Dreamed o'er the Chiliast dreams of Petersen."

This Society of the Woman of the Wilderness is said to have been composed almost entirely of students, whose peculiar opinions had driven them from the German universities. Their learning, we are assured, was prodigious. Kelpius is said to have known Hebrew, Greek, and Latin, and to have been able to write English with remarkable purity. They believed in the near approach of the Millennium, when the woman mentioned in the Book of Revelation should come up from the wilderness leaning on the arm of her beloved, and deliver the Church. They are said to have devoted themselves to the education of the poor. But at the same time they practised magic and astrology, and also ordinary fortune-telling.

These very learned Germans have been somewhat enlarged upon in recent years, and there has been a tendency to make extraordinary claims of merit for them. It has even been suggested that their wonderful knowledge and the sufferings they endured in the crowded immigrant ships entitled them to greater consideration than the Pilgrim Fathers and other English colonists. As has happened with almost every State and element of population in the Union, it has been at times hinted that perhaps these dreamers were the real creators of America, and that the peculiar features of our government and civilization must be traced to them.

The Making of Pennsylvania

When the prodigies are investigated, however, and the character and extent of their knowledge disclosed by contemporaneous evidence, we find that the learning of these astrologers was not of the effective kind. Men like Seelig, Kelpius, and others were crammed full of all sorts of book-learning, with but little genius or ability in its use. The wonderful capacity of the German for absorbing information often produces queer characters, and Mr. Charles G. Leland, from his long familiarity with the German-American, has some apt remarks on this subject :

> " America abounds with Germans who, having received in their youth a 'classical education,' have passed through varied adventures, and often present the most startling paradoxes of thought and personal appearance. I have seen a man bearing a keg, a porter, who could speak Latin fluently. I have been in a beer-shop kept by a man who was distinguished in the Frankfort Parliament. I have found a graduate of the University of Munich in a negro-minstrel troupe." (Leland's Hans Breitmann's Ballads, edition 1884, p. 5.)

The Tunkers, as they arrived, joined the Mennonites in Germantown, and the two sects built up what must have been a very pretty village, which straggled for several miles on both sides of a wide road, which is now the Main Street of Germantown. Peach-trees, bending under the weight of fruit, flourished along both sides of the road. The houses were of peculiar architecture, built usually of stone in the most substantial manner, with curious roofs and pent-eaves. Some of the houses were two stories high ; others had only one story and an attic, with their gable ends towards the road. Behind them extended large gardens full of strange plants, many of them growing for the first time in American soil. Some of these houses and the remains of some of the gardens are still to be found, together with a few descendants of the Mennonites.

They appear to have been a rather well-to-do people, of a much higher class than the immigrants that followed them. Pastorius and his learned friends had collected them in Germany, obtained from Penn the grant of land on which they settled, and it was natural that a rather better sort of people should attach themselves to leaders of such high character.

The village was at first unnamed, and called the German Town, which after a while was spelled as it now is. It was the first German settlement on American soil, and was incorporated in 1691 with a good array of Germans and Dutchmen for officers:

"Francis Daniel Pastorius, bailiff; Jacob Telner, Dirck Op den Graeff, and Thones Kunders, burgesses; Abraham Op den Graeff, Jacob Isaacs Van Bebber, Johannes Kassel, Heivert Papen, Hermann Bom, and Dirck Van Kolk, committeemen."

These worthy burghers Whittier has described as associating in easy, friendly familiarity with Pastorius, discussing the strange mysteries of their religion, and leading lives of gentle simplicity among their gardens and farms:

"Or talking of old home scenes Op de Graaf
Teased the low back-log with his shodden staff,
Till the red embers broke into a laugh."

Citizenship under such pious rulers was not to be considered a trifle, and immigrants were obliged to pay one pound sterling for the privilege. That there might be no mistake in their knowledge of the laws, the people were

The Making of Pennsylvania

to be called together on the 19th of January in every
year, and the laws and ordinances read aloud to them.
The learned Pastorius contrived a seal for their little
town, and, as most of them were weavers and had come
from a country of vineyards, he made it consist of a
clover-leaf on which were a vine, a stalk of flax, and a
weaver's spool, with the words "Vinum, Linum, Tex-
trinum."

It was difficult, however, to get these good people to
carry on a government even under such an ingenious
seal, and they finally lost their charter by failure to
elect officers under it. Like the Quakers, they were, in
theory, opposed to politics and all kinds of force, even
the force of a sheriff in serving a writ or making an
arrest. They were at first unwilling to proceed to force
even against thieves and trespassers; and until, like the
Quakers, they had had a full taste of the sweets of
power, resignations and refusals of office were somewhat more numerous than they are now in Germantown.

There was a curious character among them named
Anthony Klincken who might very well have been mentioned in Whittier's Pennsylvania Pilgrim. He seems to
have been well-to-do, like many of the others, and devoted himself almost entirely to hunting, for which the
surrounding wilderness afforded abundant opportunity.
But the best place for duck shooting, he always said,
was the little spatterdock pond close to Philadelphia,
where Fourth and Market Streets now intersect. He
usually took his gun with him when he went to Philadelphia in autumn and winter, and seldom failed to be
rewarded at the pond. He imported a German yäger
36

to assist him in his expeditions, and his home was always full of game carefully labelled with the date when it was killed.

The German village was a pleasant resort for the Philadelphians in summer, and they fled to it in great numbers after the Revolution during the epidemics of yellow fever. It was unlike Philadelphia, and remained thoroughly German until the beginning of the present century. It has continued to be a summer resort down into our own time; and many are still alive who remember the last of its old German characteristics, which have now pretty much all disappeared.

The Tunkers and the Mennonites established schools, a printing-press, and a newspaper conducted by Christopher Sauer, a Tunker elder. The old German-town Academy, which still exists, was founded in part by their efforts. For fully a century Germantown was the head-quarters of the Pennsylvania Dutch and the German-Americans. Sauer's newspaper had a wide circulation among all the Germans from New York to Georgia, and for a time Sauer also published a maga-zine, probably the first one that appeared in America.

Like the little colony at Ephrata, the Germantown people sent out their books, almanacs, tracts, and maga-zines, all in German, and all devoted to holding together the Germans as a distinct race and keeping up their language, traditions, and customs. Sauer published the first German Bible that was printed in this country. He manufactured his type, paper, and ink, and bound his own books. He also sold medicines and practised as a doctor.

Like Franklin, he greatly increased his influence by

an excellent almanac he sent out every year, and in that day almanacs had more influence with the masses than newspapers. He was the sort of character and possessed the sort of homely knowledge and skill that carried great weight among the sects, and Muhlenberg, who was the leader of the Lutherans, often complained of his power. His son, of the same name, continued his business, inherited a large part of his influence, and added two hundred books to the list of his father's publications.

Sauer had a quarrel with Beissel, the head of the Ephrata community, which is somewhat characteristic. In 1739, when Beissel had no printing-press, he got Sauer to print for him a book called "Weyrauchs Hügel," containing seven hundred and ninety-two pages of hymns. It was the first book printed by Sauer, and the first book printed in German type in America. It was dedicated, after the mystic manner of the Ephrata people, "To all solitary turtle-doves cooing in the wilderness as a spiritual harp—playing in the many tunes of divine visitation," and the thirty-seventh verse of the four hundredth hymn has been translated by Judge Pennypacker :

> " Look, look, look,
> Look upon the man ;
> He is exalted by God ;
> He is our Lord and Christ."

One of Sauer's printers told his master that in this verse Beissel intended to represent himself as a second Christ. Sauer immediately wrote to Beissel asking him if it was true, and Beissel in reply not improperly told him that he was a fool. Whereupon Sauer published a

pamphlet against Beissel, in which he charged, among
other things, that his name contained the number six
hundred and sixty-six of the beast of the Apocalypse;
that he had received something from all the planets,
—"from Mars his strength, from Venus his influence
over women, and from Mercury his comedian tricks."
By this mystic, astrologic quarrel Sauer lost for the
future all the printing of the Ephrata community. The
indignant Beissel set up a press of his own, and the only
wonder is that the quarrel did not result in a new sect.

Many of the early Mennonites were from Holland, or
from the parts of Germany adjacent to Holland, where
the Dutch language was spoken. These could have
been properly called Dutch; but the term Dutch
gradually came to be applied to the whole German
population, probably for the reason that their own
name for themselves was Deutsch. In some parts of
the United States, especially in Virginia, the country
people, it is said, still use the word Dutch to describe
anything that is foreign; and this use of the word is
no doubt a survival from colonial times, when the only
foreigners with whom the English colonists were at all
familiar were Germans, calling themselves Deutsch.

Besides Holland many of the Pennsylvania Dutch
came from the German side of Switzerland. But the
great mass of them came from Germany proper,—from
Alsace, Suabia, Saxony, and almost every principality
and dukedom of that distracted empire, and most of
them from those parts of it called the Palatinate. They
were often spoken of as Palatines, and in the passenger
lists of the emigrant ships were always described by
that name down to the year 1740.

The Making of Pennsylvania

The Lower and the Upper Palatinate were old fiefs or divisions of the German Empire which appeared upon the map of Europe for more than a hundred years. The word appears to be related to our English word palace. The master of the palace or royal household was often given the jurisdiction of cases which the king had a right to decide; and whenever the king wished to please a baron, or the holder of an important fief, he gave him the same jurisdiction as his own master of the palace and called him a count palatine. The word was often used to describe a petty prince in any country; and we find the Episcopalians in Pennsylvania complaining, at one time, that William Penn boasted that he was the Palatinate of Pennsylvania.

The Lower Palatinate lay upon the Rhine near the provinces of Alsace and Lorraine, and contained the ancient towns of Heidelberg and Mannheim. The upper Palatinate lay towards the southeast on the Danube, and its most important town was Amberg. Most of the Germans who came to Pennsylvania appear to have been from the Lower Palatinate on the Rhine, which suffered most from the persecution and invasion of the French.

The divided condition of Germany, split up into palatinates, provinces, and fiefs, from which it has been rescued by Bismarck and Von Moltke in our own time, was a grand opportunity to the French and Louis XIV. At the close of the seventeenth century, when the Quakers founded Pennsylvania, Louis laid claim to this fief or that province as suited him, invaded them with fire and sword, and offered them the choice of Romanism or persecution. The Palatinate was at different times ruled by a Lutheran, a Reformed-Church man, and a Catholic, and at each change the people had to conform or suffer. It was such troubles as these, long continued in Germany and Switzerland, that encouraged the sects as well as the Lutherans to come to Pennsylvania.

The movement of the sects was started by William Penn and the Quakers. Penn was half a Dutchman, his mother having been a native of Holland; and he made several preaching expeditions to that country, and also to Germany, where he found these people were almost in complete agreement with him. George Fox, the founder of the Quakers, had also been twice in Germany; and a large part of the Mennonite immigration was not only encouraged by the society of Quakers, but directly assisted by them with money.

For the first twenty years, from 1682 to 1702, the German immigration was comparatively slight; and Rupp says that in that time only about two hundred families arrived, who settled for the most part in Germantown. As others arrived they passed out into the country beyond, and left Philadelphia and its environs in undisturbed possession of the Quakers.

In 1702 some of the Germantown Mennonites had begun to move out to Skippack, in Montgomery County. One of them, Matthias Van Bebber, a Hollander of some wealth, had bought six thousand acres of land in that neighborhood, and gave a hundred of it for a meeting-house. He was one of the immigrants whose families finally left Pennsylvania and went to the Bohemia Manor, near the Elk River, on the eastern shore of Maryland, a place much resorted to in colonial times, and almost as productive of well-known names as the Mayflower of old china. The Van Bebbers spread through Maryland and

Virginia and became prominent in all walks of life. One of them became a famous Indian fighter on the frontier, and a place called Van Bebber's Rock on the Kanawha River marks the scene of one of his exploits.

Some others of the Pennsylvania Dutch also dispersed themselves towards the South. Most of those that went in this direction passed out by way of Carlisle and Gettysburg into the Shenandoah Valley, which they followed into Virginia, where their descendants are to be found to this day. It was to a Lutheran congregation of these people that General Muhlenberg was preaching at the outbreak of the Revolution when he decided to become a soldier. But many of those who went to the Shenandoah Valley were of the sects, and would take no part in war. Much difficulty was experienced with them in the Revolution, and again almost a hundred years afterwards in the Civil War.

The sects seem to have had no great desire to remain in Philadelphia, although it was ruled by their friends the Quakers. A few of the Lutheran and Reformed established themselves there, and Franklin tells us that signs in the streets were often in both German and English, and sometimes in German alone. The sects, with their strong love of country life, and the greater part of the Lutherans and Reformed, pressed far out into what was then the wilderness, and left the country for many miles round Philadelphia, except at Germantown, almost entirely free from their influence.

They filled the Lehigh and Schuylkill Valleys and occupied a wide segment of a circle beginning at Easton, on the Delaware, passing westward towards the Susquehanna, through the towns of Allentown, Reading, Lebanon, and Lancaster, and thence down to the Cumberland Valley, on the Maryland border, where they had a natural outlet to Virginia and the South. The tier of counties north of this circle and along the borders of New York was comparatively free from them, and was taken by the settlers from Connecticut. In modern times, although the Germans have come no closer to Philadelphia, they have permeated, in greater or less degree, almost every other part of the State,—have even in some places displaced the Scotch-Irish, and passed westward across the Susquehanna.

The last important sect to arrive was the Schwenkfelders. About seventy families came a few years after the Tunkers, and arrived at Philadelphia in the ship "St. Andrew," September 22, 1734, a day they still celebrate with religious service and sermons, calling it Gedächtniss Tag. Other migrations of smaller numbers followed, and it has been said that no representatives of the sect were left in Europe.

They had been terribly persecuted by both Catholic and Protestant in Silesia, reduced to poverty, and had been sent to Pennsylvania by the benevolence of some merchants in Amsterdam. They were a rather old sect. Their founder, Kaspar Schwenkfeld, was born in 1490, and they grew up in the times when John Huss was preaching the earliest doctrines of the Reformation. But they went far beyond Huss, adopted the views afterwards held by the Quakers, were opposed to war, oaths, and all the ancient sacraments.

Before they came to Pennsylvania they had been hunted from place to place for two hundred years, and so strong had the habit of concealment and hiding grown upon them, that for fifty years after they settled in Montgomery County they never had a church or meeting-house, but congregated for worship in each other's dwellings, as in the old days of persecution. They settled in a body on the head-waters of the Perkiomen, where they can still be found, the only Schwenkfelders in the world, with many of the peculiarities of dress and custom which they brought from Europe nearly two hundred years ago. They are said to have been more generally well educated than any of the other German sects, and were much devoted to transcribing in beautiful writing the various volumes of their religious books, which are now highly prized as curiosities.

There were numerous other sects, which it is hardly necessary to describe. The Separatists were peculiar in holding that all church government and organization was wrong; but they appear to have had no objection to their own existence. Then there were the Amish, the United Brethren, and the smaller sects of Labadists, New Born, New Mooners, Zion's Brueder, Ronsdorfer, Inspired, Quietists, Gichtelians, Depellians, Mountain Men, and in modern times the River Brethren, Brinser Brethren, and two or three divisions of the Mennonites, each emphasizing some peculiar phase of German mysticism which was deemed important.

In Lancaster County alone, the number of sects has at different times been estimated at from twenty-two to over thirty. But such lists, which have often been prepared out of curiosity, are not supposed to be complete, and it would now be, probably, utterly impossible to give a list of all the religious divisions that have existed among the Pennsylvania Germans. The German mind, at that time, was in a ferment, and threw off sects almost every day. Their own writers describe them as countless and bewildering. Many of them existed only for a few years and disappeared, and new ones were formed. Large numbers of the people were of no religion at all. "Atheists, Deists, and Naturalists," says Muhlenberg, "are to be met with everywhere; in short, there is no sect in the world that has not followers here."

They had been accustomed to a very strict paternal government in Germany; everything had been done for them; and when they found themselves free in the forests of Pennsylvania they were more disordered than ever. There was an advantage in this, however; for the feeling among them in favor of establishing a distinct German State within the English colonies was rather strong, and their great numbers might have given force to the idea if it had not been for their disunion and divisions.

Some of those who came in with the sects, and with the Lutherans and Reformed, were Roman Catholics, and it was the general belief at that time that there were more Romanists among the German settlers than among the English. In the French and Indian wars they were strongly suspected, even by some of the Germans, of being in league with the French in Canada. They could not at best have been very numerous, for all the Catholics in the province in colonial times are supposed to have been not over two thousand. Most of the English Catholics were congregated in Philadelphia at the mission of St. Joseph, on Fourth Street.

A considerable number of Frenchmen came in with the Germans. Most of them were probably Huguenots, and among them we find such names as De Turck,

Bertolet, and De la Plaine. Their descendants are still to be found in the counties of Lancaster and Montgomery. Some of them were Catholics, and among these we find Le Tort and two brothers named Besalion, Indian traders, who were always suspected of tampering with the Indians in the interest of the French in Canada.

The Mennonites, and other sects that arrived up to the year 1702, were in many respects of a better class than the German immigrants that followed them for the next sixty or seventy years. They were possessed of more property, were less uncouth, and of much better education and intelligence than the great mass of peasantry which came afterwards. It would be a great mistake to judge of the whole German immigration by what we read of the gentle Schwenkfelders, the peaceful and peculiar Tunker or Mennonite, or the men of education or prominence who accompanied them.

Many of the Lutheran and Reformed were very rough, as Schlatter and Muhlenberg discovered to their sorrow. Even among those who were fleeing from cruel persecution, and deserved the sympathy and assistance of every enlightened man, there appear to have been large numbers whose appearance was not at all unlikely to arouse prejudice among English colonists. They had come from mountain fastnesses or from obscure country districts, where they had been hiding; they had suffered hardships in reaching the sea, and still greater hardships on the two months' voyage. Their dress was peculiar; many of them were staring and strange like wild animals, carried weapons, and spoke an unintelligible dialect; they wore huge wooden shoes; and the men who settled in Lancaster were described as wearing long red caps, and the women without either hats or caps, tying a string over their heads to keep the hair from their faces.

In fact, this German migration was largely composed of peasants, many of them very much like the peasants whom we have seen in our own time landing from the emigrant ships at New York. They were the first of that class to reach American soil, and were utterly unlike the English yeomanry that settled Virginia, New England, and most of the other colonies.

The reason for the change of character in the German immigrants after 1702 seems to have been the adoption of a new policy by Queen Anne, who ascended the throne in that year. Anne and her ministry seem to have been impressed with the idea that it would strengthen the British Empire to keep the English more at home on their island and fill up the colonies with Germans, or any unfortunate and cheap people from the Continent, provided they were Protestants and hostile to France and Spain.

To this end efforts were made to collect all the discontented Germans, oppressed by war, poverty, persecution, and a disunited and broken country, and transport them to the colonies. In this attempt the Quakers as a sect do not seem to have taken much part. Their attention was confined chiefly to encouraging the peace sects who were in sympathy with themselves, and they cared nothing about the Lutherans and Reformed or the masses of the rough German peasantry.

The British government circulated books and papers in the Palatinate and other provinces to encourage emigration. The books had a picture of the queen, and a title-page in gold letters, and were long known among the poor people whom they were intended to influence as the Golden Books. They produced a great effect, and there was soon what has been called a landslide of humanity in the German population. During the two years 1708 and 1709 over thirty thousand of them crossed over to England.

The Golden Books and the devastation of war and persecution had been assisted by a very severe winter, in which birds and animals were frozen in the fields and men fell dead on the roads. For a time the government had more success with its new plan than it desired, for these people were utterly destitute, and created no little alarm and considerable riot among the lower classes. They were sheltered in tents on the commons and fields near London, and the process of transporting them to Pennsylvania, New York, and the Carolinas was begun.

Several thousand, including most of those who were Roman Catholics, were picked out and sent back to Germany. About three thousand were sent to Ireland. They settled in a part of Limerick County, where, it is said, their descendants are still to be found retaining many of their old customs and, to some extent, their language. The rest were sent to America, and nearly everybody who had a land scheme, or a colony on their hands, took a few of them as a cheap way of developing values. The famous John Law got several thousand for his project in Louisiana, and might have obtained many more if he had not allowed his first cargo to perish in the marshes of Mobile.

After the greater part of these unfortunates had been disposed of, the policy of importing other Germans

The Germans

to the colonies was continued in a more regular and systematic manner, and seems to have found favor with English statesmen for the next seventy years. Burke, in his "Account of the European Settlements of America," speaks of it approvingly, but with the qualification that the imported should be compelled to learn the English language and customs.

For many years large numbers continued to go to England to be shipped. But as time went on it became more and more the habit to transport them direct from their own country. The vessels that carried them from Germany usually touched at an English port to be cleared and have their cargo justified under the authority of the British government. A regular emigrant trade sprang up, and vessels were chartered to proceed to Rotterdam and load Palatines for Pennsylvania just as they were chartered for cargoes of rum, molasses, or negroes. The owners and captains were not altogether unlike the typical slavers, and the Palatine voyage to America was not far removed from the horrors of the middle passage.

The small snows and brigs carried from fifty to a hundred people; other vessels between two and three hundred, and the large ships between five and six hundred. In one year as many as twelve thousand arrived. By the year 1717 the traffic had so much increased that Governor Keith became uneasy, and called the attention of the Provincial Council to the great numbers of Germans, ignorant of the language and laws, that were flocking into the province, and dispersing daily throughout the country without giving any account of themselves or their intentions. They had no license from Great

99

Britain, and made no application for any to the Colony, which was a dangerous practice, and might let in enemies as well as friends.

The Council took some heed of the governor's warnings, and ordered all captains who had lately imported such people to appear and give an account of them. It was also ordered that the foreigners recently landed should take an oath of allegiance, and that hereafter no inward-bound vessel should be given an entry until her master had given a list of his passengers.

Apparently, these regulations were not enforced at all, or were not well enforced until 1727, when they were made more elaborate, and after that there seems to have been a systematic regulation. The captains turned in lists, and the immigrants were all sworn or affirmed on a long oath of allegiance. This change was brought about by Governor Gordon, who, like Keith, called the attention of the Council to the possible danger from such immigrants, who, he said, were settling the country as a distinct people. The minutes of the Council also show the same distrust:

" The Board taking the same into their serious Consideration, observe, that as these People pretended at first that they fly hither on the Score of their religious Liberties, and come under the Protection of His Majesty, it is requisite in the first Place they should take the Oath of Allegiance, or some equivalent to it to His Majesty, and promise Fidelity to the Proprietor & obedience to our established Constitution ; And therefore, until some proper Remedy can be had from Home, to prevent the Importation of such Numbers of Strangers into this or others of His Majesties Colonies it is ordered" &c. (3 Colonial Records, 282.)

The lists furnished by the captains usually contained the names of all the male passengers above the age of sixteen years. Marks are said to have been made oppo-

site those who had died or were sick; but there is some
evidence that this precaution was often neglected, which
gave the shipping-agents and sailors an opportunity to
plunder the dead.

Other lists were made on shore of those who took the
oath of allegiance. These also contained only the names
of males above the age of sixteen, and they are peculiarly interesting, because they are the autograph signa-
tures of the immigrants who could write. Those who
could not write had their names written for them by a
clerk. All these lists were preserved in the Secretary's
office; but in recent years they have been much muti-
lated, and many of them stolen. It was by copying the
autograph lists and commenting on them that Rupp
made up his valuable book, " Thirty Thousand Names of
German Emigrants." As we turn its pages and read the
entries of the vessels and other details, we seem to be
brought nearer to this old German immigration, and
realize more fully its meaning :

" Oct. 1, 1754, Ship Phœnix, John Spurrier, Captain, from Rotterdam,
last from Cowes.—Inhabitants from Franconia, the Palatinate, and Zwei-
brucken,—seventeen Roman Catholics, twenty-five Mennonites.—554
passengers."

The condition in which the immigrants reached Philadelphia was shocking. The ships were floating hospitals
and pest-houses, filled with small-pox and all the other
diseases of crowding and dirt, which gathered frightful
intensity from the voyage of two or three months. One
ship reached the coast, after a voyage of six months,
with the surviving passengers living on rats and vermin.
Vessels often lost on the passage one-third of their

human freight, and one ship is said to have arrived after having lost two hundred and fifty.

Sauer said that in one year two thousand of the Germans had died in crossing the Atlantic, and this estimate does not seem to be excessive. The Palatine ship that was wrecked on Block Island in 1738, and celebrated in Whittier's verse, is said to have started out with four hundred passengers, who at the time of the wreck were reduced by a malignant fever and flux to one hundred and five, and of this remnant ten died a few days after they were taken ashore.

The delays in the voyage were numerous. Before reaching the ship the people had to pass through thirty or forty custom-houses on the Rhine, at each of which they were delayed often several days, so that this Rhine journey usually consumed five or six weeks, and completely exhausted their slender stock of money and provisions. Other delays of five or six weeks occurred at the seaports, and the poor immigrants, starving and desperate, sold themselves as redemptioners to the captains and shipping-agents. Mittelberger, in his " Journey to Pennsylvania in 1750," has described what they suffered on the voyage.

" In Rotterdam and Amsterdam they begin to pack the people in like herring, and since the ships insist on carrying not less than four, five, or six hundred souls, besides enormous cargoes of household utensils, chests, water-casks, and provisions, many are obliged to occupy berths scarcely two feet wide by six long. . . .

" It is not, however, till the ship has raised its anchor for the last time and started on its eight, nine, ten, eleven, or twelve weeks' sail for Philadelphia that the greatest misery is experienced. Then there are heart-rending scenes ! The filth and stench of the vessels no pen could describe, while the diverse diseases, sea-sickness in every form, headaches,

The Germans

biliousness, constipation, dysentery, scarlet-fever, scrofula, cancers, etc., caused by the miserable salt food and the vile drinking water are truly deplorable, not to speak of the deaths which occur on every side.

"In addition to all this, one invariably meets with an actual scarcity of every kind of provisions, with hunger, thirst, frost, severe heat, an ugly wet vessel, murmurings, complaints, anxiety, loathsome contagious diseases, and other innumerable varieties of tribulations, such as lice in such numbers that they can literally be taken in quantities from the bodies of the passengers, especially of the sick. Forlorn, though, as the situation is, the climax is not yet reached. That comes when, for the space of two or three days, all on board, the sick and dying as well as those in health, are tossed mercilessly to and fro, and rolled about on top of one another, the storm-tossed vessel seeming each moment as if in the next it would be engulfed by the angry, roaring waves. . . .

"Even those who escape sickness sometimes grow so bitterly impatient and cruel that they curse themselves and the day of their birth, and then in wild despair commence to kill those around them. Want and wickedness go hand and hand, and lead to trickery and deception of every kind. One blames another for having induced him to undertake the voyage. Husbands reproach their wives, wives their husbands, children their parents, parents their children, and friends their friends, while all denounce the cruel Newlanders whose trade it is to steal human beings.

"Many heave deep drawn sighs, and exclaim, mournfully, 'O God! O God! if I only had a piece of good bread or one drop of fresh water!' or cry out in the anguish of their souls, 'Oh, if I were only at home and lying in my pig-sty!' The wailings and lamentations continue day and night, and, as one body after another is committed to a watery grave, those who induced their unfortunate companions to leave their old home in search of a new are driven to the verge of despair.

"The sufferings of the poor women who are pregnant can scarcely be imagined. They rarely live through the voyage, and many a mother with her tiny babe is thrown into the water almost ere life is extinct. During a severe storm on our vessel one poor creature who, owing to the trying circumstances, was unable to give birth to her child, was shoved through an opening in the ship and allowed to drop into the water, because it was not convenient to attend to her. . . .

"It is little wonder that so many of the passengers are seized with sickness and disease, for, in addition to all their other hardships and miseries, they have cooked food only three times a week, and this (it is always of a decidedly inferior quality, and served in very small quantities) is so filthy that the very sight of it is loathsome. Moreover, the drinking water is so black, thick, and full of worms that it makes one shudder to look at it, and even those suffering the tortures of thirst frequently find it almost impossible to swallow it."

The Quakers were obliged to provide for the immigrants and prepare hospitals to receive them, and the physicians who made Philadelphia famous as a centre of medical education gained some of their first experience in this way. The ships as they arrived were held at arm's-length as long as possible, detained below the city under inspection, and when allowed to come up abreast of the town, compelled to anchor in the middle of the stream and discharge the Palatines in boats. These long detentions often caused much suffering, and on at least one occasion brought on disputes between the governor and the Assembly; each charging the other with unnecessary delay.

The numbers arriving seem to have varied considerably at different times. But on the whole it was a systematic and, for many years, an almost continuous movement of immigration, with many of the characteristics to which we have become accustomed in the similar system of our own time, which has reached such huge proportions. The greater part of it was of the assisted sort, and the assistance and encouragement came in great measure from the shipping-agents, who were interested in the freight.

In the recent investigations of Congress it has been discovered that the principal part of modern immigration is induced by the steamship lines, who have thousands of agents scattered all over Europe, who paint the glories of America, persuade the peasant, and are paid a commission on the number of tickets they sell. In the German immigration to Pennsylvania there was a similar system, and a class of men sprang up usually called newlanders, and sometimes soul-sellers, who are much complained of by Rupp, Seidensticker, and other German historians. They passed to and fro and scattered themselves over Germany, working up the traffic and managing the people by every trick and device that suggested itself. They had no hesitation in getting men drunk, or getting them to sign papers they had not read, if they could accomplish their purpose, and their profits were in proportion to the number they deluded.

The early immigration of Mennonites and Tunkers that settled Germantown does not appear to have been assisted in this way, and it is probable that a large proportion of the sects came independently of any regular system of ship-owners. But, as a general rule, from the year 1705 to the Revolution most of the German immigrants were uprooted from their native soil at first by the Golden Books of Queen Anne, and after that by the systematic encouragement of men who enjoyed the profits of transporting them.

Mann, in his " Life of Muhlenberg," says that the shipping-agents had discovered that the Germans migrated more easily if they knew that one of their clergy was to go in the ship, and the agents were on the alert to persuade such men, or men who would pass as such, to take passage. This may, perhaps, partially account for the charlatan preachers who gave Muhlenberg so much trouble, and also for the large number of schoolmasters who were often half preacher.

Besides their legitimate profit in passage money, the

shipping people enjoyed the proceeds of selling many of the immigrants as redemptioners, and the poor creatures were also regularly plundered of their clothes and goods. Their money was taken from them, their sea-chests rifled, and those possessed of means compelled to pay the passage of the poorer ones. Although attempts were made by the provincial government to regulate the traffic, they were usually directed to preventing the spread of dangerous diseases on shore, and to limiting the numbers that could be carried on a single ship. The plundering and ill-treatment seem to have continued down to the Revolution, for in 1774, Lewis Weiss sent a memorial to the provincial council describing the evils as still in full force.*

Rupp has described very explicitly the method of selling the redemptioners :

"The usual terms of sale depended somewhat on the age, strength, and health of the persons sold. Boys and girls usually had to serve from five to ten years till they attained the age of twenty-one. Many parents were necessitated, as they had been wont at home to do with their cattle, sell their own children. The children had to assume the passage, both their own and that of their parents, in order that the latter might be released from the ship. Children under five years of age could not be sold. They were disposed of gratuitously to such persons as offered to raise them, and let them go free when they attained the age of twenty-one." (Rupp's Note to Rush's Manners of the Pennsylvania Germans, 8.)

This redemption system, which seems now like a species of white slavery, was not considered a very serious evil, even by people who at that time disapproved of negro slavery. There is no trace of any stigma or disgrace attaching to a redemptioner. Re-

* 4 Penna. Archives, 473.

spectable families, well thought of by their neighbors, have descended from such people; and Germans of means are said to have voluntarily sold themselves to contract labor of this sort for the sake of more quickly becoming familiar with the methods of the new country.

The way in which this assisted immigration was distributed among the colonies was very significant. It is probable that the British government wished it distributed among all of them, but, as a matter of fact, a small part of it went to the Carolinas and Georgia, some to New York, and the principal part to Pennsylvania. Americans at that time were by no means all convinced of the benefit of encouraging alien immigration. It was the general feeling to expect immigrants only from Great Britain, and they were spoken of usually as new-comers, while those of other nationalities were called foreigners, and had to be naturalized.

The New England colonies received no immigration of any importance, even from England, after 1640, became very homogeneous, and had a strong dislike for outside influence. The Germans not only received no encouragement from that quarter, but would, in all probability, not have been permitted to land there. Virginia was thoroughly English and Episcopalian, and, while not so exclusive as New England, showed little or no inclination to encourage foreigners.

New York, having been originally settled by the Dutch and conquered by the English, was already a somewhat mixed community, and held out some inducements for the Germans. Many of them went there. But the attractions of Pennsylvania were stronger. That province was already very mixed in its population, had never been homogeneous, had very liberal laws, and had given out that it was ready to receive all sorts and conditions of men. The Germans were more kindly treated there than in the other colonies, and this soon became known in the Fatherland. In New York they were by no means well received, and one flagrant instance of injustice turned the tide more strongly than ever towards Pennsylvania.

Among the Germans who were the first to respond to the Golden Books of Queen Anne, and were protected in tents on Blackmoor, near London, were about four thousand who were shipped in ten vessels for New York. Some Mohawk chiefs, then on an embassy to England, are said to have suggested their shipment and offered a tract of land west of the Hudson. The voyage consumed six months, and seventeen hundred of them died at sea. They appear to have been under an agreement to manufacture tar and raise hemp for the government naval stores to pay for their passage. They were delivered to Governor Hunter, who quartered them on Governor's Island, in New York harbor, took care of the women and sick, apprenticed the numerous orphans among the people of the province, and took the able-bodied up the Hudson to work out their contract on Livingston Manor.

The German description of this transaction makes it consist of fraud, perfidy, and extortion, from beginning to end, and even after due allowance made for all exaggerations, there remains a strong suspicion of a private enterprise on the part of the governor and his friends, who found themselves in control of some cheap and ignorant labor. As the Germans tell the story, they were obliged to remain in a state of helpless slavery for three or four years, when, having had some communication with the Indians, most of them broke away and entered on the lands promised them in the Schoharie Valley.

The governor and his friends allowed them to settle and plant their crops, and when they seemed to be somewhat advanced in prosperity they were informed that they had no title to the land and must pay for it. The price demanded seemed to them exorbitant. Some submitted and remained. Others scattered themselves over the country.

In 1723, Keith, the governor of Pennsylvania, being at Albany and hearing of their condition, intimated that there was room for them in his province. Thirty-three families of them united, cut a road through the woods to the head-waters of the Susquehanna, and floated their goods down it until they came to the mouth of the Swatara. Following up this stream, they established themselves in the wide, fertile valley of the Tulpehocken, west of Reading and south of the Blue Mountains, where their descendants are still living. The long years of suffering they endured before they found this retreat were well known in Germany, and their countrymen who were compelled by the course of immigrant vessels to land at New York usually crossed the Jerseys and entered Pennsylvania.

All classes and sects of the Germans became farmers, and in that occupation, Dr. Rush assures us, they excelled the Scotch-Irish, and all the other settlers in the province. They took better care of their cattle, had better fences, and often built their barns and stables before they built their houses. They were good judges of land, always selected the best, and were very fond of the limestone districts. They never avoided a tract because it had on it great forest trees which would require unusual labor to remove, for they knew that a heavy growth of timber showed the richness of the soil. They were also shrewd enough to buy land which had already been cultivated by unskilful settlers, and were often known to grow rich on farms where their predecessors had starved. In this way they drove out many of the English, and in North-ampton County and the Cumberland Valley displaced some of the hardy Scotch-Irish.

Their economy was extraordinary. The other colonists usually destroyed the forests by girdling the trees, and after they had fallen to the ground, burnt them. But to the Germans this seemed a wicked waste and they seldom resorted to it, but cut down each individual tree, and preserved every stick of it as though it were gold.

The other colonists built their houses with a chimney at each end and with two huge open fireplaces, in which in winter they threw mighty logs and sat round them, their faces burning hot and their backs cold. The Germans had only one chimney, which saved expense in building, and they heated their houses with stoves which burned comparatively little wood, and saved the time and labor of cutting it. Their use of stoves is said to have given their houses an even temperature, which enabled their women to work at various useful occupations in the long winter evenings, which were passed by the wives and daughters of the other settlers in idleness, with benumbed fingers, shifting places round their romantic and wasteful fires.

The Germans

Most of the Germans hated debt, and were, as a rule, very punctual in their engagements. They worked their farms with their sons, daughters, and wives, and had very few slaves. They developed a fine breed of heavy draught horses called Conestogas, from a stream near Lancaster where they were first bred. The same name, Conestoga, was applied to their wagons, strong and solid as a fortification, and covered with a great canvas roof like the prairie schooners of later times. Until far down into the present century these wagons were one of the most typical scenes on all the highways of eastern Pennsylvania, as, filled with chickens, turkeys, and all kinds of the best country produce, they rolled slowly towards the towns.

It is to be feared that many of the Germans too often followed that rule, of selling everything, giving what was left to the pigs, and what the pigs would not eat taking for themselves, by which, it is said, a farmer is sure to grow rich. Both in colonial times and after they have probably often injured themselves with too much economy. Dr. Rush mentions the opinion, as prevailing in his time, that they abstained so much from animal food as to lose their vigor early in life.

The church people, as they are called, the Reformed and the Lutherans, did not begin to arrive in great numbers much before 1725. The sects, especially at first, usually came in united, organized bodies. But the Reformed and Lutherans were, for the most part, disconnected and irregular in their migration, and had to be afterwards organized with much difficulty by Schlatter and Muhlenberg. At first the sects far outnumbered the church people; but long before the Revolution the two divisions were about equal. After that the church people increased rapidly, and are now a great deal the more numerous.

The Reformed and the Lutheran Churches of Europe, if not founded by the teachings of Zwinglius and Luther, respectively, may be said to have had those men for their earliest representatives. The Reformed has had various names in the countries where it has prevailed, as the Dutch Reformed in Holland, the German Reformed in Germany, and now with us the Reformed Church in the United States. In Switzerland, Calvin became its most striking leader, and some of its most characteristic doctrines have been called by his name. In England and America these doctrines and the general principles of the Reformed Churches have usually prevailed among the Presbyterians and Congregationalists.

The members of the Reformed Church of Germany are sometimes spoken of as German Calvinists, and in old books of Pennsylvania history are often called simply Calvinists. They also appear to have been sometimes spoken of as Presbyterians, a name which, in colonial times, was often applied to the New England Congregationalists. These terms are, of course, all misleading, and we shall confine ourselves to the word Reformed, which always identifies them.

The Reformed in Germany were not very much given to the doctrines distinctively known as Calvinism, and those of them who came to this country were still less inclined to such principles. They differed from the Lutherans in being, perhaps, more metaphysical or speculative, and more severe in their forms of worship. The Lutherans permitted images, altars, tapers, private confessional, and had a belief which somewhat resembled the doctrine of the real presence. All these were rejected by the Reformed. The Lutherans were closely connected with the state in Germany, while the Reformed were always independent of it.

About four hundred of the Reformed came to Pennsylvania in 1727, under the lead of the Rev. George Michael Weiss, and settled along the Skippack. Others followed, and in 1747 the Rev. Michael Schlatter organized all the Reformed in Pennsylvania as part of the synod of Holland, under which they remained until 1793, when they became an independent American church.

The Lutherans, who began to arrive soon after, became much more numerous, and in time were double the numbers of the Reformed. Their leader, Muhlenberg, was a man of great executive ability, and a natural organizer. Schlatter seems to have been less efficient in this respect, and was continually involving himself in difficulties.

Muhlenberg, who became the leader of the Lutherans not only in Pennsylvania, but in all the other colonies, belonged to the Pietist party in his church, the party which was called radical, and which seems to have been more fervid, more given to philanthropy and the alleviation of suffering, and more apt to rely on feelings and excitement than the conservatives, who had become perfunctory in their devotion to dogmas. There was also among the Pietist party a tinge of that subjectiveness and quietism which had created the Mennonites and the Quakers. But, at the same time, they considered themselves as still holding to the ancient landmarks of the Lutherans.

They had many affinities with the Episcopalians, who at that time looked upon them as likely to become a church in communion with themselves, if not actual converts. Muhlenberg was invited to preach in Episcopal churches, and was a trustee of the Church of England Society for the relief of the widows and children of its clergy. When his son Peter was called to a Lutheran congregation in Virginia, where under the law he could have no standing unless he was a clergyman of the Church of England, he, without the slightest hesitation, went to England and was ordained. He had no intention of giving up his convictions as a Lutheran, and the Lutheran Synod saw nothing objectionable in his course.*

When Muhlenberg arrived among the Pennsylvania Germans, in 1742, he found he had to deal with a very rough, suspicious, and disorderly people. The Moravians were cutting into them and claimed them all. Many of them were falling under the influence of the sects and Christopher Sauer. Vagabond preachers and frauds of all kinds were wandering among them, extorting money at the communion-table, and turning them into a disorganized rabble at the mercy of every new eccentricity that the learned and mystic German mind could invent. A large part of Muhlenberg's life was spent in fighting off these creatures, many of whom were mere scamps and adventurers.

" At the present time old and young self-appointed pastors, offended keepers of inns and groceries, silversmiths and beerhouse fiddlers, dancing-masters, entire companies of recently-arrived Nethinim (1 Chron. ix. 2), and the insane rabble of Sichem (Sirach i. 28), gather together, throw dust into the air, and raise, with their cursing and blaspheming,

---

* Mann's Life of Muhlenberg, 390, 427.

such a confusion that the town-clerk himself might be perplexed (Acts xix. 23–40). The sum and substance amounts to this: we are called Halle Pietists, Moravian rogues, impostors, thieves of collection-moneys, etc., etc. The German newspapers supplement the deficiencies of this fermentation. The civil authorities in this free latitude cannot take any steps in our behalf unless there should be gross acts of violence and personal injury; lawyers look upon us with contempt, since we have no money to engage their services." (Mann's Life of Muhlenberg, 299.)

When Muhlenberg arrived he found five congregations of Lutherans in the province, but three of them had been won over to the Moravians, who at that time believed themselves a part of the Lutheran Church. He had to content himself at first with the two that remained, New Hanover and New Providence. Out of these he rapidly built up a strong following, and soon overcame the efforts of the Moravians.

He was by far the ablest and most liberal-minded man of all the German immigrants. We hear no stories of his prodigious learning or many languages. He had had a university education at Göttingen which, instead of overwhelming his faculties, had broadened and enlightened his native shrewdness and strengthened his high character and integrity. Yet among his own countrymen in Pennsylvania he was almost to his dying day the victim of all sorts of petty, dirty tales. His morals were attacked. He was accused of stealing, turning papist, drawing double pay, collecting contributions from his parishioners and at the same time receiving a secret salary from Germany. That he rose superior to all these difficulties, which overwhelmed Schlatter, and out of them succeeded in organizing a powerful church, not only in Pennsylvania, but all over the Union, is one of the many proofs of his strong character.

The Making of Pennsylvania

In colonial times it may be said that there were three leaders of opinion among the Germans,—Sauer, with his newspaper for the sects, Schlatter for the Reformed, and Muhlenberg for the Lutherans. Of these, Sauer was in some respects the most powerful, and his influence among his own people was more complete. He controlled, through his journal, not only the sects, but many who properly belonged to Schlatter and Muhlenberg.

Sauer's adherents always voted and sympathized with the Quakers, were averse to war, and in the Revolution were sometimes in danger of being roughly handled by both patriots and Tories. When that contest closed in favor of the Americans, some of them refused to live under a government founded on force, and moved to Canada.

The followers of Schlatter and Muhlenberg were always quite friendly with each other. Many of them took part in the Revolution, and Muhlenberg's son, Peter, who had gone to Virginia, became a famous general. But the mass of the Germans, whether of the sects or of the church people, were always regarded with more or less suspicion by the English, both in the French and Indian War and in the Revolution. Muhlenberg complains with much bitterness of the way in which the militia jeered at him and called him a Hessian.

Both Schlatter and Muhlenberg, however, were firm believers in the supremacy of the English race in America, and in the importance of all the Germans learning English and becoming Americanized as soon as possible. Muhlenberg taught English, and was careful to have his sons educated in it before they were sent to Germany to study for the ministry. Schlatter, after

being several years in the province, was so convinced
of the illiterate and disordered state of his countrymen
that he made a special report to Holland and Germany.
His report was translated in England and attracted much
attention. He received money from Germany and Holland, six young ministers to assist him, and the interest
on a fund of twelve thousand pounds. Prominent people
in England became convinced of the great importance
of teaching the Germans English. Funds were raised,
and under the leadership of Provost Smith, Franklin,
Chief-Justice Allen, and others, a system of English
schools for the Germans was instituted in 1755.

Schlatter was made the general supervisor of these
schools, and Muhlenberg gave them his hearty encouragement and active support. At the height of their
success they contained about seven hundred and fifty
pupils, and they may be said to have been successful for
seven or eight years. But the strenuous opposition of
Sauer and the confusions of the French and Indian Wars
destroyed them. A somewhat similar attempt was continued for a long time at the college of Philadelphia by
having a special German department, and it was hoped
that it would accomplish great things among the Germans, but its success was very trifling.

The mass of the Germans, especially the sects, were
determined from the beginning to keep their own language, literature, and customs, and create a little Germany
in the midst of Pennsylvania. In this they have been
largely successful. In colonial times the services in
their churches were conducted in German, and the
majority of the people were unable to speak English.
German is still the language of most of their churches,

and great numbers of the people whose ancestors have been in the country more than a hundred and fifty years cannot yet speak English.

The German they speak has degenerated into a patois called Pennsylvania Dutch, and is described as a dialect of South Germany with an infusion of English. This strange form of speech is still the spoken language of a large part of the population of Pennsylvania. Many speak it fluently and speak English with difficulty, and the English spoken is generally a sad mixture, of which the best that can be said is, that like the Irish brogue it often affords much amusement. In the towns of Lancaster, Lebanon, York, Reading, Allentown, Easton, and Harrisburg, Pennsylvania Dutch is constantly heard, and in some of these towns there are comparatively few people who speak English exclusively.

In clinging to their customs many of the Germans have been equally successful, and it has been said that in some parts of Pennsylvania there is more of the old Germany of two hundred years ago than in the German Empire itself. Many of them still refuse to vote or take any part in government. Some of them still love to have their religious books bound in old-fashioned, deeply-stamped white vellum with great brass clasps. They could hardly believe a religion that came out of any other sort of book.

Their maxims and traditions are most conservative, and of high rank among them is that one which instructs a son not to attempt to improve on the ways of his father. The sects continue to administer their sacrament of feet-washing, and their religious services often last all day. One division of them, the Amish, distinguish themselves from the others by fastening their clothes with hooks and eyes, instead of buttons. They still use a hymn-book that was written three hundred years ago, and still sing of Felix Mantz, who was drowned at Zurich in 1526, and of Sattler, who had his tongue torn out the next year.

The persecution in the Reformation was more relentless on the continent than in the British Islands, and these German sects were visited with fire and torture, compared with which the sufferings of Puritan and Quaker count for almost nothing. Under the rule of Philip II. of Spain six thousand are said to have been put to death, and the final persecution of 1659 almost extinguished some of the heresies. There are many families among the Pennsylvania sects that can trace themselves back to an ancestor burned at the stake.

They have always had, and still retain, a strong prejudice against education. In colonial times the men are said to have been usually able to read and write, and the women to read, but not to write. The autograph immigrant lists in which they signed the oath of allegiance seem to show, however, that a large number of the men could not write. Many of the names are written by a clerk. In these lists printed in Rupp's book the names of those who could not write are marked with a star, and any one can easily see by turning over the pages that in many of the lists more than one-half are illiterate.

In early times in Pennsylvania it was quite common for their churches to have schools of a very low grade connected with them; and a large number of schoolmasters are reported to have come over in the immigrant ships. Some of them gave up teaching and took to preaching, and many of them are admitted to have been worthless scamps. Schlatter and Muhlenberg describe the ignorance and illiteracy of their people in very strong language. There were certainly a few schools among them here and there, but the best of them were usually very inferior.

Christopher Dock, one of their school-masters on the Skippack, has been in recent years unearthed from his long obscurity, and the pretty story of his humble but earnest life told by the Hon. Samuel W. Penny-packer. He was famous for his skill, and Sauer, who had something of the enterprise of modern journalists, finally persuaded him to write out for publication his rules and methods of instruction. It is impossible to read the homely, simple language of the essay without loving the good master who was so devoted to the children and so ingenious in his way of teaching.

"HOW I RECEIVE THE CHILDREN IN SCHOOL.

" It is done in the following manner. The child is first welcomed by the other scholars, who extend their hands to it. It is then asked by me whether it will learn industriously and be obedient. If it promises me this, I explain to it how it must behave, and if it can say the A, B, C's in order, one after the other, and also by way of proof can point out with the forefinger all the designated letters, it is put into the A-b Abs. When it gets this far its father must give it a penny, and its mother must cook for it two eggs, because of its industry ; and a similar reward is due to it when it goes further into words, and so forth." (Pennypacker's His-torical and Biographical Sketches, 100.)

He had little presents for them of his own besides the eggs the parents were to boil. He drew birds and pic-tures for them, was much more sparing of the rod than was usually the custom in those times, and he had the plan of getting the children to teach each other. But he had a rough, unruly set to deal with ; his instruction was confined to the simplest sort of spelling, reading, and arithmetic, with much instruction in the Bible, which was an important text-book in those times among the English as well as the Germans. His efforts had to be directed more to conduct than to mental training; and he seems to have had his hands full in keeping some of his young charges from swearing and stealing. He drew up elaborate rules, which were evidently intended for the children of a very rough peasantry, who had to be prevented from living like wild animals and throwing the bones they had gnawed under the table.

Sauer's son wrote some very sensible generalizing on education, which reads well, and to which no one can take exception. Rupp assures us that the numerous school-masters among the German immigrants were in the habit of reading a book on education, entitled " Gedanken, Vorschläge und Wünsche zur Verbesserung der Öffentlichen Erziehung als Materialien zur Pädagogick, herausgegeben von Friederich Gabriel Resewitz," which was in four huge volumes, and must certainly have exhausted the subject.

Like the Quakers, these people had many new ideas in their heads which were to simplify many problems, war and government, as well as education. But none of them were very practical, and none of their efforts can for one moment be compared to the vigorous intellectual training given in the colonial schools of the Presbyterians, which produced such good results.

The Germans, unfortunately, stand in the history of

The Making of Pennsylvania

Pennsylvania as the enemies of all attempts at good education. There was great difficulty in introducing the public school system among them, and in some cases it was resisted by indignation meetings and litigation. Many of them professed to consider it tyranny, and attempted to pose as martyrs by refusing to pay the school-tax, and allowing their property to be taken by the sheriff. The Tunkers, although on their first arrival they made some efforts in behalf of schools, afterwards degenerated so far as to boast that there were scarcely any educated men among them, and at one time they would not admit such persons to their society. Many of them were inclined to destroy all books that were not religious.

An exception must be made, however, in favor of some of the Reformed and Lutherans. Their leaders, Schlatter and Muhlenberg, never resisted education. On the contrary, they deeply regretted its absence, and made every effort to have it. But they were thwarted in colonial times by their own people. After the Revolution the Reformed and Lutherans combined in establishing Franklin College at Lancaster, in 1787, under the notion, unfortunately very prevalent at that time in Pennsylvania, that different religious bodies could go into partnership in a college.

The plan failed, of course, and the college was closed in 1821. About eighteen years afterwards it was revived into a respectable academy, and in 1850, the Reformed having bought out the Lutheran interest in it, they united it with a college of their own called Marshall, which they had established at Carlisle in 1825. The combination, now known as Franklin and Marshall, at

Lancaster, is prosperous and hopeful, and shows the conservatism which has always marked the Reformed, by adhering to the old-fashioned course of classics and philosophy. The Reformed have also Albright Institute, at Myerstown, and Ursinus at Collegeville. The Lutherans have Thiel at Greenville, Muhlenberg at Allentown, Pennsylvania at Gettysburg, and Susquehanna at Selin's Grove.

The sects, however, remain unchanged, although the Quakers, who once held almost the same opinions about higher education, have in recent years branched out into three flourishing institutions, Haverford, Swarthmore, and Bryn Mawr.

Wickersham, in his "History of Education in Pennsylvania," while he laments the persistent hostility of the German population to education, insists that on their arrival as immigrants they were not so much opposed to it, and on the whole would have compared favorably in this respect with English immigrants of the same class. Their rapid degeneration was due, he thinks, in great part to their refusal to learn English, which isolated them and cut them off from the social, political, and commercial currents of the time.

Their habit of sequestering themselves on farms, and their division into numerous sects, each one too poor to have good educational means of its own, and too much at variance with the others to unite with them in a general system, tended to intensify the narrowness and isolation of their language. They were unaccustomed to local self-government, had not the Englishman's instinct for acting as an organized community, and were used to having education provided for them by a higher authority. Christopher Dock seems to have some such idea as this in his mind when he says, "It was before known to me that school-teaching in this country was far different from in Germany, since there the school stands upon such pillars that the common people cannot well overthrow it." *

The reasons that the Germans themselves have given for their opposition are, that in their experience, in the old world, learning was always connected with the states and churches that persecuted them; some of the most learned men had been their bitterest enemies, and had led the worst and cruelest attacks on their lives and liberty. Colleges were closely connected in their minds with theological schools, and theology was an evil. That occasional individuals, like St. Paul, might combine learning with Christianity was possible. But St. Paul, before his conversion, had used his knowledge for nothing but persecution, and such men were at best uncertain lights.

Many of them said, bluntly, that schooling made boys lazy and gave them a dislike for farming. They also feared that high learning, which with many of them began at grammar and geography, would destroy some of the peculiarities of their religion. Some of them, true to their suspicious instincts, saw in the schools nothing but a conspiracy of lazy people to get salaried positions for themselves out of the hard-earned savings of the honest farmer and mechanic.

It is impossible to form any exact estimate of the numbers of the Germans. All calculations of the Pennsylvania population in colonial times are but little better

---

* Pennypacker, Historical and Biographical Sketches, 98; Wickersham, History of Education in Pennsylvania, 123.

than guesses. Some insist that up to the Revolution fully half the people of the province were German. One estimate places their numbers for 1730 at thirty thousand. Governor Gordon's estimate of the whole population for the same year was forty-nine thousand, which gives the Germans considerably more than half. Seventeen years later another governor gives them three-fifths out of a total of two hundred thousand. Other estimates give them ninety thousand in 1750 out of a total of two hundred and seventy thousand, and one hundred and forty-four thousand six hundred and sixty in 1790 out of a total of four hundred and thirty-four thousand three hundred and seventy-five. In recent years it has generally been believed that about one-third of the people of the State are German, or of German descent. Franklin's rule of thumb, by which he always estimated the colonial population of the province as one-third Quaker, one-third German, and the remaining third miscellaneous, was probably not very far wrong.

As the Germans kept arriving in increasing numbers, not a little hostility was felt towards them by the English. It was feared that they might come in such swarms as to change the character of the colony, and it was several times suggested that they be permanently disfranchised. The governors of the province, though compelled at times to regulate their admission, were, on the whole, in favor of them, for the proprietors could have no strong objection to such numerous purchasers of land who usually paid for what they took, and seldom attempted, like the Scotch-Irish, to exercise squatter sovereignty.

The opposition to them, such as it was, usually came

from the assembly or from men like Franklin and James Logan. Franklin was always very outspoken in his dislike, called them " Palatine boors, the most stupid of their race," and believed that their refusal to adopt the English language and customs was a serious injury to the province. Sometimes he said they would take no interest in politics, and at other times sweep everything before them. He busied himself to make application to the British government to prevent their coming, but nothing was accomplished except the imposition of a small head-tax. He joined in every plan for their education, and at one time went so far as to add a set of German types to his printing establishment in the hope of publishing a German newspaper and German books in the English interest.

One of their most earnest advocates and friends was the eccentric Dr. Rush. His first argument was that if they continued to cling to their language it would be the channel through which the knowledge and discoveries of the wisest nations in Europe would be brought to America, and his second, that the more they learned their own language the more they would become acquainted with English. Both assertions have been abundantly contradicted by experience.

It is not to be supposed that the Pennsylvania Germans were in any sense disloyal to America. In colonial times, when the French occupied the present site of Pittsburg and threatened to press on to the Susquehanna, the Germans were seriously suspected, but apparently without much foundation. In modern times their feeling and position are beyond question. They readily joined the Native American movement of 1850, and usually show considerable contempt for the modern German immigrant who is forever talking of the fatherland.

As they are American at heart, it is all the more reason why they should become American altogether, and give up the mere sentimental devotion to the language and ways of a country which they deserted two hundred years ago because they could not endure it. They have more to gain by helping to make Pennsylvania a homogeneous united commonwealth, than by clinging to the mere shell and appearance of a system and nationality in which they long since ceased to believe. We can easily forego the great amusement of hearing negroes, in some of our counties, speaking Pennsylvania Dutch, and we can also forego the unpleasant spectacle of white men speaking debased and barbarous German-English. The attempt to maintain two languages in the same community inevitably ends in injuring both and rendering them useless for the best purposes of literature.

By refusing to adopt English ways the Germans injure themselves more than they injure the State. They often bring upon themselves unnecessary poverty, ignorance, and suffering, and exclusion from advancement and pleasures. The Huguenots, who were more easily assimilated than any race that has ever come to us, losing all their foreign characteristics in the first generation, have reaped their reward, and can, it is said, trace their blood in more prominent and important men, in proportion to their numbers, than any other element of the population except the English.

The modern German immigrants often stand out against assimilation in the same way as their brethren in Pennsylvania. Where they are well scattered among the native population their efforts usually fail. But where they get together in bodies, as in Pennsylvania, and as recently in some of the Western States, they are able to accomplish a large part of their purpose; and some of them have been visionary enough to suppose that they could in time make German the language of the United States.

The consequence of these attempts has been that, as shown by statistics, the Germans in America, in proportion to their numbers, have produced fewer remarkable and prominent men than any other division of the people. The race is not in itself deficient. But when it isolates itself in an American community it is cut off from the best development of that community, and also from its old associations in Europe, and inevitably deteriorates.

In Pennsylvania the Germans themselves have at times been conscious that they have not done all that was to be expected from their numbers, and their writers and orators have made excuses for them, and sometimes complained that justice had not been done them. But in attempting to offset criticisms by enlarging on the services the Germans have rendered America they often go too far and claim too much. As with all other foreign elements of the population, the hint is, of course, thrown out that in some mysterious way they were the real creators of the United States. Rupp, in his notes to Rush's " Germans in Pennsylvania," goes so far as to say, " It was to the German farmers America owed her independence."

As a separate, distinct nationality living among us the Germans have accomplished comparatively little, and they have only themselves to blame for not mingling more with the rest of the people. There has been, it is true, a good deal of assimilation accomplished, especially in parts of the State where the Germans were few and well scattered among the rest of the people. Most of the families that settled in Philadelphia and German-town have been long ago absorbed, and in other places a steady, though very slow, process of amalgamation can be noticed.

Many of the names gradually became anglicized. Bossert becomes Buzzard; Fluck becomes Fluke; Op den Graeff, Updegraff; Conderts, Conrad; Scherker, Yerkes; Tissen, Tyson; and Schmidt, plain, honest Smith. In some places the curious phenomenon is seen of a large family, part of whom retain their name in the old German, while the rest are gradually anglicizing it, to the great confusion of the sheriff's jury-list and the tax-assessor.

But in the counties where the Germans have always lived in masses there is comparatively little change; and, judging by the trifle that has been accomplished in a hundred and fifty years, complete absorption and a homogeneous population are still five hundred, if not a thousand, years away. The public school system, from which something was expected, has thus far accomplished but little. In fact, nothing will be of any avail except such a breaking up as will produce a great deal of intermarriage. It has long been a common and careless boast with us that we could quickly absorb any foreign element. So we can, and so can any nation when the foreign element is well scattered; but where it congests in masses we are as slow with it and perhaps slower than other people.

The Making of Pennsylvania

Those of the Pennsylvania Germans who had the good sense to drop Germanisms and Americanize themselves, and especially those who are the result of intermarriage with English or Scotch-Irish stock, are as good as the best. Conrad Weiser was among the Germans who fled to the Tulpehocken Valley from the injustice they were suffering in New York. His name is now almost forgotten; but during the period of the French and Indian Wars it is to be found on almost every page of the "Colonial Records." He was the proprietary interpreter, Indian agent, and negotiator of treaties, and as such played a most important part. Like Muhlenberg and every other German who has become prominent, he adopted America without qualification, and was one of the trustees of the society for establishing English schools among the Germans.

Muhlenberg's family is a striking instance. A thorough believer in the English, he was careful to have his children taught their ways. They were put in charge of an English woman for that purpose, and were well repaid for it. Peter Muhlenberg became one of the distinguished generals of the Revolution. Frederick was the first speaker of the National House of Representatives, and had a long and honorable political career. His grandson, the Rev. Dr. Henry Augustus Muhlenberg, became a clergyman of wide influence and distinction in the Episcopal Church. Not only has the family had these well-known members, but in its numerous branches throughout the Union is often found in positions of prominence and importance.

Throughout the State and in Philadelphia, numerous instances can be found of Germans who, having been

willing to emerge from the nationality of the country
they had deserted, have become distinguished in the
paths of science, business, or politics. They have furnished governors for the State, professors for colleges,
and German families have become well known in social
or fashionable life. Dr. Gross, one of our most distinguished physicians, and Dr. Leidy, a very distinguished man of science, were of the Germans. Seven
of our governors have been of the same stock,—Snyder,
Hiester, Shulze, Wolf, Ritner, Shunk, and Hartranft.
It was under Governor Wolf's administration, and with
his assistance, that the public school system was adopted
throughout the State, although most of his countrymen
were opposed to it, and a memorial gate-way at Easton
commemorates him as the father of the public schools.

Rittenhouse, the first American astronomer, and one
of the famous astronomers of the world, was brought
up among the old Mennonites, near Germantown, and
was half Hollander and half Welsh. Dr. Caspar Wistar,
who upheld the fame of Philadelphia for remarkable
physicians during the beginning of the present century,
was half German and half English, and, in fact, the Wistar
and Wister families, very well known and of much
eminence in Philadelphia, are an interesting instance of
what may be the result of blending the German and
English stocks.

There were also two very remarkable Pennsylvanians
who, although the Germans do not appear to have
claimed them, had, nevertheless, some of the blood in
their veins. Jeremiah Black, in some respects the ablest
man Pennsylvania has produced since the Revolution,
traced his lineage partly from the Scotch-Irish and partly

from the Germans. Bayard Taylor, the only man of any real literary genius born on our soil, was half Quaker and half German.

The Camerons, so long in possession of political control in the State, were also partly Scotch-Irish and partly German. In fact, wherever the Germans have emerged from their isolation, either by intermarriage with the English or by adopting English ways, they have been the gainers by it, and have still been able to retain any sentiments for their origin that were valuable. The Muhlenbergs, though completely Americanized, have always been noted for their affection for the past; and Governor Wolf found that he could love his ancestors and at the same time favor public education.

But to most of our Germans greatness still means to have a great farm. They cling to the land and to country life more persistently than even the Scotch-Irish, and it has been said that fully eighty per cent. of them are farmers. Scattered all through the State, and in the majority in many counties, they have stamped the country population, and, perhaps, the typical Pennsylvanian, if such a person is possible in so mixed a community, with many of their characteristics. Their heaviness, however, has its advantages. They are generally a most thrifty, conservative people, always husbanding their resources, qualities which, if the State ever becomes homogeneous and they are amalgamated with the rest of the people, may produce very great results.

Their farms are often found to have descended from father to son for more than a hundred years, in many cases untouched by a mortgage, and they are among the most skilful and successful farmers in the world. Albert

The Germans

Gallatin once said of them, "In Pennsylvania the Germans are the most ignorant, but the best political economists. They give any price for the best land, and hold it all."

Travellers on the Pennsylvania Railroad are often surprised, as they pass through Lancaster County, at the enormous size and peculiar construction of the barns. New Englanders, coming from a rocky soil, where all the crops that are ever gathered can be stored in an ordinary stable, are always very much amused, and think it a foolish waste of money for a farmer to build a barn fifteen times as large as his house. They are not aware that they are passing through one of the garden spots of earth, and if they knew the nature of our German they would have no fears of his spending a dollar or enclosing a square foot of space that was not absolutely necessary for the housing of his enormous crops.*

---

* Cassell's History of the Mennonites; Rush's Germans in Pennsylvania (with Rupp's notes); Pennypacker's Historical and Biographical Sketches; Rupp's Thirty Thousand Names of German Immigrants; Mann's Life of Muhlenberg; H. A. Muhlenberg's Life of General Peter Muhlenberg; Ayres's Life of W. A. Muhlenberg; Harbaugh's Life of Schlatter; Harbaugh's Fathers of the Reformed Church; C. Z. Weiser's Life of Conrad Weiser; Wickersham's History of Education in Pennsylvania; Haldeman's Pennsylvania Dutch; Martin's Mennonites; Pennsylvania Dutch and other Essays; Mittelberger's Journey to Pennsylvania; L. T. Reichel's Early Moravians; Rosengarten's Pennsylvania Dutch, Nation, vol. ix., 583; Pennypacker's Colonial Reports; Sachse's German Pietists of Pennsylvania; Heydrick's Genealogical Record of the Schwenkfelders.

CHAPTER V.

THE Moravians deserve mention separate from the other Germans; for, although they belonged to the pietist movement, their origin was different, and they were also in other respects very unlike the rest of their countrymen.

Their sect was originally not German at all. Their proper title was Unitas Fratrum; and they arose in Bohemia, and the neighboring province of Moravia, about the beginning of the fifteenth century, more than a hundred years before the Mennonites were heard of, and two hundred years before the advent of the Quakers. They were the result of that early outburst of the Reformation inspired by the preaching of John Huss. They studied the Bible and held the doctrine, which characterized so many of the early reformers, that the efficiency of a sacrament depended on the righteousness of the officiating priest.

At first they were inclined to be very fanatical. They could not allow themselves to take an oath, go to war, fill any civil office, or even carry on a mercantile business which involved the sale of anything but the bare necessities of life. They held the seven sacraments of the Roman Church and many of the usual doctrines, but explained them in a Protestant way, which took them entirely outside of Romanism; and they also preached that awful heresy, liberty of conscience.

As time went on they broadened themselves, and when the movement under Luther came they had three or four hundred churches and about two hundred thousand members. At that time they became more like the other Reformed churches on the continent and dropped five of their sacraments. They grew with the growth of Protestantism in Bohemia; and so well did Protestantism prosper there that in 1620, out of three million inhabitants, there were only about two hundred and fifty thousand Roman Catholics.

But the Roman Catholics of that time still retained some of the old mediæval courage of their convictions. They lived their dogmas logically and were not obliged to fritter away their meaning to suit a modern liberalism. Within two years they completely wiped out of existence the whole of that luxuriant growth of Protestantism in Bohemia. They had learned some lessons in the Reformation and were careful to make as few martyrs as possible, so that only twenty-seven of the leaders were put to death. The rest of the procedure was a model of thoroughness and success.

Every Protestant church was confiscated and either levelled with the ground or turned into a Catholic church. Every Protestant clergyman was banished. The property of all prominent Protestants was confiscated. Commissions were sent roving through the country banishing all the common people who would not recant. Laws were passed by which none but Catholics could be citizens, none but Catholics could marry, and all Protestant inmates of hospitals were

expelled unless they recanted. Every Protestant book
and every book in the Bohemian language that could
be found was destroyed, and one Jesuit attained great
honor because with his own hands he had burned sixty
thousand volumes. When Bohemia got through with
this conversion and the thirty years' war that followed,
her population of three millions was reduced to eight
hundred thousand.

What was left of the Unitas Fratrum scattered itself
in Poland, Hungary, Transylvania, Prussia, and Silesia,
grew weaker and weaker, and finally seemed to have
nothing left but the succession of its bishops. It would
soon have disappeared forever had it not been revived in
1722 by Count Zinzendorf, a remarkable young German
nobleman, who adopted religion as the occupation of
his life. About three hundred people who had maintained the old faith in secret in Moravia migrated to the
count's estate in Saxony, and from these the sect was
renewed.

The three hundred emigrants were of the Slavonic
race; for Moravianism had up to that time been exclusively a Slavonic religion. But the aftergrowth was all
German. Zinzendorf was a German Lutheran of the
pietist type, and the Moravians became engrafted on the
pietist movement. Henceforth they were a German sect,
and soon began to adopt ideas and feelings which would
have astonished their Slavic originators. The old race
knew them no more, and the change was rather curious.
There are many instances in history of a race changing
its religion, but comparatively few of a religion changing
its race.

Like every other German sect, they of course took

their own view of pietism, and to say that they were Pietists is a very vague description of them. Muhlenberg's followers among the Lutherans were also Pietists, and yet very different from the Moravians, and by no means friendly with them. Indeed, the Moravians stood more aloof from the rest of the German population in Pennsylvania than any of the other German sects.

They had the general pietistic principle of revolt from formal and systematic theology. They adopted the feet-washing ceremony, or sacrament, of the other sects, and had somewhat of the same leaning towards communal life which appeared among the Tunkers. They were opposed to all kinds of warfare, and took no interest in politics and government, and they had a system for watching each other's conduct and administering discipline in families very much like that of the Quakers.

They were at one period of their history overwhelmed by a flood of emotionalism, and used expressions which were extravagant and almost unintelligible in German, and seem still worse when translated into English. They dwelt upon the sufferings of Christ, his wounds, and the scenes of his passion, in a way which seemed fanciful and childish even to people from the continent of Europe, and to English and Americans irreverent and shocking. They made an extraordinary use of the highly figurative language of love in the Song of Solomon, and appeared to be attempting to realize the Saviour by an effort of the imagination, falling in love with his image as one falls in love with an earthly sweetheart. In this they resembled some of the other pietist Germans.

They had the same devoted love for music as the

Ephrata people, and took the same delight in composing hundreds and hundreds of hymns, some of which when translated into English seem very extraordinary. In fact, they had a very large measure of those mystic German feelings in religion which are so strange and fantastic that they can hardly be understood by people of English stock.

Although they had a decided tendency towards communal life, they were not believers in celibacy, like the Germans at Ephrata. On the contrary, they exalted marriage into a very sacred duty. All souls, they held, were in their essence feminine, and the male was simply a temporary office created for the probationary period of this world. But although his existence was ephemeral, his duties were none the less clear and positive. As Christ was the true spouse of every woman, so her husband was his representative and the saviour of his wife in this world.

They regulated their marriages very strictly, and the church often took the part of match-maker, helped the man to choose his wife, and communicated his proposal to her. In this, as in many of their other deliberations, they often resorted to casting lots. Indeed, the lot was relied upon by them for their most important decisions, and by it missions were established and ministers appointed. Like the Quakers, they have never made any rules about divorce, and yet to this day, it is said, divorce is practically unknown among them.

They seem to have been more inclined than the other German sects to develop liturgies, and they had one which has attracted some attention, and is known as the Litany of the Wounds. They have now a regular

liturgy which is printed with their hymn-book, and together with their hymns has a strong resemblance to the services of the Church of England. They were indeed a curious blending of qualities of their own and qualities which resembled those of the Quakers, Mennonites, Tunkers, and various other forms of pietism.

They showed comparatively little of that strong tendency of the other Germans to cling to their language and customs. They readily adopted English, and in colonial times were always on closer and more congenial terms with the English than with their own countrymen; and their modern ritual and customs have always proved attractive to people of English religion.

A few years of American life had a great effect in changing their emotionalism; and, it is said, they have been afflicted with its worst forms only once in this country while under the rule of Bishop Cammerhof. They have long since frankly repudiated all such excitements, and, in the preface to a recent edition of their hymn-book, describe them as belonging to a time of sentimental fanaticism. They now more nearly resemble the original church in Moravia, which, before it was destroyed by the Romish persecution, was Episcopal and not unlike the Church of England. Indeed, the Church of England has long since recognized the succession of the Moravian bishops as apostolic, and the two churches are in communion with each other.

The Moravians date the beginning of their renewal when they became a German sect, from the 17th of June, 1721, when the first tree was cut down for them on Count Zinzendorf's estate, but the date usually given is 1722. It was the era of sect-making, and they increased

rapidly, spread all over Germany, the United Provinces, Great Britain, and sent missionaries to Greenland and the West Indies. In 1749, less than thirty years after their renewal, they are said to have numbered at least thirty thousand members, with over a thousand missionaries.

They began to come to America in 1734, and settled in Georgia on some land which had been offered to the Schwenkfelders who preferred to come to Pennsylvania. The Moravians might possibly have continued in Georgia, if they had not been obliged by the government, contrary to their religious scruples, to take up arms against the Spaniards.

The first of them began to appear in Pennsylvania about 1739, and they settled on a tract of land near Nazareth, a few miles north of the Lehigh River. This land belonged to Whitefield, the famous preacher, who was also interested in Georgia. He had named the place Nazareth, and had intended to establish a negro school there. It was within one of the Penn manors which has often attracted attention, because it was held by one of those curious old English tenures which required the delivery every year of a red rose. This manor had also attached to it the privilege of Court Baron, and was capable of being developed into a little principality. The Moravians selected it for this reason, as their intention was at first to live by themselves and have a colony of their own. They, however, never made use of the privilege of Court Baron, and their exclusiveness in government was confined to their communal system.

The remaining Moravians soon arrived from Georgia, and, the Indians becoming troublesome, the whole body moved a few miles south to the banks of the Lehigh, and in 1741 founded Bethlehem, where they have remained ever since. They spread out to Philadelphia and other parts of the State, but their head-quarters were always at Bethlehem, and Bethlehem is still the metropolis of their church in America.

It was there they established their communal system. Personal property was not surrendered, but the church owned all the land, and received into its treasury the results of the combined labor of the community, giving to each member in return the necessities of life, instruction for his children, and protection in sickness and old age.

They provided houses in which the bachelors lived together, other houses for the single women, and others for the widows. Some of these houses can still be seen in Bethlehem, and are of curious and interesting architecture. So independent and self-sustaining were they that they owned one or two ships, with captains of their own faith, in which their immigrants were brought over in ease and comfort, and avoided the dirt, crowding, and disease which destroyed so many of the other Germans.

About thirty trades were carried on for the benefit of the church. There were button-mills, grist-mills, saw-mills, tanneries, potteries, linen weaving, stocking weaving, rope-making, bakeries, butcheries, and even chimney-sweeping and shoe-cleaning. Some of the products of their industry became well known for their excellence, and were sent to Philadelphia in considerable quantities. The profits being all concentrated in the community and not dissipated among individuals, The Economy, as they called their communal establishment, became very prosperous and successful.

The Making of Pennsylvania

Their intention was not merely to separate themselves from the world and afford retreats where men could hold undisturbed communion with God, but to make of themselves more efficient missionaries. One of their principal objects at first was the conversion of the Indians. The number of missionaries among them was always very large in proportion to the laity, and those who came to Bethlehem seem to have been unusually earnest. Communism seemed to them an economical way of uniting their efforts so as to enable the greatest number to give time and energy to the conversion of the heathen.

The story of their Indian missions is a long one, and would fill a volume in itself. They were among the first who carefully studied Indian customs; they formed successful communities among the savages near Bethlehem, and also as far west as Ohio. But the coming on of the French and Indian Wars destroyed the fruits of all their efforts, as it destroyed all that Penn and the Quakers had done. The flourishing Indian community of the Moravians in Ohio became suspected of being in league with the hostile tribes, and was destroyed by the white settlers at the close of the Revolution.

In 1762, at the time of the Indian wars, the communism at Bethlehem was largely abandoned. The church retained as its property only a few farms, trades, and the old Sun Inn. But it still controlled the land, and would sell it to none but Moravians until 1844. At that date the town was thrown open to strangers, and soon began to develop those enormous industries in the manufacture of iron, which have now made it one of the richest and most prosperous towns in the State.

In December, 1741, when the settlement at Bethlehem

was begun, Count Zinzendorf appeared in Pennsylvania, and remained for a little over a year. He spent much of his time at Philadelphia and Germantown, and also visited nearly every other part of the colony. He made several excursions among the Indians, and was the first white man to penetrate the Wyoming Valley. His daughter accompanied him on these rather daring expeditions, and he has left us in his journal an interesting account of their wanderings and dangers.

He seems to have aroused much enthusiasm among the Moravians; but other people were by no means favorably impressed with him. The English thought him disagreeable and eccentric. Muhlenberg complained very bitterly of his attempts to convert Lutherans, and accused him of resorting to artifice and trickery unbecoming a man of religion.

He was certainly a very extraordinary character, full of the strangest sort of German emotionalism, and difficult to understand. His own disciples have admitted that he was governed more by his heart than by his head. He decided everything rapidly and on the spur of the moment, and was constantly changing his mind. He seemed to be giving utterance to every thought, vague, subtle, or eccentric, that occurred to him, and often resorted to several languages to express himself. He had, however, unquestioned force of character, and a commanding influence over his followers.

The appearance of his face in the best portrait that has come down to us is certainly most striking and powerful. He had boundless energy and industry, and was indifferent to hardships and fatigue. He bustled about in the towns and forests of Pennsylvania in a way that was astonishing, and few men then living could have covered so much ground, seen so many people, white and red, and expressed so many extravagant notions in the same amount of time.

One of the objects he seems to have had most at heart, was to organize the whole German population of all sects and classes into a sort of league of religions which he called the Church of God in the Spirit. He seems to have considered himself in a certain sense a religious statesman. He had taken up religion as a great general subject of infinite importance, and certainly the one which at that time was strongly attracting the attention of the German people.

By birth and associations he was a Lutheran, deeply convinced of the benefits of the pietist movement. When the remnant of the Moravians appeared he had taken them under his care, settled them on his estate, and become one of their bishops, not because he was a Moravian more than anything else, but because he believed they were one of the sects that were travelling upon the right path. He always proclaimed that he had not ceased to be a Lutheran by becoming a Moravian.

He came to Pennsylvania because the Germans there had been represented to him as in a state of great disorder, split up into innumerable divisions, without leaders and yet willing to be led, and anxious to be organized into some form of evangelical religion. He was bitterly disappointed when he found that each sect was as hard set in its prejudices as a Presbyterian or a Catholic ; that instead of a soft mass of enthusiastic German sentiment, waiting for a great man to mould it, there were a score or more of hard crystallized divisions, more distinct than in their native land, and suspicious of every one but themselves.

Before coming to Pennsylvania he announced that he had laid aside for the present his office of bishop among the Moravians, and wished to be known simply as a Lutheran clergyman. When he arrived in the province he called a meeting of the governor and prominent citizens in Philadelphia, and in their presence, and asking them to be witnesses, he laid aside his title as count. He was going into battle, he said, and was ready and willing to be attacked and hit, but wished to avoid having his family name dragged about in the conflict. He tried to give himself various other names,—Dominie de Thürstein, Friend Lewis, Brother Ludwig, and Ordinary. But his formal resignation of a title was a failure, caused much amusement among the English, and his original name always clung to him.

Thus prepared and assisted by Antes and other Germans, he began to call together delegates from the sects. The first synod was held in Germantown, January 7, 1742, and representatives appeared from the Reformed, Lutherans, Mennonites, Tunkers, Hermits, and a few others. The object was to establish a league, or spiritual union, in which all would agree in essential points, and yet each remain true to his own denomination. It was to be a Christian Union on almost exactly the same plan that has been much talked of and recommended in our own time.

The difficulty was to agree on what were essentials and to avoid having the essentials adopted consist too exclusively of the essentials of one of the parties to the contract. The Separatists were the hardest to deal with, for they held it to be sinful for believers to have close fellowship. The strenuous advocacy of any idea was, they thought, an uncharitable reflection on those who differed from it. Zinzendorf's spiritual union, as an attempt to make a sect which should not be a sect, seemed to be in their line, and yet they were afraid of it, and ended by calling Zinzendorf the beast of the Revelation, and persuaded Sauer to use his newspaper against him.

The Tunkers and their offshoot, the Ephrata people, were also in the synod, and could not be restrained from occasionally taking a turn at each other. Zinzendorf was greatly grieved, but was himself very little better than the rest. He finally announced in one of the synods that Lutheranism was the true principle, and that Lutheranism would gradually absorb the Reformed and also all the other sects, including the Moravians, and that would be the true church.

This ideal of union among the Protestant divisions of Germany remained long in his mind, and was afterwards attempted by others, sometimes with a little success. The union, however, when analyzed, meant that the Moravians were to be the centre of the unity; that all other denominations were to recognize them as the connecting link, and after that be allowed to retain their own peculiarities; certainly a noble position for Unitas Fratrum. In other words, Zinzendorf's conception of Christian unity was about the same that has been entertained in our own and every other time.

The synods he established for the purpose in Pennsylvania continued to meet every few weeks and lasted for about five years after he returned to Europe. But the sects one after another withdrew, and finally they became synods of the Moravian Church alone, to which Zinzendorf, in spite of his protests, really belonged.

At the same time that he was managing the synods of the Church of God in the Spirit he was organizing the Lutherans and Reformed as his own people. With the Reformed he had comparatively little success. But the Lutherans flocked to him. They had then no regular head or leader in Pennsylvania, and the count easily persuaded them. He was made pastor of their church in Philadelphia, and several other congregations recognized him as the superintendent of the churches of the colony, with power to appoint ministers.

Whether he could finally have turned them all into Moravians is difficult to say, for he had been at work among them only about a year, when Muhlenberg appeared and soon put a stop to his course. It has been supposed by some that information of his success had reached Germany, and was one of the chief reasons why Muhlenberg was sent. Muhlenberg's authority as a Lutheran clergyman seems to have been more regular than the count's. At any rate, the people more readily recognized him, and though at first he had only a minority as followers, he soon acquired control of pretty much the whole body. Zinzendorf's Lutheranism he regarded with contempt, as a mere cover to advance the Moravians, and Muhlenberg's writings are not the place to look for praise of the count.

The count, however, had secured a few recruits. The Moravian Church in Philadelphia appears to have been made up principally of Lutherans and English converts, and in several other places in the province the Church of God in the Spirit seems to have proved itself a valuable ally. For many years afterwards the Moravians continued to keep a watchful eye on the Lutherans and Reformed, and encouraged any tendency among them that seemed to lean in the right direction. A catechism was written for those who inclined to Moravian doctrine. The Moravian Church had also an officer who was called Vice-Inspector of the Lutheran Church in America, and he is said to have ordained a Lutheran pastor-elect at Tulpehocken. Moravian missionaries continued for some years to organize congregations among both the German and the Swedish Lutherans and also to some extent among the Reformed.

The explanation of this apparently loose state of affairs is, that the German pietist movement had not at that time crystallized. Most of the Lutherans in Pennsylvania were pietists of one form or another, and the Moravians were also pietists, and most of them had been born Lutherans. It was disputed whether the Moravians were in the Augsburg Confession with the Lutherans, and in Germany it had been decided that they were. The Moravians were really a pietist party in the Lutheran Church, and the real dispute between Zinzendorf and Muhlenberg was whether the Pennsylvania Lutherans should take the Moravian form of pietism or adopt Muhlenberg's Halle pietism. In the end Muhlenberg prevailed, and the Moravians separated and became a distinct division.

When Zinzendorf arrived in Pennsylvania, in December, 1741, the Moravians were a mere handful, who had just built a log-house at Bethlehem. He visited them there, but for the first six months or so his efforts were chiefly devoted to the conversion of the Lutherans and Reformed. Having done what he could for these, he turned his attention to his own proper people and the Indians, who sufficiently occupied his time during the remainder of his visit.

His presence caused much excitement and controversy, and produced a long list of pamphlets and polemical literature. The Quakers were not opposed to him, and the Episcopalians had no very serious objection. His worst opponents were the Presbyterians, and some of the German sects like the Separatists. To the Presbyterians of that time Moravianism seemed either ridiculous or loathsome. They had no hesitation in saying so, and Zinzendorf, in his turn, seldom hesitated to say what he thought of Calvinism. He accordingly found himself accused of drunkenness, his daughter, who was with him, described as a child he had kidnapped, and his followers as " locusts from the bottomless pit."

But he returned to Europe, and the land had rest. His life and work, in spite of all his peculiarities, were an important episode in the history of the Moravians. He restored and renewed them when they were about to perish, and there are few things in history more romantic than this young nobleman expanding under the religious movement of his time, filled with broad ideas of unifying the disordered sects of his country, adopting a persecuted and helpless sect of another country which he believed was in the right, and sacrificing all his estate and fortune to help it. The story is still more complete when we know that within recent years the Moravians have paid back to the count's family every cent he expended for their benefit, with interest to date.

After the count returned to Europe the Moravians settled down at Bethlehem, increased in numbers, and began to develop what became a very beautiful and quiet life. We read of no stories of dirt and disorder, which the colonists so often charged against the other Germans. On the contrary, the Moravians were more like the Schwenkfelders and the early Mennonites, who settled Germantown under Pastorius,—orderly, neat, neither poor nor rich, self-respecting, respecting others, and liked by everybody. They were far removed from the rabble, nominally Lutherans and Reformed, which Muhlenberg and Schlatter complained of, and still farther removed from that nondescript mass of ignorant peasantry which had been picked up in Germany by the newlanders and shipping-agents and exported to Pennsylvania for what it would bring.

Bethlehem became a garden. Like the Mennonites at Germantown, the Moravians were very fond of fruit-trees, and planted them everywhere. The streets were lined with them, and far down into the present century the stranger passing through the town could help himself and enjoy a great variety. They became famous for their inns, and added to the already high reputation of the colonial tavern in Pennsylvania. The Nazareth, the Rose, and the Crown were outside of Bethlehem, but well known, and each has had its history, and the Moravian historians have spared no pains to celebrate their merits. The best one of all, however, was the Sun, which was within the town, and familiar for nearly a hundred years to all the people of the country from Massachusetts to the Carolinas.

The reason for this was, that the principal line of travel between Boston and the Southern colonies passed through Bethlehem. Travellers from the South usually came to Philadelphia, thence to Bethlehem, thence through what were called the Minisink settlements in northeastern Pennsylvania to Kingston, on the Hudson, which was crossed, and a straight road followed to Boston or any other part of New England. There was another line of travel from the South which went to New York City through New Jersey, and was convenient for any one going to that place. But those going to Massachusetts usually followed the Bethlehem and Kingston route.

It is doubtful if we shall ever again in this country see any of the old-fashioned comforts that were enjoyed in that inn. It had private suites of apartments, most of them consisting of a sitting-room with two bedchambers, with a special servant. An Englishman who was there at the time of the Revolution describes how he was received, led at once to his private apartment, the key given him, the special servant assigned to him, and he felt at once as if he were in his own home.

At different times the inn has entertained beneath its roof nearly all the signers of the Declaration of Independence, most of the members of the Continental Congress, and all the Presidents of the United States down to Lincoln. That the wines were remarkable, and that the inn had its own brand of Madeira, goes without saying. The early Moravians lived largely on game and cultivated a great variety of vegetables. Deer and grouse were very abundant on the barrens in the Manor of the Red Rose. It was long a favorite sporting-ground for Philadelphians, and the resort of colonial governors. The wayfarers at the inn lived on all these delicacies in the greatest abundance, together with the famous fruit, trout, shad, and wild strawberries. Foreigners who stopped there invariably declared that the inn was fully equal to the best in Europe. It was owned and managed by the Moravian Church as part of its communal system. Let us hope that other religions may arise that will keep such inns.

One of the chief amusements of the travellers was to stroll out from the inn and visit the establishments of the Moravians, the widows' house, the brothers' and sisters' houses, and the schools. Every one was not only pleased, but strongly attracted; and many wished to intrust the education of their children to these simple, well-ordered souls. Such visitors have continued to be numerous down into our own time, and the church has been often obliged to appoint a special person whose business it was to show such people the town.

In colonial days, and long afterwards, distinguished men of the country and distinguished foreigners were constantly appearing. Some of them travelled by stage, but most of them were in their own carriages or on horseback. Hotel registers, in which the guest signs his name and says nothing about himself, were not used then, but a much more interesting book was kept by the clerk who entered descriptive memoranda. In some of these books at the Virginia Springs there are curious records of the old plantation life, when whole families were in the habit of invading the springs, bringing their coach- and saddle-horses and slaves, and one book is said to have the significant entry, "The Hamptons, 32 horses." The entries at the Sun were somewhat similar.

> " 1801 June 20. A gent. & lady in a chair.
> " July 4. A gent. in the stage. One glass of punch.
> " July 12. A lady dressed in black.
> " " 15. A company of French gentlemen with a servant. Four suppers, four breakfasts, four dinners. 5 bottles porter, 2 bowls punch, 1 pint Lisbon.
> " Nov. 28. General Lee, 6 horses, and 4 servants. Five dinners, 1 bottle Madeira, 5 quarts beer, 5¼ pints brandy.
> 1802 Sept. 18. The President of Cambridge University."

During the Revolution, troops were constantly passing and repassing through Bethlehem. It was inland and out of the way of the British, who usually confined their movements to the lines of travel through New Jersey. After the battle of the Brandywine was fought, September 11, 1777, Washington was uncertain whether Howe would be content with taking Philadelphia, or would follow up his success by pursuing the Continental army. Bethlehem was selected as a place secluded and easily fortified, to which the army could retreat and make a stand. The stores and ammunition were sent there, and seven hundred wagons with their horses and attendants encamped opposite the town where South Bethlehem now stands. The houses of the brothers and sisters were taken for a hospital. Lafayette, wounded in the battle, was sent there, and spent several weeks, by no means unpleasantly, recovering, and reading many books. Congress also made it their refuge, and the town was several times the head-quarters for the Continental hospital.

The Making of Pennsylvania

In all the accounts of this occupation the respect with which Congress and the officers of the army treated the Moravians, and the care that was taken not to inflict too heavy burdens upon them, are quite remarkable. The Moravians were. opposed to war, but, like the Quakers, they often made exceptions. They had no objection, of course, to caring for the sick and wounded. On the contrary, they were glad to do it. Their women prepared a beautiful silk flag, which they presented to Pulaski's regiment, an event celebrated in a poem by Longfellow. In their dealings with the Indians they had not hesitated to carry arms for protection, and in the Revolution they declared their principles in such a way that while they were placed in the position of noncombatants, they were, at the same time, shown to be favorable to the American cause.

From the time of the Revolution until after the Civil War Bethlehem was a summer watering-place for Philadelphians, and also for people from New York, who not only found the climate agreeable, but were interested in the ways of the Moravians, their buildings, their antiquities, and their history.

Soon after the Revolution the school for girls at Bethlehem began to receive pupils of every creed from all parts of the Middle and Southern States. The Moravians had always been remarkable for their success in a certain kind of elementary education. One of their bishops, Comenius, in the beginning of the eighteenth century, wrote books on education, which contained suggestions a hundred years in advance of his time, and which have only lately been put into practical use. These principles, as well as those enforced at Bethlehem, were of a kind intended to affect conduct, rather than to accomplish a very high intellectual training. But so far as they went they were very successful, and among the five or six thousand alumni of the school can be found the names of prominent people from almost every part of the Union, together with the names of daughters of Continental officers and others, who became familiar with the peace and rest of Bethlehem in the Revolution.*

---

* De Schweinitz's Unitas Fratrum; L. T. Reichel's Early Moravians; W. C. Reichel's Memorials of the Moravian Church, Moravian Seminary, Essays, etc.; Henry's Moravian Sketches; Martin's Moravian Church; Ritter's Moravian Church in Philadelphia; Memoirs of the Moravian Historical Society.

CHAPTER VI.

BESIDES being the chief seat of the Quakers and the Germans in colonial times, Pennsylvania was also the home of the Presbyterians,—the place where their first American Presbytery was established in 1705, and the first place on the continent where they became numerous and powerful. There were two divisions of them. The Eastern Presbyterians lived mostly in the eastern part of the province, and, while largely Scotch-Irish, had many English among them. The Western Presbyterians were almost exclusively Scotch-Irish, always sought the frontier, and advanced with it westward. In religion there was but little difference between the two divisions, but in character and temperament the Western Scotch-Irish were more excitable and violent.

It would be hard to conceive of a greater contrast in thought and feeling than was presented in these Presbyterians living in the same community with the Quakers. The eagle and the dove, the lamb and the lion, suggest themselves at once as proper similes. But, curiously enough, in this instance the dove was in power, and all through the colonial period kept the eagle in control. The dove was not inclined to be at all tyrannical to her enemy, but at the same time her love of peace was very exasperating to the men who were passionately fond of war.

The Scotch-Irish and the Presbyterians

The feelings of dislike or hatred on one side and contempt on the other usually spent themselves, when occasion arose, in abusive language and pamphlet warfare. The Scotch-Irish in one instance, however, seem to have had the full intention of attacking the Quakers for protecting the Indians, and they marched with arms in their hands to Germantown. The Quakers were ready for them, and had no hesitation in arming themselves and fortifying Philadelphia, for the chance of a shot at a Scotch-Irish Presbyterian was too much for their scruples of religion.

In the minds of the Quakers the Presbyterians in Pennsylvania were a part of the Massachusetts Puritans who had whipped Quakers at the cart's tail and put four of them to death, and they were human enough to want to square that account. But besides this very strong cause for dislike, and the continual attacks of the Presbyterians on their peace policy with the Indians, the Quakers saw in the religion of their opponents all that was contrary and shocking to their own. The Presbyterians had been one of the conservative sects of the Reformation, and were far behind the Quakers in advanced ideas. They were a part of the great Calvinist or Reformed movement which during the sixteenth century spread over a large part of Europe. In England people who inclined to this mode of thought were called Puritans while they remained a party within the Church of England. When separated from it some of them became known as Presbyterians and others as Independents and Congregationalists.

The Calvinists differed radically from the Quakers in being by no means ready to get rid of dogmas. It is true they rejected a great deal of the Middle Age methods, the Pope and his temporal power, image worship, ceremonies, ritual, tradition, modern miracles; and they gave their laity a share in church government, and confined their worship to hard-headed, logical preaching. Yet to the one or two dogmas which they retained they clung with a persistency which made them the most dogmatic of all the divisions of Protestants. They could not give up, and some of them cannot yet give up, the central idea of the old system,—the doctrine of exclusive salvation. They simply transferred it from the Roman Church to themselves.

They also took one of the dogmas of the old belief and carried it to new conclusions. It had always been held in the Middle Ages, that by the fall of Adam the whole human race had become corrupt, and every individual of it would be consigned to eternal fire unless he were saved by baptism and faith in the creeds of the Church. This taint from Adam was called original sin. The Calvinists went a step farther and said that not only were the descendants of Adam naturally corrupt, but they were completely and utterly so, and that it was impossible for them, unless elected and saved by grace, to escape the tortures of hell. Thus original sin became total depravity.

The development went on. God, it was said, being omnipotent and all-wise, had from the foundation of the world foreseen and foreordained the fall of Adam and the subsequent corruption and damnation of all his descendants, and had arranged the fate of every individual beyond the power of change. This was predestination. And then was added the next step, the doctrine of election, which held that out of this rotten and lost mass of humanity some were by God elected or foreordained at the foundation of the world to be saved, and the rest were foreordained to be damned; that those chosen to be damned would be damned in spite of good deeds, and those chosen to be saved would be saved in spite of evil deeds. Such, it was maintained, was the pleasure and will of God.

But if our fate in the future life, as well as all our actions in this, are foreordained beyond the possibility of change, what is the use of prayers, and strivings, and good deeds? And the answer usually given was, that the prayers, and strivings, and good deeds were also foreordained, and therefore, must be performed. The arguments in favor of predestination are of great force until they reach the question of moral responsibility, when they become extremely subtle. They are, however, a valuable mental discipline to those who indulge in them, and, indeed, the whole Calvinistic theology was well calculated to develop keenness of mind.

It was also, in the doctrine of election, productive of a severe and cruel tone of thought; for, in order to have the whole theory consistent, the Creator was made to appear vindictive and furious. God, as the Calvinists described him, was a monarch who, for the gratification of his pleasure and absolute sovereignty, had foreordained a large part of mankind to torture. He delighted not only in the eternal punishment of sinners, but also in the eternal burning of innocent children who had died unbaptized.

These Puritans, who fled from kings and professed to have a holy horror of arbitrary government, ascribed

The Making of Pennsylvania

to the God whom they worshipped qualities which made him more arbitrary, tyrannical, and absurd than any earthly monarch that ever reigned. Jonathan Edwards, whose whole life was passed in benevolence, delighted, nevertheless, in describing the fierceness and the relentless cruelty of God. He loved to depict his Maker as trampling on the sinners, and "staining all his garments with their blood." He had gradually wrought his mind into such a state that he believed that he loved a God of this sort, and declared he would willingly be damned to gratify his rage.

It is the fashion now to ridicule these old Calvinistic doctrines, and the sects that once held them are softening them down and adopting changed beliefs. But they had their advantages. They made men hard and stern, it is true, but they also made men strong. There was no dreamy spiritualism about them. No one could be a saint in that religion, no one could say that he had achieved any excellence until he had convinced himself that he was willing to go to hell for the sake of those who should be saved, and for the glory of God.

Whatever may be our opinion of the divine origin of such doctrine, it was certainly a powerful means of discipline. It created self-contained, steadfast, aggressive natures, who remained of that character long after they had lost faith in the belief which created it. Such people have formed and still form a large and important part of the English-speaking race, and have had a vast influence on the destinies of America. The thought and enterprise of New England have been built up entirely by Congregationalists, well on to one-half of the social fabric of Pennsylvania has been built up by Presbyterians, and there is scarcely a State in the Union where the influence of Calvinism has not been powerfully felt.

But the Quaker could not persuade himself to look at it in this light. To his spiritual mind such belief was horrible and disgusting, and when he saw some of the results of it, the whipping and hanging of his own sect in Massachusetts, the Salem witchcraft, not to mention the banishment of Roger Williams and Mrs. Anne Hutchinson, together with other cruelties, his dislike and disapproval were turned into a violent feeling for which he scarcely had a name in his gentle vocabulary. He must have often, in his secret heart, regretted that he had founded his colony on the broad principles of religious liberty. It was bad enough to see the Episcopalian and the ordinary English Presbyterian enter under the protection of that beneficent law; but when the Scotch-Irishman came, with his violence and contempt, and his belief that the Old Testament was still in force and commanded the destruction of the heathen Indians, the patience of the Quaker was sorely tried.

The Scotch-Irish were Scotch and English people who had gone to Ireland to take up the estates of Irish rebels confiscated under Queen Elizabeth and James I. This same James, who was King of Scotland as James VI., encouraged his Presbyterian subjects to emigrate to Ireland and occupy the confiscated lands. The migration was numerous, and began in the early part of the seventeenth century, about seventy-five years before the founding of Pennsylvania. Towards the middle of the same century the confiscation of Irish lands by Cromwell increased the emigration to still greater proportions, and after this many Englishmen joined the movement.

The Making of Pennsylvania

These people, English and Scotch, who occupied Ireland in this way have usually been known in England as Ulstermen, and with us as Scotch-Irish, and are, of course, totally different in character as well as in religion from the native Irish. Even those who came to Ireland from Scotland were not Celtic Scotch but people of English stock who had been living for many generations in Scotland, so that neither the name Ulstermen nor the name Scotch-Irish is at all descriptive of them.

They became famous in history for their heroic defence of Londonderry against James II. They were more thrifty and intelligent than the native Irish. They took the land on long leases, and began to make it blossom like a garden. They were, however, soon put to a severe test by the persecutions of Charles I., who, after coming to the English throne in 1625, attempted to force the Scotch people in both Scotland and Ireland to conform to the Church of England. At the same time the native Irish rose to expel the Scotch, and succeeded in killing a few thousand. So between their two persecutors these settlers, already sturdy from their race and religion, were not without the additional discipline of suffering and martyrdom.

Many of them emigrated to America, especially when the long leases on which they held the Irish land began to expire. The movement began about the year 1700 and continued for forty or fifty years. Some of them went to Maryland and a great many went to Virginia, where they still constitute a distinct element in the population. In Virginia, as elsewhere, most of them sought the frontier. In fact, in colonial times, they could be found on the whole American frontier from New Hampshire to Georgia.

The Scotch-Irish and the Presbyterians

They did not, however, all seek the frontier, as has been sometimes supposed. Many of them, especially in Pennsylvania, remained in the East. In modern times many of them have settled in the southwestern section of Philadelphia, which is now largely populated by them. But city life has a very quieting effect on their temperament. They flourish better in the country, and best of all on the frontier. Their most striking and peculiar qualities seem to have been developed by contact with the wilderness, and the frontier Ulsterman has become so conspicuous that his less demonstrative, though probably equally efficient, brother has been thrown into the shade.

They wanted the land as their own, and would have no neighbors but their own people. When the Germans began to move into some of their settlements in Pennsylvania, it was found difficult for the two nationalities to live together, and the proprietors asked the Scoth-Irish to move farther west, a suggestion which they always eagerly accepted. They were delighted when, in 1768, the land west of the Alleghanies was opened for settlement, and they immediately began to throng through the mountain passes to reach it.

The larger part of the Scotch-Irish migration to America appears to have come to Pennsylvania attracted probably by the fame of the colony for religious liberty and fertile soil. They scattered themselves to some extent all over the State, and members of the race can now be found in almost every part of it. A large number of them went up on the Lehigh. Some of the first arrivals went into Bucks County and Lancaster County. They also occupied Octorara Creek, Pequea, Donegal, and

The Making of Pennsylvania

Paxton. But the greater part congregated in what is now known as the Cumberland Valley. This valley was, in colonial times, known as the Kittochtinney, afterwards changed into Kittatinney, and now Cumberland. It includes that triangular shaped country in the southern central portion of the State, with the Susquehanna on one side, the Tuscarora Mountains on the other, and the Maryland boundary on the south. It is the same country which the Union and Confederate armies trampled over in manœuvring for the battle of Gettysburg, and contains the flourishing towns of Chambersburg, Gettysburg, Carlisle, and York.

Fighting had become part of the religion of the Scotch-Irish, as peace was part of the religion of the Quakers, and they used the rifle to settle difficulties with the Indians which the Quakers settled by a treaty. Rough, independent, and vigorous, they sometimes carried these qualities to excess, and became connected with a great deal of the disorder which marked the history of the colony. They were the instigators of the Whiskey Rebellion, which Washington put down soon after the Revolution, and in the records of the colonial period we usually find them described as uncivilized and cruel. In his "Introductory Memoir to the Journal of Braddock's Expedition," Sargent has a passage which, although the Scotch-Irish have objected to it, is a very fair description of them at that time :

"They were a hardy, brave, hot-headed race, excitable in temper, unrestrainable in passion, invincible in prejudice. Their hand opened as impetuously to a friend as it clinched against an enemy. They loathed the Pope as sincerely as they venerated Calvin or Knox, and they did not particularly respect the Quakers. If often rude and lawless, it was partly the fault of their position. They hated the Indian while they despised him, and it does not seem, in their dealings with this race, as though there were any sentiments of honor or magnanimity in their bosoms that could hold way against the furious tide of passionate, blind resentment. Impatient of restraint, rebellious against everything that in their eyes bore the semblance of injustice, we find these men readiest among the ready on the battle-fields of the Revolution. If they had faults, a lack of patriotism or of courage was not among the number."

There is no doubt that the Scotch-Irish were rough, but roughness is not always a serious vice, and there are various degrees of it. They had had the lands of the Irish rebels given to them; they had entered on them with a strong hand, and they had grown accustomed to maintaining themselves among a hostile population from whom they expected but little consideration. They were not much addicted to politeness, or to asking leave for what they took, and they entered Pennsylvania in a manner that was rather irritating to the proprietors. Large numbers of them marched to the " York Barrens," in what was then Lancaster County near the Maryland boundary line, without first offering to buy the land from William Penn. When spoken to on the subject, they replied that Penn had solicited colonists and they had come accordingly. A more serious offence was their settling without purchase on the lands of the Indians, an intrusion which is generally believed to have caused several massacres.

In 1743 the proprietors began to eject them from the unpurchased lands, and as a preliminary proceeding ordered a careful survey to be made. The surveyors and their assistants were resisted, their instruments broken, and they were compelled to retire. The Scotch-Irishmen insisted that the land was theirs, because they had expended time and labor in its improvement. But when legal proceedings were begun, they submitted, accepted leases, and in the end many of them purchased the land ; and this submission has been considered by some of their descendants as an act of remarkable graciousness.

Shortly after the French and Indian Wars they discovered that some traders were crossing the Alleghany Mountains with a supply of goods for the Indians, consisting largely of lead, hatchets, knives, and gunpowder, although there was a law of the colony, passed only a few years before, which strictly prohibited any one from furnishing the savages with weapons or military stores. A party of Scotch-Irish pursued the traders and begged them to desist. They refused, and another party followed them, shot the horses, and burned the goods. The traders appealed to Lieutenant Grant, a royal officer in command at Fort Loudon, who promptly arrested a number of people in the country who had been in no way concerned in the affair. Immediately three hundred armed rangers appeared before the fort, and Grant had to surrender his prisoners. He kept some of their guns, however, and shortly afterwards, on going into the country, he was seized by the inhabitants and held till he gave up the guns.

On another occasion a German, Frederick Stump, together with his German servant, barbarously murdered ten Indians, four men, three women, and three children. There was no doubt of his guilt, and he was arrested and confined. But a warrant was issued from Philadelphia commanding him to be brought to that city to answer for his crimes. Immediately the spirit of the

Scotch-Irish arose. Murdering Indians was not a very serious offence in their minds, and in this attempt to remove Stump they saw an attack on their civil rights. If the guilty could be taken to Philadelphia for trial, so could the innocent, and liberty would be in jeopardy. Seventy of them went to the jail, released Stump and his servant, took them to a place of safety, whence they fled to Virginia, and could never again be found.

They could take care of themselves, these Scotch-Irish. They became impatient and rebellious at the first suggestion of injustice, and raised their rifles at the slightest provocation. But their culminating offence, the offence for which their most ardent admirers can find but slight excuse, was what was known at the time of its occurrence as the Western Insurrection, afterwards called the Whiskey Rebellion. It occurred about ten years after the Revolution, and was an organized and deliberate attempt to overthrow the laws of the United States, persisted in for a period of three years.

But though entirely unjustifiable, there was one characteristic of it for which the Scotch-Irish deserve credit. Though very fond of tarring and feathering their opponents, they did not take a single human life. They lost some of their own number,—the two or three killed in the attacks on the revenue-inspector's house, and the two killed by the army on its march to Carlisle. But they showed no desire to avenge themselves for their losses, and when their enemies fell into their hands they allowed them to escape. Indeed, although they had no respect whatever for the life of an Indian, they had great regard for the life of a white man. This may seem like rather doubtful and negative praise; but it appears in better light when we consider the frightful disregard of human life that has been shown in modern times in Pennsylvania. To relate the history of all the rioting and disorder that have troubled our Commonwealth would be a long task and not a very pleasant one. But it is some satisfaction to know that most of the worst outrages have been committed by foreigners.

A few years after the Civil War our mining regions were infested by an organized association of murderers known as Molly Maguires. These men were not Scotch-Irish Presbyterians, but native Irish Catholics of the lowest type. They had not the excuse of oppression; they had no laws to complain of; no government was interfering with them. They simply indulged themselves in gratuitous murder from spite, prejudice, and often from no cause at all, except that their society had issued an order that a mining boss or some other person should be killed. Everybody knows that these wretches terrorized whole counties for years. The government of the State was absolutely helpless before them, and they might be flourishing to this day if it had not been for the courage and intelligence of President Gowen, of the Reading Railroad, whose triumph over a lawlessness which should have been impossible in Pennsylvania and in the nineteenth century is still too fresh in our recollections to be related here.

The Molly Maguires are gone, but large sections of the State are still troubled by swarms of Hungarians, Poles, and Italians, imported for their cheap labor and their ability to submit to degradation and dirt. Their tempers are uncontrollable, and their hands instantly follow their tempers to a knife or a revolver. If the report from those counties can be trusted, homicide has become so common that the people have long since ceased to wonder at it.

It is hardly necessary to refer to the numerous riots in Philadelphia between 1835 and 1850, or to the Pittsburg strike and riot of 1877, or the Homestead affair of 1892, in all of which many lives were lost and a vast amount of property destroyed, and in almost any one of which more lives were lost and more property destroyed than the Scotch-Irish are responsible for in the whole course of their history. Our civilization of the last hundred years has accomplished wonderful things in science and material wealth. But so far as keeping the peace and preventing bloodshed and murder are concerned we cannot boast. And when we consider some elements of the population we have among us, we would gladly enough bring back again the genial Scotch-Irishman in the worst form of his primitive roughness.

The best description we have of the colonial Scotch-Irish is by the Rev. Dr. Joseph Doddridge, who began life as a Methodist minister, but afterwards became a clergyman of the Church of England. He studied medicine under Dr. Rush in Philadelphia, and maintained himself on the frontier by the practice of it, while at the same time he was preaching. He travelled over Western Pennsylvania, Western Virginia, and Ohio for many years after the Revolution, and laid in those regions the foundations of the Episcopal Church. No man was more generally and more intelligently familiar with frontier life, not only from having seen it, but from having lived it. As a boy he had worked in the clearing and taken his place at the port-hole of a stockade to fight the Indians.

He was born on the east side of the Alleghanies, but removed when very young to the west side, and lived along the Monongahela River. That part of the country was settled about the year 1772, and a large part of the early settlers came from northern Maryland and northern Virginia. Many of them came in over Braddock's trail, which, before entering Pennsylvania, passed through northern Maryland. Many of them were English stock. Some were Scotch-Irish. Large numbers of the Scotch-Irish east of the Pennsylvania mountains joined them, so that the community was Scotch-Irish in tone, and it was altogether Presbyterian.

The country, when they arrived in it, was heavily timbered, damp, and cold, and Doddridge assures us that in his own lifetime he witnessed decided changes of climate caused by the removal of the forests. The summers were at first short and cool, frost lasted until May, the winter began early, and the snows were deeper than any that were afterwards experienced.

Game was abundant. Herds of buffalo and elk wandered through the woods. There were enormous migrations of squirrels. Sometimes they became so numerous as to threaten the destruction of the crops. Then, as if by common consent, they would begin to move, swimming the rivers in countless numbers, and becoming sickly and poor, with large worms attached to their skins. Wolves were also numerous, but so shy that they were seldom shot. Suddenly they began to disappear, and the cause was discovered to be the spread of hydrophobia among them. Doddridge attended as physician several men who were bitten by rabid wolves and died in great agony. Rattlesnakes and copperheads were almost as much dreaded as the Indians. It was no uncommon thing to kill six in one day while cutting a field of grain. They lived in dens among the rocks, several hundred together, and the neighbors would often join in an attack on these places. One of the dens was found in an old Indian burying-place, the skeletons of hundreds of snakes that had died in past years mingled with the skeletons of the Indians.

The settlers found numerous remains of a former population,—stone hatchets, earthenware, huge fortifications, and sepulchral mounds. Arrow-heads were so plentiful all over the country that they could be picked up almost anywhere, and showed that the former population had been numerous. For many years they were used as flints for guns, and were preferred to the imported ones.

The settlers dressed in what was called a hunting-shirt, a garment something like a frock-coat reaching half-way down the thighs and belted round the waist. The bosom was made large, and lapped over a foot or more, so as to be used as a sort of knapsack for carrying provisions. There was a cape on the shoulders, which was usually fringed. The belt carried a hatchet, scalping-knife, and bullet-pouch. Moccasins were worn instead of shoes. Some of the men dressed their legs, like the Indians, in a breech clout, which left the thighs and hips entirely bare, and in this costume they often went to church.

Their wedding ceremonies were characteristic, and show the state of their civilization. These frolics were the delight of old and young, and were the only gatherings at which there was not the labor of reaping, log-rolling, building a cabin, or planning some scout or campaign.

The wedding company assembled at the house of the groom's father prepared to march, so as to reach the house of the bride by noon. They were dressed without the aid of a store or tailor within hundreds of miles, and their horses were also unaided by either blacksmiths or saddlers. Any buckles, rings, or buttons among them were relics of old times, family pieces from grandparents.

As they marched in double file along the narrow trail they were apt to be ambuscaded by surprise parties, who sprang out and fired to alarm the horses. As the cavalcade neared the bride's house, two of the young men usually started on a race to bring back the whiskey-bottle, which was standing ready for them. The victor seized it, and returned to pass it about among the company. The feast was beef, pork, venison, and bear's meat, and if table-knives were scarce the scalping-knives were drawn from the belt and used. Immediately after dinner the dancing commenced, and was kept up till the next morning. As soon as one became tired another stepped in to fill his place. Whoever stole off to get some sleep was hunted up, dragged out on the floor, and the fiddler ordered to play "hang on till to-morrow morning."

At nine o'clock some of the young women stole off the bride and put her to bed. Then some young men seized the groom, and, says Doddridge, "placed him snug by the side of his bride."

The dancing continued. If seats were scarce, every man was expected to offer his lap to a girl, and the offer was never refused. Later in the night, refreshments were sent to the bride and groom, together with Black Betty, as the whiskey-bottle was called, and they were compelled to eat whether they were ready or not.

The feasting and dancing continued at other houses after leaving the house of the bride, and were often kept up for several days. The thirsty one called aloud, " Where is Black Betty ? I want to kiss her sweet lips." And when the bottle was brought he said, " Health to the groom, not forgetting myself, and here's to the bride, thumping luck, and big children." In that natural state of society children and many of them were much desired. The Indians were hostile and numerous, and their depredations increasing. Children became soldiers and the sinews of war, and the family that had their quiver full of them were not afraid to meet their enemies in the gate.

Among such people a word was quickly followed by a blow, and quarrels and fighting were frequent. But in these encounters no weapons were used. They settled all their difficulties with their fists ; and a man who was clearly no match for his antagonist was allowed to employ a friend to fight for him. There was no assassination, none of that murderous shooting at sight which has been so common on the frontiers of modern times. They had, however, one disgusting practice called gouging. This consisted in holding an adversary down and forcing his eye out with a thumb or finger. The atrocity was introduced from Virginia, where it was by no means uncommon. Although Doddridge mentions it as occurring in Western Pennsylvania, it is believed to have been rare, and to have been unknown east of the mountains.

The Making of Pennsylvania

The laws passed by the colonial legislature, sitting in Philadelphia, of course applied to the frontier. But the distance made it difficult to administer them, and in most cases impossible. The people became a law unto themselves, had their own customs, and administered their own punishments, which usually consisted of a flogging, administered with hickory sticks by the person aggrieved or by the neighbors who knew about the offence. Such discipline was called a " laced jacket," was sometimes made severer than usual by counting nineteen strokes as a dozen, and was very apt to be followed by a sentence of exile. Whipping was also resorted to as a torture to force confessions of guilt.

Besides that relic of the Middle Ages, the people showed their nearness to the old civilization of Europe by their songs and tales. Lore-telling was popular, and Jack the Giant-Killer and romances of knight-errantry favorite stories. Their songs were mostly ballads of Robin Hood. They enjoyed themselves through their hospitality, which was boundless, and their friendships, which were ardent. They were fond of sports, running, wrestling, and jumping, and when they had enough ammunition they shot at marks. They had that same skill in shooting a squirrel through the eyes which afterwards was so often heard of among the Kentuckians, and their rifles at short ranges within a hundred yards were fully as accurate as modern weapons.

After the year 1755 all these people, men, women, and children, lived in a continual state of war with the Indians. There were few boys so young that they could not fire a rifle through a port-hole, and few women who could not cut bullet patches and carry water. Doddridge describes the preparations he witnessed for the defence of a fort, in which the women worked as hard as the men, showed no signs of alarm, and enjoyed the excitement.

Until about the year 1755 the frontiers, owing to the pacific policy of the Quakers, enjoyed peace. But from about the middle of the eighteenth century, when the French began to tamper with the Indians, war set in and continued with short intermissions for forty years. It lasted, in fact, until the famous campaign of Wayne some years after the Revolution. Wayne moved the scene of conflict farther westward, and relieved forever afterwards the frontier of Pennsylvania. So accustomed did the people become to a life of continual bush-whacking that Doddridge says they accepted it as the natural state of man, and never hoped to be free from it.

The cruelty and brutality of their warfare are almost beyond belief. Both sides scalped each other and both sides killed prisoners; the white man reserving to him-self the merit of never torturing prisoners, and seldom killing women.

The settlers' only season of respite was during the winter, when the snow and cold prevented the Indians from campaigning, and forced them back into the fast-nesses of Ohio to cower over the fires in their wigwams. The balmy air of spring and the sunshine of summer brought no pleasure to the border population. The melting of the snow was a sign of terror; they knew their enemy would soon be upon them, and the people of each district all retired to their fort, where they lived huddled together in great discomfort until November. From the fort the men went out almost every day in armed parties to cultivate their farms. Their arms were stacked in the middle of the field, and sentries stationed in the woods.

The coming of frost and snow was hailed with delight. Each family retired to its home. But often in November, after the winter had apparently set in, there came those mild, smoky days, which we all know so well. This was a fresh alarm. Some families went back to the fort, and only the boldest remained at home. Hence, says Doddridge, arose the expression " Indian Summer," a phrase which is now of pleasant association, but which in its origin could make the most light-hearted frontiersman grave.

At the end of January, or the beginning of February, there was apt to be a thaw of some days, or a week or two. Such weather was called " paw-wawing days," because it was then the Indians were supposed to hold councils to plan the spring campaign, and if this weather continued long enough they would start on a foray. As one melting day would succeed another, the women in the cabins would grow restless, and the men would cease from all labor and watch the woods.

It was a wild life and a rough one, but it had its compensations. The people were hardy, vigorous, and full of strong animal enjoyment. They were masters of their own destinies. No one was unsexed and degraded ; there were no sweating-systems ; no mill work ; no man devoted his whole life to making pin-heads. Every one was a Jack-of-all-trades, his own blacksmith, his own carpenter, his own cooper, his own gunsmith, and his wife his own weaver of linsey cloth. Jacks-of-all-trades are not the most effective means of organizing a rapid material civilization, but they often bring great happiness to the individual Jack.

Nor was it altogether a monotonous life. The continual excitement of forty years of war, the rapid development of the frontier, the growth of new settlements, the varied exertion required, left little room for sameness. Men grew old early from the privations and hardships. But they never complained that life seemed dull. And the Quakers in Philadelphia would probably have added that life must have been exciting enough to people who were continually engaged in so much mischief and disorder.

The Whiskey Rebellion closed the disorderly period of Scotch-Irish history. In the hundred years that have since intervened they have lost that crudeness of spirit which produced such unruly outbursts. They are no longer isolated. They no longer have to contend with the violence of the Indian on one side of them, and the placidity of the Quaker on the other. They are no longer hunters and rangers, and the rifle has disappeared from its resting-place across the chimney. Railroads and the levelling tendencies of modern times have polished the rough oak, and the grit and strength remain.

With all their faults they have been a great people, and have had a great and valuable influence in the development of Pennsylvania. Some of the most agreeable, genial, and accomplished of our citizens are to be found among them. In colonial times they were repressed by the Quakers, and displayed themselves only in opposition to the existing order of things. The Revolution was their great opportunity. They entered it heart and soul, and it has been said that there was not a single Tory among them.

The Making of Pennsylvania

So great was their success at that time that they completely turned the tables on the Quakers and the Episcopalians and got possession not only of the State, but of Philadelphia, which may be said to have been ruled by their influence all through the Revolution. While fresh in the possession of this power and elated with victory, they committed not a few excesses, the worst of which was the destruction of the charter of the old college of Philadelphia and the confiscation of its property. Their absolute rule in Philadelphia ceased after the Revolution, though their influence remained large. In the State they are still a very important element, and it has been said that no man can have a long career in Pennsylvania politics without their support.

Their excesses in modern times are confined for the most part to somewhat fulsome eulogies of their own merits in the past; and if we can believe what their orators say we must conclude that all that was best in the United States waited for the Scotch-Irish to create it.

It is very true, however, that some remarkable men in our history were of Scotch-Irish origin, or had some of the blood in their veins. Grant, Jackson, Buchanan, Monroe, Greeley, Blaine, and others are among the number. Grant and Jackson were both of them typical Scotch-Irish characters. The race always shines in war, and usually shows certain distinctive traits. They care but little for manœuvring, and never hope to conquer merely by holding strategic positions. Their objective point is always the army of the enemy; to get at that and annihilate it, or be themselves annihilated, they consider the main object of war. This, it will be remembered, was one of Grant's most striking characteristics, as it was of Jackson, and also of General Stark, of the Revolution, who was also a Scotch-Irishman.

General Wayne has been usually classed as a Scotch-Irishman, and he undoubtedly had many of their characteristics. He was descended from one of the English families that migrated to Ireland, and in religion he belonged to the Church of England. There were many of these English families in Ireland; and it has been said that fully half the Ulstermen were from England and belonged to the Established Church. In temperament and character they differed but little from the Scotch-Irish Presbyterians; for the Scotch who migrated to Ireland were not Celtic Scotch, but of the same races as the English.

General Arthur St. Clair, like Wayne, a distinguished Pennsylvania soldier, and James Wilson, the constitutional lawyer and judge, have also sometimes been called Scotch-Irishmen; but they were both Scotchmen whose families had never lived in Ireland.

In Pennsylvania, among the famous Scotch-Irish governors are Curtin, Geary, Johnston, Pollock, and Pattison. But the most interesting and characteristic men they have produced are the three great chief justices, McKean, Gibson, and Black. McKean was born in Chester County, in the eastern part of the State, and, though of Scotch-Irish descent, he was not of the frontier class. He had that same ferocious aggressiveness and indomitable, emphatic temper that characterized General Jackson. He was chief justice of the State for twenty-two years, from 1777 to 1799, and he was afterwards governor. He made a deep impression on the conduct of affairs both State and national from the outbreak of the Revolution almost up to the War of 1812, and the story of his life bristles with anecdotes which show the Scotch-Irish strain.

While presiding in court at Harrisburg a mob outside disturbed him, and he ordered the sheriff to disperse them.

" I cannot do it," replied the frightened sheriff.

" Then why do you not summon your posse ?" roared the judge.

" I have summoned them, but they are ineffectual."

" Then, sir, why do you not summon me ?"

" I do summon you," said the trembling officer.

Instantly the chief justice rushed out in his scarlet robes, seized a couple of rioters by the throat, and the rest retired.

On another occasion a man in the court-room made an offensive remark intended for his ears. He appeared not to hear it. But presently adjourning the court, he stepped off the bench and striding up to the fellow said, "Sir, on that bench up there I am the chief justice of Pennsylvania, and unable to take notice of merely personal impudence, but on this floor I'll have you know that I'm Thomas McKean, and ready to break your neck or give you any other satisfaction of the sort you please."

When governor he appointed, as chief justice, William Tilghman, who afterwards became one of the ablest and best known of Pennsylvania judges. But the appointment was very much disliked, and some representatives of the Democratic party waited on the governor to object. The governor, with a profound bow and mock courtesy, asked what the great Democracy desired.

"The appointment of a man," they said, "more in accordance with our wishes."

"Indeed," said McKean; "inform your constituents that I bow with submission to the will of the great Democracy of Philadelphia, but, by God! William Tilghman shall be chief justice of Pennsylvania."

Chief-Justice Gibson belonged to the frontier Scotch-Irish, and was born and bred in the Cumberland region. He had a grandfather six feet and eight inches in height, and he himself was over six feet. He was brought up in the mountains on deer-hunting and wrestling, and had the usual excitable temperament, which in his case showed itself in vigorous and incisive language. Winthrop Sargent said of the Scotch-Irish that they always clothed themselves with curses as with a garment. Certainly most of the anecdotes of them which have come down to us contain profanity, and Gibson's life adds a few more. One of the best-known stories about him describes an application which was made to him while judge, to compel a Roman Catholic priest, by a writ of mandamus, to admit a woman to the privilege of the Eucharist. "You had better," he said, "take out a God-damn-us."

But this love of vivid language, when harnessed and controlled in the written opinions of a court, produced some wonderful results, and gave the Supreme Court of Pennsylvania a high and world-wide authority. The opinions and decisions of Chief-Justice McKean were much admired by Lord Mansfield, and laid the foundation for the greatness of the court. Gibson's opinions were greatly admired in England, and at least one of his sentences passed into a legal maxim.

Very often the only difference between a very distinguished judge and an undistinguished one lies in the power of expression. The great judge expounds the law and states it in language either so clear or so beautiful that it becomes valuable to his profession and to mankind. The inferior judge may decide the same case in the same way, or other cases with equal justice, but, for want of the divine art, he remains unknown. Black said of Gibson that he had one faculty of a great poet, that of expressing a thought in language which could never after be paraphrased.

Black himself was a continuation of Gibson, and showed the same characteristics. But he was a more distinguished man, and of wider activities. Besides his remarkable career as chief justice, he was an orator, an advocate in the most important cases of his time before the highest tribunals of the country, and to some extent a statesman. He practised law only as it can be practised by the great. He had no office except in his hat. He kept no papers and no accounts. He argued causes when people insisted upon having him, and he usually tried to avoid them, preferring the fields and orchards of his farm. It is to be regretted that his opportunities in politics were not greater. But his ability was so striking, his opinions so pronounced, that he utterly failed to fill some of the requirements of a politician.

He was an epitome of Scotch-Irish qualities, and had all their homely fondness for domestic life and nature. When at home on his farm, drinking in the fresh delights of spring or the sombre tones of autumn, he would refuse to open his letters for weeks, fearing a call to Washington to argue some important cause. He had his race's intense courage of conviction and fierce love of independence which led him to champion without fee or reward any cause where he thought civil liberty was in jeopardy. His earnest warnings against the encroachments of corporate power and his efforts to purify politics and check the tide of legislative corruption will long be remembered in this commonwealth.

He also had the Scotch-Irish aptness in the use of language, and went beyond Gibson in this respect. Speaking of a rather notorious railroad promoter, he said of him, "If he would take an oath that he was a liar I might believe him." Who but a Scotch-Irishman would have tied such a knot of words? He had a quaint ancestor who always carried a heavy cane, for the purpose, as he never failed to announce, of punishing those who lied in their conversation.

Of all the sects and nationalities that have affected the destinies of Pennsylvania, the Scotch-Irish alone furnish pithy anecdotes that can be quoted. The colorlessness and diffusiveness of the Quakers and Germans are a barren field for anything pointed.

Black's judicial opinions are, for power of expression, among the most remarkable in the English language, and may be found interesting to the laity as well as to lawyers. Perhaps the most typical specimen of his judicial style is a quotation from an opinion in which he dissented from the rest of the court.

"The judgment now about to be given is one of 'death's doings.' No one can doubt that if Judge Gibson and Judge Coulter had lived, the

The Making of Pennsylvania

plaintiff could not have been thus deprived of his property. . . . It is a melancholy reflection that the property of a citizen should be held by a tenure so frail. But 'new lords, new laws' is the order of the day. Hereafter, if any man be offered a title which the Supreme Court has decided to be good, let him not buy it if the judges who made the decision are dead; if they are living, let him get an insurance on their lives, for ye know not what a day or an hour may bring forth.

"The majority of this Court changes once every nine years, without counting the chances of death and resignation. If each new set of judges shall consider themselves at liberty to overthrow the doctrines of their predecessors, our system of jurisprudence (if system it can be called) would be the most fickle, uncertain, and vicious that the civilized world ever saw. A French Constitution, or a South American Republic, or a Mexican administration would be an immortal thing in comparison to the short-lived principles of Pennsylvania law." (2 Phila. Rep. 417.)

Many examples of his eloquence might be given, especially passages from his open letter to President Garfield, which for power of statement and stinging sarcasm has seldom been equalled. There is a passage from a speech he made in a famous Kentucky case which shows the quieter side of his oratory.

"It is not from the exercise of despotic power, nor yet from the headlong passions of a raging people that we learn our duty to one another. When the Prophet Elijah stood on the mountain side to look for some token of the divine will, he did not see it in the tempest, or the earthquake, or the fire, but he heard it in the 'still small voice' which reached his 'ears after those had passed by. We have had the storm of political debate, we have felt the earthquake shock of civil war, we have seen the fire of religious persecution. They are passed and gone; and now, if we do not hearken to the still small voice which speaks to our consciences in the articulate words of the Constitution from the graves of our fathers, then we are without a guide, without God, and without hope in the world."

The Presbyterians of Pennsylvania, whether Scotch-Irish or English, always showed a stronger leaning to-

The Scotch-Irish and the Presbyterians

wards the best sort of education than either the Quakers or the Germans. Their surroundings and circumstances often seriously interfered with them; but even on the frontier they made efforts to have good schools, and Doddridge speaks of two institutions which they founded in the wilderness on the extreme verge of civilization, one an academy at Cannonsburg, which afterwards became Jefferson College, and the other Washington College, in the county and town of the same name.

The Eastern Presbyterians were equally enthusiastic in the pursuit of knowledge. Primary schools were not enough for them, and, except the Church of England, they were the only religious division in Pennsylvania which in colonial times was willing to encourage higher education. One of them, William Tennent, a Presbyterian minister, established on the Neshaminy, in Bucks County, in 1726, a school, which became known far and wide as the "Log College." Such were the vigor of this man's instruction, and the inspiration of his character, that some of his pupils established similar schools, and the name Log College, whether applied to a man or to an institution, became in Pennsylvania a synonyme for excellence in mental training and some little culture. From these log-college men can be traced several excellent academies, Dickinson College, at Carlisle, also the important university at Princeton, in New Jersey, and the lesser lights, Hampden-Sidney, in Virginia, and Washington and Jefferson, in Pennsylvania.

Dickinson College, from its foundation, in 1783, until 1833, when it was turned over to the Methodists, had a hard struggle for existence. The trustees were continually quarrelling among themselves and with the faculty.

The Making of Pennsylvania

At two different times the college was closed for several years, and yet among its little company of alumni are to be found President Buchanan and Chief-Justice Taney, Justice Grier, of the Supreme Court of the United States, two district judges, Chief-Justice Gibson, and three associate judges of the State Supreme Court, five United States senators, ten members of the House of Representatives, about twenty-three presidents of other colleges, seventy professors in other colleges, Bishops McCoskry and Cummins, of the Protestant Episcopal Church, two Postmaster-Generals, Professor Baird, of the Smithsonian Institution, and Governor McClelland, of Michigan, who was at one time Secretary of the Interior. Governor Curtin, of Pennsylvania, was a graduate of the Law School, as was also one of the governors of Minnesota.

The statistics of Washington and Jefferson University are equally remarkable. Besides sending an unusually large number of learned men into prominent positions in the Presbyterian ministry, it has produced sixty-four presidents of colleges, ninety-five judges, twenty of whom were on the Supreme Bench of their respective States, over sixty members of Congress, ten senators, ten governors, and five cabinet officers.*

---

* Morrison's Among the Scotch-Irish; Proceedings of the Scotch-Irish Society in America; Chambers's Tribute to the Scotch-Irish; Doddridge's Settlement and Indian Wars of West Virginia and Pennsylvania; Fourth Annual Meeting of Pennsylvania Scotch-Irish Society.

CHAPTER VII.

THE CHURCH OF ENGLAND MEN.

WILLIAM PENN'S principles were very liberal, but all the circumstances of the founding of his colony indicated that its government would be largely controlled by the Quakers. They were the most earnest advocates of religious liberty that had ever appeared in England; but their sincerity had never been put to the final test. The men of those times were very familiar with sects which preached religious liberty when they were persecuted and practised quite the reverse the moment they got their hands on political power. The officers of the Crown were bound to protect the established religion, and accordingly we find a clause in the charter to the effect that whenever twenty persons should petition for a Church of England parish it could be established. The National Church, which was a part of the British government that created the charter, was thus protected from any attempt to nip it in the bud, if it should show signs of life in the province; but Presbyterians and other dissenters were left to take their chances with the Quakers.

Penn, in one of his letters to James Logan, seems to imply that the English Church attempted to get more protection for herself than the clause which was finally inserted in the charter. " The Bishop of London," he says, " at the passing of my patent did what he could to get savings for the Church, but was opposed by the Earl of Radnor." If the bishop tried for anything more than the provision finally adopted, it was unnecessary, for the clause as inserted proved to be amply sufficient.

The Episcopalians, after some years, attained to a very strong position in the province, and when the proprietors joined the Church of England, members of that Church were soon in control of the executive portion of the government. But at first they were few in numbers, and there was no attempt to present a petition for a parish until 1695, thirteen years after the founding of the colony. Christ Church was established in that year, and a building erected with a bell hung in the crotch of a tree. The brick building so interesting for its architecture, and which still stands on Second Street, was begun in 1727, and finally completed with its steeple in 1755. It was the sole rallying-point of the Churchmen for more than fifty years, or until the founding of the college which gave them an additional stronghold. Intrenched in these two institutions and under the leadership of the provost of the college, Dr. Smith, they became an element of great political importance.

As soon as the petition for a parish was presented in 1695, the Quaker magistrates arrested the attorney who drew it and several of the principal signers. This persecution, and the imprisonment of William Bradford for publishing Keith's pamphlet, are the only instances in which the Quakers violated their extreme principles of religious liberty. For the sake of the truth of history these instances must be mentioned. But when we consider that the Quakers controlled the government of Pennsylvania for nearly a hundred years, allowed and encouraged people of all sorts of creeds to come to them, these two outbursts of irritation count for very little. We should indeed rather welcome and rejoice in them. The conventional books of history, from which most of us get our ideas, always represent the Quakers as utterly stupid in their perfection. Anything that shows them to have been human is a valuable discovery, and, like the one or two instances in which Washington lost his temper and swore, should be carefully preserved.

Such exhibitions of human feeling on the part of the Quakers were not calculated, however, to soften the hearts of the Churchmen, and there was considerable ill temper between the two faiths. They stood apart in political matters, never acted in concert and often in violent opposition. The letters and documents of the Churchmen during the first forty or fifty years are full of the most virulent abuse of the Quakers and their " many notorious, wicked, and damnable principles," as they called them.

On the other hand, the Quakers never appear to have expressed themselves so violently. They disapproved of the Churchmen ; but they preferred them to the Presbyterians, for whom they had a most intense dislike. In fact, it has been said that many of the Quakers were willing to encourage the Church of England, and even favored an English bishop, as an offset to Presbyterianism, which they feared would overrun their colony.

Who were the first Churchmen and when they came is unknown. Doubtless some of them arrived soon after the first Quakers who came over in the " Welcome" with William Penn. A school-master named

The Making of Pennsylvania

Arrowsmith seems to have been their first clergyman, and he sometimes obtained the assistance of the Rev. Richard Sewell from Maryland. The Rev. Thomas Clayton was, however, the first regular incumbent, and began his labors in 1698, three years after Christ Church was built. The Quakers called him "the minister of the doctrine of devils;" but still he had great success in converting them. He was followed by the Rev. Evan Evans, who met with even greater success. The readiness with which the Quakers joined the Church of England in Pennsylvania was contemporaneous with the founding of the colony, and has continued down to the present day.

The relations of the church with the Swedes were very friendly. The Swedes were Lutherans, and their clergy often exchanged pulpits with Episcopal clergymen, and on at least one occasion took charge of an Episcopal church in the absence of its rector. Gradually the Swedes were all merged in the Church of England, and for a long time it was expected that the German Lutherans would follow them. The beautiful old Swedish churches, Trinity at Wilmington, and Gloria Dei at Wicaco in Philadelphia, besides several others, became the property of the Episcopalians, in whose hands they still remain.

In the early days, under Arrowsmith, Clayton, and Evans, the Churchmen developed rapidly, not only in the city, but in the country districts. In a few years, however, this rapid development in the country ceased, and many of the missionary stations fell into decay, and after that the advance in the country was comparatively slow. The cause of this is somewhat obscure, but may

have been the decision some of the clergy reached
to dispense with vestries. But the churches in the city
always flourished, and in colonial times the city was the
chief stronghold of the Episcopalians, as the counties
were of the Presbyterians.

The Churchmen were much increased by the Keithian
controversy, which within a few years sent five hundred
Quaker souls into Episcopacy. The Church grew
steadily all through the colonial period, gaining not only
by immigration, but by the recruits it received from the
Quakers and the Swedes.

The rapidity and ease with which the Quakers joined
it in preference to all other divisions of Christendom
were quite remarkable, and have always been somewhat
of a surprise to historians. The explanation, however,
is easy if the fundamental principles of the two religions
are kept in mind. The Church of England has never
been a very dogmatic body, has never been much
devoted to systems or theologies, and has always given
ample room for the development of individual opinion.
In colonial times, and up to the middle of the present
century, it was in the low-church stage, especially in
Pennsylvania, and in some respects more free from
dogma than now. In fact, it was sometimes very close
to what is now known as old-fashioned unitarianism.
It satisfied the Quaker instinct for religious liberty
and faith without formula. It had the additional advantage of allowing him to dress and spend money as
he pleased, and contained a large measure of the delicate
spirituality which characterized his own religion.

The Churchmen for a long time felt themselves in
a very uneasy position, outnumbered in a dissenting

community; and they appear to have been not altogether satisfied with religious equality. Some of them
would have preferred to see their faith established by
law and their clergymen given the dignity and position
which they had in England and Virginia. They had
been accustomed in England to snub Quakers and
Presbyterians, and now they found themselves in a
colony where to snub a man for his religion was a
penal offence. They felt this to be such a deprivation
of ancient privileges that they called it persecution, and
sent long complaints to the home government.

The truth of the matter was, that the Quakers had
turned the tables and were snubbing the Churchmen.
They believed themselves the makers of Pennsylvania,
and their religion the established one, and they treated
the Churchmen as dissenters.

" The Holy principles of our religion teach us not to resent such affronts,
but it grieves us at this time that all Church of England men should be
stigmatized with the grim and horrid title of treacherous and perfidious
fellows, dissenters, and schismaticks from the established Religion, which
is Quakerism, Intruders and Invaders in the Province, and, above all,
that our Proprietor and Governor is resolved, and will be, *aut Cæsar, aut
nullus.*" (Perry's Collections, American Church in Pennsylvania, 4.)

George Ross, a clergyman at Chester, writes, in 1712,
that the Quakers are a " haughty tribe," and nowhere
" more rampant " than in his parish. Penn was certainly
a good deal of a Cæsar in his way. He intended himself to be the first in control, with the Quakers second,
and other religions freely tolerated, but in a subordinate
capacity. He considered it fair, and in accordance with
his plans, to let the Churchmen hold a few of the offices
within his gift, but not many, and their aggressiveness

was very offensive to him. "They misrepresent all we doe," he says, "and would make us dissenters in our own country." He complained that they took advantage of his principle of toleration. "Their present minister," he says, "brought over printed books and broad sheets in great quantities to be pasted up in their Houses; is this submission to Government?"

The Churchmen professed to regard the Quaker control of the province as a great evil, not only to themselves, but to the British empire. The Quaker objection to war prevented the establishment of a militia. The colony was in a defenceless condition, and might at any time fall into the hands of his majesty's enemies. They were careful not to lose this cause of complaint, and when it was proposed to organize a militia they voted against it. Not only was the province unprotected, they said, by the stupid Quaker government, but even civil justice could not be administered. The Quaker laws required no oaths; a simple affirmation was the only form used in judicial proceedings and in accepting public office, and a man might be tried for his life by a judge, jury, and witnesses not one of whom had been sworn.

Their remedy for this state of affairs was to have the colony taken away from the Quakers and turned into a royal province, under the direct government of the king, and doubtless many of them foresaw in such a change a chance to have their church established by law. When the Jerseys, which were largely Quaker, became a royal province in 1702, the Pennsylvania Churchmen regarded it as a precedent in their favor and had great hopes of success. When Lord Cornbury, the first royal governor of Jersey, came out, they entertained him in Philadelphia, presented him with an address of welcome, and urged him to use his influence to obtain a royal government for Pennsylvania. In the same way they tried to obtain the assistance of Governor Nicholson, of Virginia, and left no stone unturned in their endeavors.

It was characteristic of the constant changes that were taking place in the position of parties in Pennsylvania that some years afterwards the Churchmen held just the opposite of these opinions, and became very much opposed to direct royal jurisdiction. When the sons of Penn, who were proprietors of the province, became Episcopalians, the Quakers deserted the proprietary interest, and the Churchmen joined it. In other words, the two parties exchanged sides. In the year 1764 it was the Quakers who were attempting to turn the colony into a royal province, and the Churchmen who were opposing it.

In the early days, when the Churchmen favored a royal government, they were led by Colonel Quarry, at one time governor of South Carolina, whose name is still to be seen engraved on the communion set which he gave to Christ Church. He represented the Crown in the province, and was Judge of the Court of Admiralty, which had been established to adjudicate maritime causes, enforce the navigation laws, prevent direct trade with foreign countries, and, in general, look after the royal interests. He considered it part of his duty to send complaints of all kinds to the Board of Trade in England, and report irreverent and disloyal speeches. He was a great nuisance to Penn, who was almost willing to give up the province for the sake of getting rid of him.

The Church of England Men

Under the leadership of Quarry the Churchmen made, in 1703, what they considered a very clever move. They obtained an order from Queen Anne, which, while it allowed Quakers to affirm, compelled all others to take oath. The Quakers had as much objection to administering an oath as to taking one, and, armed with this order, Colonel Quarry was in a fair way to compel the resignation of every Quaker who held public office. Some resigned, others remained in office and administered oaths, and both received an indignant rebuke from Penn, who said that they should simply have disobeyed the order. It was an unfortunate affair for the Quakers. Such orders were probably unconstitutional, and in the end could not have been enforced; but they pointed out a method of annoyance which, though never entirely successful, was several times attempted.

Soon after the death of Penn, when his sons had become Episcopalians, there seems to have been a feeling that the deputy-governor was head of the Church in Pennsylvania, as the king was head of it in England. One or two governors certainly gave themselves airs of this sort. But the idea was never very fully carried out, and probably for the reason that the Churchmen saw that if the governor's authority in this direction was much developed, his interference might at times become very inconvenient.

In " Perry's Collections" there is a curious letter written in 1727 by one of the clergy, William Becket, to the Bishop of London, in which he suggests a very ingenious plan for the advancement of the Church. The title to the three lower counties, as Delaware was then called, was, he said, in dispute. Penn claimed it, and also Lord

The Making of Pennsylvania

Baltimore. The probability was that neither of them owned it, and it belonged to the king. Why not, then, give it to the Church as a manor ? There were said to be two hundred thousand acres of cleared and improved land in it, and the rents from this would easily support an American bishop, missionaries, and many other things which the Society for the Propagation of the Gospel might judge expedient.

The desire for a colonial bishop was always present with the Churchmen, and always more or less under agitation, but never accomplished. In the Middle and Southern colonies, the opposition to it among the dissenters was not very serious. But in New England it was regarded with horror, and on the outbreak of the Revolution one of the strongest arguments which the Puritan ministers urged upon their people was, that unless they achieved their independence there would be an American Episcopate, with another Laud at its head, who would hang them up by the thumbs every morning, put their legs in Spanish boots, with all the other tortures of the inquisition.

But after all, the bishop might not have been such a serious evil as was supposed ; and if Delaware had been given him as his see and manor, he could have lived in a most princely state from the rents of its fertile farms, become a most striking and remarkable character, and added an exciting interest, not only to the annals of Delaware but to the history of all the colonies.

The pettiness of conduct which marked the early history of the Pennsylvania Churchmen passed away. By the year 1750 they had adopted broader views, were no longer peevish in their treatment of the Quakers, had

The Church of England Men

learned to accept religious equality as a blessing, and soon after gained an abler leader than Colonel Quarry. The rest of their history in colonial times is the history of an institution and a man. The institution was the College of Philadelphia, and the man was the Rev. Dr. William Smith, its provost or president.

It would be out of place to enlarge much further on their position. They were not isolated like the Scotch-Irish, Germans, Moravians, or Connecticut people, who led a more or less distinct life of their own, and appeared only at intervals in the general history of the colony. The Churchmen, on the contrary, were largely the makers of that history. Most of them lived in Philadelphia or its immediate vicinity, the seat of government and the scene of all political conflicts. They were the head and front of the proprietary party and the bitter opponents of the Quakers and Benjamin Franklin.

Their clergy were not very numerous in Pennsylvania. Up to the time of the Revolution there were never more than eight or ten of them, and four of these were in Philadelphia. They had three churches in the city,—first, Christ Church, and afterwards two offshoots from it, St. Peter's and St. Paul's. St. Peter's, founded in 1761, was a sort of colony of Christ Church, and the two were long known as the United Churches of Christ Church and St. Peter's. St. James, a colony of St. Peter's, was added to the Union in 1809. St. Paul's, established in 1760, though also an offshoot of Christ Church, was the result of a disagreement, and was never in the Union. Outside of the city they had Trinity, at Oxford, nine miles to the north, and St. David's, about eighteen miles to the west, at Radnor, and St. Thomas, at White Marsh.

The Making of Pennsylvania

The buildings of Trinity and St. David's, dated respectively from 1711 and 1714, still stand, and are among the most interesting relics in the country of the old colonial architecture. They also had congregations at Chester, Bristol, Perkiomen, Pequea, Lancaster, Huntington, and other places. The eight or ten clergymen had to supply all these in turn, and one man often had charge of three or four congregations.

Far out on the frontier, among the Scotch-Irish and Germans, they had a mission in charge of the Rev. Thomas Barton, a courageous, devoted man, who, with the Presbyterian ministers, was ready at any time either to preach and pray or to lead his congregation to war against the Indians. He was a firm believer in the importance of establishing the English control of the continent as against the French. He was close to Braddock's defeat and Fort Pitt, and familiar with every movement of the enemy. It seems to have delighted him when his congregation appeared at service with their muskets, and he reported the event to England with evident satisfaction. His situation at first was nominally at Carlisle, but he appears to have ranged the whole country and even penetrated into the interior of New York. His descendants formed for a long time a well-known family in Philadelphia.

In a certain sense all the clergy in Pennsylvania were missionaries. They were sent out by the Society for the Propagation of the Gospel, which paid them their salaries, and they were supposed to be under the jurisdiction of the bishop of London.

The number of the laity is not known, and any attempt to state it would be a mere guess. They

The Church of England Men

formed a part of that third which Franklin described as the miscellaneous fraction of the population. They were most numerous in Philadelphia, where they shared the control with the Quakers. As in all the Middle and Southern colonies, they naturally assumed to themselves the leadership in society, and it was readily accorded them. When the proprietors became of their faith they had the additional advantage of being part of the government, and the offices within the proprietary control were usually distributed among them.

An interesting essay might be written on the different ways in which little aristocracies were developed in the different colonies. In Virginia and in Massachusetts, where the population was homogeneous in race and religion, where there was no proprietary government, and where the people had enjoyed at times a large measure of independence, the better and more intelligent classes gradually became small aristocracies in what seems to have been a very natural way. Their roots went down among a united people, who gave them support and much respect.

In Pennsylvania, however, there was a very curious condition of affairs, and the aristocratic class was divided among the Quakers and the Churchmen. The Quakers, as the creators of the province, were entitled to the first place, and many of them took the position. Religious scruples about dress and amusements, of course, held back many of them from such a life, and they formed a distinct society of their own, with a great deal of good living and enjoyment, and their own rules about dress. Those who entered the fashionable life of the Episcopalians were very apt to join that faith. In the government of the colony the Quakers controlled the assembly, and the Churchmen controlled the executive offices in the gift of the proprietors; social life was divided up in very much the same way between the two religious bodies; and they have always formed two distinct societies in Philadelphia.

The men who formed the Church of England aristocracy, as it may be called, had many fine traits. The Chews, Provost Smith, Richard Peters, Judge Peters, Robert Morris, the Binghams, the Willings, the Hamiltons, William Moore, of Moore Hall, and others were all accomplished, talented men, full of public spirit and enterprise, who, so far as they were allowed to shape the community, did it wisely and well, and would have been men of note in any city of that age. We might add to them Chief-Justice Allen, who, though a Presbyterian, always acted with them, and was one of the leaders of the proprietary party, and very lavish of his wealth in every public improvement. John Dickinson, a Quaker, was also of the proprietary party, and, like Allen and the others, of unquestioned high character and ability.

Unfortunately, these men depended for part of their position upon the proprietary interest, or were believed to depend upon it, which, so far as results were concerned, was the same thing. The proprietorship was not popular, and the rest of their hold, the Church of England, was equally unpopular, and the Quakers were against them. They had the misfortune to live in a very mixed commonwealth, where any position they had must be given them by a mere faction. They had no broad roots extending all through the community like the aristocracies in Virginia and Massachusetts, and when the Revolution came they went to pieces and disappeared. In Virginia and Massachusetts, on the contrary, the colonial aristocracies went through the Revolution without harm, played a large and important part in it, and afterwards flourished more abundantly than ever, and produced the greatest statesmen in the Union.

In a previous chapter we called attention to the striking individualism of the Scotch-Irish, and mentioned their three great chief justices, McKean, Gibson, and Black. It may be well, therefore, by way of contrast, to speak of another great chief justice, William Tilghman, who was not the product of Scotch-Irish and Calvinistic influences, but was bred among Church of England people in Maryland and afterwards in Pennsylvania. He was the very opposite of McKean, Gibson, and Black. He had none of that excitable aggressiveness, no instinct for impressing everything with his individuality. He was colorless, retiring, modest. He had no vividness, originality, or picturesqueness, either in language or manner. Like Washington, Hamilton, and Jefferson, who were also bred as Churchmen, his style, though showing ability in conception, was rather dry and uninteresting. Yet his judicial opinions are generally regarded as equally as sound, consistent, and valuable as the work of either McKean, Gibson, or Black.*

---

* Perry's Collections, American Church in Pennsylvania; White's Memoirs of the P. E. Church; H. W. Smith's Life of Provost Smith; Perry's History of the American Episcopal Church; Dorr's History of Christ Church; Records of the Society for the Propagation of the Gospel; Wickersham's History of Education in Pennsylvania.

CHAPTER VIII.

THE WELSH.

For the first fifteen or twenty years after the founding of Pennsylvania, in 1682, the Welsh were the most numerous class of immigrants, and they have left many traces of themselves for many miles round Philadelphia in the names of places. Their migration, however, soon ceased, and after 1700, with the incoming of English, Germans, and Scotch-Irish, they became comparatively few in numbers, and of less importance and influence. But still they were a distinct element, and increased for a time the incongruous and mixed character of the colony's population.

Most of the Welsh that came were Quakers, with a sprinkling of Baptists and Churchmen. They spoke their own language, and scarcely any of them had mastered English. When William Penn preached among them at Haverford, in 1701, very few could understand him.

As descendants of the ancient Britons, who had been driven into a corner of England by the Saxon and Norman invaders, they felt that they were still a separate people, and, like the Germans, they hoped to have a country of their own in Pennsylvania. For the first half-century of the colony's existence it afforded the rather unusual spectacle of an English province in which the three languages, German, Welsh, and Swedish, were spoken by quite a large portion of the people. During that time, when the

The Welsh

Germans were upbraided for not learning English, they always asked why no complaint was made of the Swedes or Welsh. But the Welsh, like the Swedes, were soon absorbed, and their language disappeared.

They had, however, been assisted in retaining their language and customs by an agreement they made with Penn before they emigrated. He had promised them a tract of forty thousand acres, where they could have a little government of their own, and live by themselves. When they began to arrive, in 1682, the tract was surveyed for them west of the Schuylkill, and it included that beautiful stretch of country which has now become very familiar to Philadelphians for its suburban homes along the line of the Pennsylvania Railroad.

There was something peculiarly suitable in giving the Welsh this tract, for it more nearly resembled their own country than any other land that could be found near Philadelphia. That it was given for this reason does not appear, but it is not at all unlikely that the woodsman's instinct of the first Welsh explorers led them to follow that ridge of high land, which is the water-shed between the western side of the Schuylkill and the Delaware. This ridge, which is more or less of a table-land, several miles wide, rises steadily from the west bank of the Schuylkill for about twenty-five miles until the summit is reached, near Paoli, about six hundred feet above the level of Philadelphia. As we advance along it westward the country becomes more and more diversified, more rolling and hilly, with longer vistas, and the climate cooler and dryer. On the northern side very extensive views are obtained over what we now call the Chester Valley, and the descent into it becomes steeper and steeper as we approach Paoli. The Welsh called it Duffrin Mawr, or the Great Valley.

They insisted that their forty thousand acres constituted a barony, or county palatine, and it was known as the Welsh Barony until modern times changed it to Welsh Tract. It was a manor with the right of Court Baron, like the one occupied by the Moravians on the Lehigh, and if circumstances had been favorable it could easily have been developed into a sort of palatinate. It was certainly a magnificent domain of hill and dale covered with enormous oaks, sycamores, and poplars, which the greatest earl or duke might have envied. The red-haired, freckle-faced Owens and Winns were well content with it. They enjoyed most heartily the game and sport it afforded, and their descendants still hunt the fox there as of old. Most of them had some means, and were of the gentleman-farmer class. In fact, the few glimpses we have of them in the old records imply an amount of enjoyment and expenditure for dress and entertainment unusual on a provincial frontier.

They might have made a most interesting place of their barony if they had been allowed to go on in the course they had chosen. They undertook to rule it in their own way, and had none of the usual county and township officers. Their Quaker meetings exercised civil authority, and this curious system prevailed for eight or nine years. In 1690 the three townships within the tract, Merion, Haverford, and Radnor, were organized in the usual way, and the jurisdiction of the Quaker meetings was abolished.

As time went on and immigration increased, the Welsh spread out into other townships,—Newtown, Goshen, and

The Welsh

Uwchlan. Some of them spread out into Montgomery County, north of the city, where places like Gwynedd and Penllyn still stand as their memorials.

Their tendency to cling together and retain their language was largely overcome in 1685, when Merion was separated from Haverford and Radnor, and made a township of Philadelphia County. Up to that time they had been a controlling influence in Chester County. But the change placed them in the minority in both counties and hastened their assimilation. They resisted the change very strenuously, and for a time refused to pay taxes.

They were also much annoyed by having the barony thrown open to settlement for people who were not Welsh. This was done because they refused to pay Penn quit-rents on the whole forty thousand acres. They contended that they should pay rent only on the land they used or cultivated; but as the returns from this were small, Penn insisted on rent from the whole barony, and, when it was refused, destroyed the autonomy of their little empire. It was just as well, perhaps, for the Welsh; the direct descendants of the ancient Britons were English in sympathy, and it was useless to keep up a distinction which had long since ceased to be anything more than a barren sentiment.

Most of their names are now Anglicized. Ap Humphrey has become Pumphrey; Ap Howell, Powell; and Ap Hugh, Pugh. Such names as Roberts, Owen, and Thomas remain as they were, and there are still townships called Tredyffrin, Eastcaln, and Uwchlan. The Pennsylvania Railroad has also helped to preserve the remembrance of these ancient Britons in the names of its stations Merion, Wynewood, Haverford, Bryn Mawr, Radnor, St. David's, and Berwyn. Some of these names are very old in Wales, and go back to the twelfth and thirteenth centuries. Merion, the name of an old British prince, Meyreon or Meiriawn, appears often in Wales in the form Meiron, Merioneth, and Merionethshire. Montgomery County was also named from the Welsh.

The patron saint of the Welsh was St. David, and this name was given to the little Episcopal Church which has now survived nearly two hundred years in one of the most charming and secluded valleys of Radnor. The touching, simple beauty of its architecture and surroundings inspired one of the poems of Longfellow, but he hardly did the subject justice. The great overshadowing oaks, the deep impression of the past, the quaint graves of the old colonists, with William Moore and General Wayne resting in their midst, seem to have been unable to arouse the great poet to his best. Several of his verses are querulous and belittle the subject, and only one verse, where he touches on the impression of rest and seclusion, is of any merit.

Members of the Welsh element in our population can still be found in prominent positions in many of our industrial enterprises; but they have produced few very remarkable men. In the early days of the colony, however, previous to 1700, all the physicians in the province appear to have been Welshmen. Thomas Lloyd, several times deputy governor under Penn, was a Welshman, and so was David Lloyd, the leader of the popular party in the assembly, and afterwards chief justice. In the Revolution and more recent times, the Welsh names of Cadwalader and Meredith have been of much distinction.

The Welsh

It was through this Welsh barony, and following close to the highest points of the ridge, that the great western highway of colonial times, now long known as the Lancaster turnpike, took its way. Begun by the footsteps of the first wandering Welshman, for a time a trail in the woods, then a rough road leading to clearings, then a better road, improved here and there with logs, and afterwards with cobble-stones, always pointing westward to the Pacific, it grew and grew until it reached the Susquehanna, crossed it and wound through the Alleghanies to Fort Pitt, its terminus for many years. Though not always on the same line as the present Lancaster turnpike, it followed the same general route, and it always was, and still is, one of the highways to the boundless West. When the Pennsylvania Railroad was built, the engineers found they could make but little improvement on the Welshman's skill, and they laid their tracks along the summit of the ridge, close beside the turnpike, and perpetuated the old colonial line of western travel, which has now become one of the throbbing arteries of civilization.

In colonial days its throbs were less hurried and nervous, but equally full of life, and perhaps more picturesque. A class of hardy humorous characters grew up who were the teamsters and wagoners to Fort Pitt, and afterwards to Pittsburg. Horses were bred for the service, and the great canvas-covered wagons became a familiar sight on the highway of the barony.

People who can remember the old days of stage travel in England assure us that it had its compensations and some advantages. The turnpikes and mail routes, always kept in thorough repair, were lively scenes, thronged with coaches and private travelling carriages, with excellent inns every few miles. Each inn had its own peculiar characteristics and reputation, and travellers in their own wagons made their day's journey as long or as short as they pleased. The old Lancaster road to the west was somewhat similar.

Not in such good repair as the roads in England, and wilder and rougher in every way, it still must have often reminded the colonists of highway scenes in their old home. The inns on the eastern end were very numerous. At one time there were sixty-two between Philadelphia and Lancaster, which was an average of one to each mile. They were of all grades, high and low. Pressy Robinson's, otherwise known as the Blue Ball, seems to have been decidedly low. There were quarrels, and traditions of strange disappearances, which were confirmed in 1877, when some workmen dug up a number of uncoffined human remains from the old orchard. On the other hand, the Paoli Inn, which still survives, was of the highest class, and has entertained beneath its roof some very distinguished men.

The people living along the old turnpike have always had interesting stories to tell of its scenes. It was not so very long ago that some were alive who remembered the troops marching westward to suppress the Whiskey Rebellion of 1791. Those who could remember the recruits straggling along the road to join in the War of 1812 would now be hard to find. But there are still some who saw the companies from the Alleghanies as they marched to the war with Mexico.*

* Histories of Chester County and Delaware County; Glenn's Merion in the Welsh Tract.

CHAPTER IX.

THE EARLY DEVELOPMENT OF SCIENCE AND THE MECHANIC ARTS.

THE peculiarities of the Pennsylvania population, the freedom from dogma of most of the sects which composed it, and their extreme advancement in the line of the Reformation seem to have produced certain results which gave the province a character of its own totally different from what we find in the other colonies.

One of the first and most natural results was a constitution and laws unusually liberal for that time. The credit of this is due to Penn and the Quakers, for they made the laws, and continued to have a controlling influence in them for nearly a hundred years. Religious liberty was the law of the land in Pennsylvania at a time when in Massachusetts and several other colonies there were statutes punishing heresy with death. Treason and murder were the only crimes punished with death in Pennsylvania at a time when in England there were over two hundred capital offences, the same number in New York, and over twenty in Massachusetts and South Carolina. Prison reform, hospitals, and charitable institutions of all kinds were flourishing in Pennsylvania long before they were regarded as desirable in the other colonies.

The general tone of the whole province was free. The Quakers were inspired with the latest ideas of liberty, and the large German population, whatever their ignorance and faults may have been, were all unquestionably in favor of liberty and free conscience, and lived up to their belief. The Episcopalians and Presbyterians, even if they had other inclinations at the beginning, were soon carried along by the others.

In the other colonies the population belonged to older and more conservative forms of religion, like the Church of England or the Puritans. The New England colonies, though independent and vigorous, were very illiberal, and at the time Pennsylvania was founded had only recently finished persecuting the Quakers, and were just about entering on the witchcraft delusion. In Virginia the Church of England was established by law, and dissenters were treated with no little severity.

Philadelphia and Pennsylvania stood out conspicuously as the home of American liberalism, and for a hundred years and more occupied a very important position, and claimed an unusually large share of the attention of the civilized world. They were regarded as the most remarkable and successful instance of liberalism that had yet appeared, and such instances were valuable. The leaders of advanced thought in those, as in all other, times were supposed to be impractical theorizers, and when they could point to an instance of practical success their triumph was great. Men like Voltaire hailed Pennsylvania with delight, and looked to it as a refuge and an asylum. They called it the home of philosophers; and when Franklin began to make his discoveries in electricity, they were more convinced than ever.

Voltaire was always very much attracted by the Quakers. When he was in England he sought them out and investigated their religion, which astonished

him. If their habit of trembling when they spoke in
their meetings and some other customs could be abolished, he declared that they were of all men the wor-
thiest of respect. "In my life," he said of one of them,
"I have never seen a presence more noble nor more
engaging."

Their stiffness and solemnity occasionally troubled
him, especially when he dined with Claude Gay, a Philadelphia Quaker, in Paris. But he never would give up
his ideal, and he clung to Pennsylvania and her founders
to the last.

"Their colony is as flourishing as their morals have been pure. Philadelphia, or the city of the Brothers, their capital, is one of the most
beautiful cities in the universe; and they reckon that in 1740 there were
one hundred and eighty thousand men in Pennsylvania. These new
citizens are not all primitives or Quakers; half of them are Germans,
Swedes, and people of other countries, who form seventeen religions.
The primitives, who govern, regard all those strangers as their brothers."
(Parton's Voltaire, vol. i., 470.)

He compared Pennsylvania with the other colonies,
most of which he despised, especially the New England
settlements. At one time in his life, when exiled and persecuted, he thought quite seriously of taking refuge in
the Quaker paradise, as Priestley afterwards did, and he
never altogether gave up the idea. "It was," he said,
"the only province on earth to which peace had fled,
banished as she was from every other region."

"I love the Quakers; yes, if the sea did not cause me an insupportable
sickness, it would be in thy bosom, O Pennsylvania, that I should finish
the remainder of my career, if there is any remainder! Thou art situated
at the fortieth degree, in a climate the most mild and favorable; thy
fields are fertile, thy houses commodiously built, thy inhabitants industrious, thy manufactures esteemed. Unbroken peace reigns among thy
citizens. Crimes are almost unknown, and there has been but a single

example of a man banished from the country. He well deserved it; he was an Anglican priest, who, having turned Quaker, was unworthy to be one. This wretch was doubtless possessed of the devil, for he dared to preach intolerance. George Keith was his name; I know not where he has gone, but may all the intolerants go with him.

" So, of the three hundred thousand people who live happily in Pennsylvania, there are two hundred thousand foreigners. For twelve guineas you can acquire a hundred acres, and within those hundred acres you are a veritable king, for you are free, you are a citizen. You can do no harm to any one, and no one can do harm to you; you think what you please, and you say it without any one's persecuting you; the burden of imposts continually doubled, you know not; you have no court to pay; you do not dread the insolence of a consequential subaltern." (Parton's Voltaire, vol. ii., 171.)

It would be easy to fill several pages with quotations from Kalm and other travellers and writers describing the position then occupied by the province, and its wonderful advancement. It was not merely the fertility of soil and the mildness of climate, but the liberal laws and customs which, in their opinion, had attracted settlers and forced on development.

At that time the opinion was rapidly gaining ground that liberty of conscience was not only right in itself, but that it had an important effect in encouraging trade and commerce. Even James II. seems to have been convinced of this result, and Penn often called attention to it in his writings, and gave Holland as an instance of unusual material prosperity as the result of extending religious liberty. His own province of Pennsylvania soon proved to be another instance.

Her material development and increase in population were, in colonial times, very rapid, and in this respect she surpassed the other colonies. She was almost the youngest of all, for her founding, in 1681, was more than half a century after the beginnings of Virginia and Massachusetts, five years after Bacon's Rebellion in Virginia, and many years after the difficulties of Massachusetts with Roger Williams, Anne Hutchinson, and the Quakers. In fact, all the other colonies, except Georgia, were firmly established and far advanced on their course before Pennsylvania began.

But in spite of this late beginning, Pennsylvania, within a few years, outranked most of them, and before the time of the Revolution stood third, coming immediately after those two great and leading commonwealths of the colonial period, Virginia and Massachusetts. In the present century, New York, which was far behind in colonial times, has risen to the first place, and Pennsylvania now stands second.

Being so far advanced in liberal laws and philanthropy, we naturally find Pennsylvania prominent in that other great result of liberty and the Reformation, science and scientific research. In fact, she was the only one of all the colonies where modern science was at all prominent or pursued with anything like ardor and success.

We do not always realize that what is now known as science is only about three hundred years old. It all dates from the Reformation, and from a rather late stage in the Reformation. It is, of course, impossible to fix an exact time for the beginning of such a great movement of thought, which started in numerous and at first imperceptible roots, and grew by steady accretion. But the year 1600 is as convenient a date as any, for it was after that year that Galileo, Kepler, Newton, and Harvey made their great discoveries.

Since then have been discovered all those laws of

heat, light, and electricity which nowadays every school-boy must learn. All that is valuable in chemistry, surgery, and medicine has since then come into exist-ence. Geology is of still later date; and to the same period since 1600 are to be assigned botany, biology, comparative anatomy, and a host of other subjects too numerous to mention. When we come to the inventions which are the fruits of these sciences, the steam-engine, telegraph, telephone, and the wonders of mechanical and civil engineering, they are all within the present century, and many of them within the memory of persons now living.

About the year 1730 a climax seems to have been reached in the progress of science. There was a sudden outburst of scientific investigation all over Europe, which has continued unabated and even stronger than ever down to our own day. It was at that time that the rakish, witty, verse-making, play-writing Voltaire sud-denly, at the age of forty-one, turned himself into a man of science, and for four years spent laborious days among drugs, test-tubes, and filters. But when this spirit of inquiry, which was expanding France and England, crossed the Atlantic for new fields of conquest it could effect an entrance at first into only one colony, Pennsylvania.

It is interesting to speculate on what would have been the probable effect on Franklin's mind if, instead of migrating to Pennsylvania at the age of seventeen, he had remained in Boston, where he was born. It is not likely that he would have become a man of science at all, and the discovery that lightning and thunder and the aurora borealis were forms of electricity would have been connected with some other name. We have a complete history of these seventeen years which he spent in Boston, and there is nothing to show that at that time he had any inclination or taste for science, or that there was anything in his surroundings which would draw him in that direction.

During those years from 1706 to 1723, Boston and Massachusetts were still thoroughly theological, and continued so, though with less and less intensity, until after the Revolution. The theology was of the objective, dogmatic type, in which facts must yield to principles. It is true that during Franklin's boyhood there was a small coterie of Deists in the colony who gradually developed the unitarianism which in the next century became the prevailing form of Massachusetts religion. Franklin, though a boy, belonged to this set, and it was by them that his religious opinions were formed. But they were few in numbers and seldom dared to express themselves openly.

Franklin is described by his biographers as always at war with the prevailing tone of thought he found in Boston. If he had remained in Massachusetts he might have helped to force an earlier development of unitarianism. But he would never have become a man of science, for his whole energy would have been absorbed in merely clearing the ground for the admission of the scientific method, freedom of thought. In Pennsylvania he found the ground already cleared for him, and in all his numerous writings there is not a sentence in which he complains of any lack of liberty in his adopted colony. On the contrary it suited him perfectly, and he flourished in it.

The Making of Pennsylvania

In Pennsylvania, in colonial times, the men who became conspicuous in the most advanced science of the age, who made original investigations in it and gained a world-wide reputation, were numerous and quite distinguished. First among them, of course, was Franklin, who, in 1752, made the wonderful discovery that the thunder and lightning of the summer storms and the aurora of the winter were manifestations of the same mysterious fluid which shows itself when glass or amber is rubbed with silk. He proved this by a series of ingenious and dangerous experiments which were repeated all over Europe, and would alone have made him immortal.

He was thoroughly possessed of the new spirit and method. His mind was free, and his whole life was passed in original research. He could not live or move without making some sort of investigation. He arranged his house with a set of lightning-rods, connected with bells in such a way that the bells would ring whenever the air was unusually charged with electricity, or a thunder-storm passed over, often to the great alarm of his wife.

He invented the lightning-rod. He discovered the phenomenon of positive and negative electricity. He explained for the first time the action of the Leyden jar. He studied storms and their causes, the wind, rain, atmosphere, water-spouts, and whirlwinds. By careful observations he established the fact that the northeast storms of the Atlantic coast usually move against the wind, and he was the first to call attention to other similar phenomena which are now familiar to every one.

There is scarcely a single one of the modern sciences

the elements of which were not more or less developed by him. He was the first man who wrote in English on the modern science of political economy, and he suggested some of the principles which are now elementary in it. It was a chance sentence of his that aroused Malthus to develop his peculiar theory of population, and when that theory was attacked some of its opponents thought that the surest way to weaken it was to strike at the original source, and prove not that Malthus, but that Franklin was wrong.

The unrestrained condition of thought in Pennsylvania affected a large part of the community, and aroused other men besides Franklin. He had three intimate friends, Ebenezer Kinnersley, Thomas Hopkinson, and Philip Syng, who experimented in electricity, sometimes in company with the great master, and sometimes by themselves. Indeed, Franklin was at one time accused of having stolen some of his discoveries from Kinnersley. They undoubtedly gave him much assistance, and made many small discoveries, no one of them very important in itself. But science is largely made up of an aggregation of trifles. Thus, Hopkinson revealed the power of points to throw off electricity as well as to receive it, and Syng invented a new electrical machine. But the important thing to notice about these men was, that they were entirely devoted to original research and discovery, and cared for past knowledge only as it contributed to progress.

The man who ranked next to Franklin in Pennsylvania science was David Rittenhouse. On his father's side he traced his ancestry to Holland, but his mother was a Welshwoman. He was a mathematical genius, invented the metallic thermometer, developed the construction of the compensation pendulum, and made valuable experiments on the compressibility of water.

But the most prominent act of his life was the part he took in observing the transit of Venus in 1769. Up to that time this interesting phenomenon of such rare occurrence, and so important to astronomers, had never been carefully observed, and accuracy in it had become more necessary than ever, because, as had been pointed out, it would afford the best data for calculating the dimensions of the solar system. Elaborate preparations were made in Europe; and the various governments dispatched astronomers to Hudson's Bay, Otaheite, California, and Pekin.

At the suggestion of Rittenhouse, Pennsylvania alone of all the American colonies decided to take observations of her own; and it is another striking instance of the wide spread of the scientific spirit in the colony that the whole community were interested in the undertaking.

The Legislature, the public institutions, and even the economical proprietor, Thomas Penn, supplied funds and apparatus, and the preparations were in charge of the Philosophical Society of Philadelphia, the only organization of its kind in the colonies. Three points of observation were selected,—Cape Henlopen, Philadelphia, and Norriton, the home of Rittenhouse; and apparatus was obtained for all three. When the reports were sent in, not only from the three Pennsylvania observations, but also from the others in different parts of the world, the practical skill of Rittenhouse as an observer became so apparent, that he at once achieved a world-wide reputation. He had constructed with his own hands all the apparatus he used at Norriton, and, not content with that, had, immediately after the emergence of the planet, made the first correct determination of a solar parallax.

He excelled in every undertaking which required the practical application of astronomy. His orrery was an advance on all others, and instead of giving only the apparent movements of the stars, as had formerly been done, it gave their actual movements. This achievement added greatly to his fame abroad. His first orrery was bought by Princeton College, and he had to build a second to be bought by the University of Pennsylvania. The Legislature of Pennsylvania then voted him three hundred pounds as a testimony to his mathematical genius, and also appropriated four hundred pounds to buy from him an orrery of double the dimensions of the other two.

Another Pennsylvanian who gained a world-wide reputation in science was John Bartram. He was the first botanist who described the plants of the new world, and in this pursuit he explored the whole country from Lake Ontario to Florida. Botany at that time had received an immense impulse and had been turned into a modern science by the classification of plants invented by Linnæus. His classification extended beyond the sphere of botany, and he advanced the whole subject of biology by showing for the first time the true principles for defining genera and species. Linnæus and Bartram were almost exact contemporaries, being born within six years of each other, and dying, Linnæus in 1778 and Bartram in 1777.

On the banks of the Schuylkill, within the present

limits of Philadelphia, Bartram established the first botanic garden in America, and the remains of it are still to be seen. He was appointed by the crown American botanist to the king, with a small pension, and Linnæus pronounced him the greatest natural botanist in the world.

Bartram's botanic garden was laid out on part of his farm at Gray's Ferry, where the highway from Philadelphia to the south and west passed over a floating bridge on the Schuylkill. The garden is now preserved as one of the city parks, but is in an unpleasant neighborhood, surrounded by gas-works and factories. In Bartram's time, however, and long afterwards it was an attractive spot and one of the favorite drives from the city. Travellers to and from the Southern States always passed that way. Washington and the other great Virginians often crossed that floating bridge, and were frequently guests at Bartram's house.

For many years his house was the resort of all the distinguished foreigners who came to Philadelphia; and they usually went away charmed with their Quaker host's intelligence, learning, and simplicity. Franklin, Rittenhouse, Wilson, Rush, Shippen, and all the early distinguished physicians of Philadelphia were his friends. The "Washington Room" in the house is still pointed out. There is still in the garden an enormous cypress, which he brought home from one of his trips to the southern swamps; also a cider-mill and a horse-trough, both hewn out of solid rock, and near by can still be seen the head-stone which marks the grave of a favorite slave, whom he is said to have buried with his own hands.

Early Development of Science and Arts

Thomas Godfrey was a mathematical genius who might have been almost the equal of Rittenhouse if it had not been for his habits of intemperance and his early death in his forty-fifth year. Besides showing great brilliancy in unimportant matters, he succeeded in making a permanent improvement in the quadrant, for which the Royal Society gave him two hundred pounds' worth of furniture,—a form of reward which, it was hoped, might not be consumed in drink.

There were, of course, other men in the colony who were much interested in science, without becoming world-wide in their reputation, like Bartram, Rittenhouse, and Franklin. For example, Dr. Benjamin S. Barton, after practising medicine with great success for many years, was appointed in 1789 to the professorship of botany and natural history in Philadelphia College, now the University of Pennsylvania. This was the first professorship and he was the first professor of these subjects in America. He wrote a number of books, which are said to have laid the foundations of the American school of natural history. Among his works are the first American book on elementary botany and the first American book on materia medica. His nephew became a distinguished surgeon, and lengthened the long list of Philadelphia's famous physicians.

Alexander Wilson, the first American ornithologist, should be mentioned in this connection. He was born in Scotland in 1766, and came to Pennsylvania when he was twenty-eight years old. He cannot be claimed as altogether a Pennsylvanian, but it is noteworthy, that, although he showed some taste for natural history while in Scotland, he never did any serious work in it until he had lived for some time in this commonwealth, and conversed with Bartram, who turned his attention towards birds.

Wilson started on his first expedition into the woods in 1804, and from that time the volumes of his work began to appear. He was the first man to describe, from actual scientific observation, the birds of North America. Books have since appeared which perhaps excelled his in the engraved plates, although even in this respect Wilson's drawing was admirable. But no writer on the same subject has excelled him in power of description, and to this day he remains a classic.

Audubon, the other distinguished American naturalist of that time, was also closely connected with Pennsylvania. He was born in Louisiana in 1780, but came to live in Pennsylvania with his parents when he was eighteen, having previously spent a couple of years in Paris, where he learned to draw under David.

Pennsylvania had the same effect on Thomas Nuttall as upon Wilson. Nuttall was a journeyman printer, born in England, who came to Philadelphia in 1808, when he was about twenty-two. He was brought in contact with Professor Barton, who persuaded him to study the trees of North America, and he very soon began travelling over the continent, and penetrated to the Pacific Ocean, a great feat at that time.

He returned by sea from the coast of California on the same ship in which young Richard Henry Dana, of Boston, was a common sailor. He is described in Dana's "Two Years Before the Mast," from the point of view of a Jack-tar who had a supreme contempt for the seedy and sea-sick professor. But Nuttall survived it. He was at one time curator of the botanic gardens at Harvard, and his three volumes of "North American Sylva," together with his other books, are still standard authorities.

It is, perhaps, a significant fact that Joseph Priestley, a very distinguished man of science, who discovered oxygen, furnished the means of discovering several other gases, and who is often spoken of by his eulogists as the creator of modern chemistry, sought Pennsylvania as a refuge. He was so outspoken in his views, he carried the deductions of science so far in advance of his time, and he was so radical in politics that he was persecuted in England, and on one occasion the mob destroyed his house, library, and manuscripts. He fled to Pennsylvania in 1794, and spent the remainder of his days at Northumberland, at the forks of the Susquehanna.

The favorable conditions which existed in Pennsylvania for the growth of science are further shown by the rapidity with which the study of medicine was developed there. The great discoveries in medicine and surgery, as in every other science, have been made since the Reformation, and are the result of the new mode of reasoning which it introduced. What was known before that period is mere nothing to what has been discovered since.

By the beginning of the eighteenth century, the advancement in this most useful of occupations was considerable, and among the colonies in America, Pennsylvania was the first to be affected by it. The first American book on a medical subject was a little volume by Dr. Thomas Cadwallader, treating of the iliac passion, and written and published in Philadelphia in 1740. The first American hospital was established in Philadelphia in 1751, by the efforts of Dr. Bond. The first separate dispensary was also founded there in 1786, and there had previously been one connected with the hospital.

To the same city is also due the honor of the first medical school and the first systematic teaching of medicine. The medical department of the University of Pennsylvania was started in 1765. But a regular course of medical lectures had been delivered since 1762.

All this was in advance of any of the other colonies. New York followed closely after with a medical school attached to King's College in 1767. But it was suspended by the Revolution, and not started again until 1792. It was not by any means successful until 1813, when, several other medical schools springing up, it was united to the College of Physicians and Surgeons, which has now become famous.

Boston had no medical school until 1783, no dispensary until 1796, and no general hospital till 1811. New York started a hospital in 1773, but before the building was entirely completed it was burnt, and, the Revolution intervening, it was not rebuilt till 1791.

Boston, however, must be given the credit of introducing inoculation for the small-pox as early as 1721. But it was introduced by the ministers, headed by Cotton Mather. There was only one regular graduate in medicine at that time in Massachusetts, Dr. William Douglass, and he opposed it.

Dr. Rush, Philadelphia's first great physician, has been frequently called the Father of American Medicine. He was a curious man, very much devoted to the practice and teaching of his profession, and yet at the same time taking considerable part in politics. He signed the

Declaration of Independence, and was a member of the cabal which attempted to deprive Washington of the command and put Gates in his place. He was positive in his opinions, reckless and violent in stating them, and got into some fierce medical controversies, especially on the subject of the yellow fever. Most opposite opinions of him have been expressed. His admirers describe him as " a brilliant star in the galaxy of American worthies," and associate his fame with Howard, Sydenham, and Washington. Others, who happened to dislike his theories, describe him as a writer of " utter nonsense and unqualified absurdity," of " unintelligible and preposterous assertions."

But his reputation went far beyond his own State and country, and his fame in Europe was by no means trifling. Since his time Philadelphia has never been without one or more physicians of national and European reputation. The line begins with Rush, Morgan, and Shippen, and comes down unbroken through Wistar, Jackson, and Barton, to Mitchell, Gross, Agnew, and others of our own time. All through the colonial period, and down to the middle of the present century, Philadelphia was the centre of medical education in this country, and still retains a large part of this pre-eminence.

The first scientific society in America was founded at Philadelphia, and called the American Philosophical Society. It still exists, though it ceased to be of much importance after the Revolution. It was organized at the suggestion of Franklin in 1744, but was rather unsuccessful for some years, until, in 1769, it was joined by the famous Junto, another society of very much the same character, also founded by Franklin. He was for a long time the president of the Philosophical Society, and was succeeded by Rittenhouse. Thomas Jefferson and other prominent persons throughout the colonies were members, and during the colonial period it was the only society of its kind in the country, and held a very prominent position which it has now entirely lost.

Philadelphia is still the home of learned societies. The Academy of Natural Sciences, founded there in 1812, is the oldest as well as the most complete institution of its kind in America. The most prominent names in American science are on its rolls. It has the largest collection of shells in the world, and until within a few years had the largest collection of birds. Its library is also unrivalled.

It has been built up by the individual efforts and donations of Philadelphians, and by the natural interest in science which has always existed in the city. Until within the last few years it had received no assistance from the State. Taken as a whole it is equalled only by institutions in Europe which have received frequent aid from the government.

It has taken active part in several important Arctic expeditions, among them that led by Dr. Kane in 1852 and the one led by Dr. Hayes in 1860. Both Kane and Hayes were Philadelphians and members of the academy.

When we examine carefully into the early history of this institution, which grew so rapidly to such large proportions, we find that it was not founded by professional and distinguished men of science, nor by men of wealth who were seeking to perpetuate their names, but by plain, ordinary persons who represented the average ability and feeling of the city.

Early Development of Science and Arts

The founders were John Speakman, an apothecary, and Jacob Gilliams, a dentist. They were young men who had a taste for natural history as amateurs. They were joined by others, also apparently average men. At their first meeting they decided that the " operations of nature demanded unprejudiced attention and severe scrutiny;" that sectarians had always been "prone to oppose the promulgation of any newly discovered fact which seemed to militate against their dogmas;" therefore they excluded from their debates all discussion of religion or even reference to it. They also put politics under the same ban.

They began in a small room over a milliner's shop, on Second Street, where they placed their first few specimens and books. Other young men have often begun similar collections, but their seed was not sown in such fertile soil. The score or so of rocks and bottles of the young dentist and the young apothecary drew their vigorous life and rapid growth not so much from their first owners as from the fruitful, scientific feeling of the city in which they were placed.

The Franklin Institute, devoted to the promotion of the mechanic arts, and established in 1824, is another Philadelphia society of wide reputation. It is interesting as marking a turning-point in the advancement of science.

Some writers place the beginning of modern science since the year 1800, and they are right, so far as concerns the practical application of science to the mechanic arts and to useful inventions like the steam-engine and telegraph. Science began by being theoretical. The theorists had to clear the ground, discover the elementary laws of matter, and start the habit of observing nature as she actually existed, and not as the theologians supposed she ought to exist. But by the beginning of the present century the work of the theorists was so thoroughly done that the applications of science to everyday affairs became very numerous. A new class of institutions sprang up for the purpose of giving instruction and information to the men engaged in such employments. The polytechnic schools and the schools of mines in France and Switzerland were among the first of these. But the want was felt everywhere, and it is noteworthy that during the years 1823 and 1824, when the Franklin Institute was being founded in Philadelphia, the first mechanics' institute was being founded in England.

During the colonial period, and for some time afterwards, Pennsylvania, like the rest of the scientific world, had been engaged in discovering the elementary laws and in developing the preliminary theories, and in this she led all the other colonies. When the theories were absorbed into practical applications, and modern science in the full sense of the word began, Pennsylvania was again at the head, and established the first American institution for diffusing a knowledge of the new spirit of the age among mechanics and manufacturers.

The Franklin Institute, in its early days, conducted some important investigations in water-motors, the causes of the explosion of steam-boilers, and the strength of materials, subjects which are now fully developed and commonplace enough, but at that time comparatively new and untried. The institute also, from time to time, gave a large number of medals and premiums to encourage investigators and inventors. These are still given in the same careful manner, are eagerly sought for, and when obtained, carry respect for their holder all over the world.

The journal of the institute, published every year since its foundation, is an authority and a source of quotation wherever modern science is taught. Descriptions of the first twenty-nine hundred patents issued by the United States government are to be found only within its covers, and from its first volume to its last it is generally regarded as an almost complete history of the growth of applied science.

Under the auspices of the Franklin was reared Thomas U. Walter, the architect of the capitol at Washington, who began life as a bricklayer; also Alexander Dallas Bache, a combination of two well-known Philadelphia names, who was finally appointed superintendent of the United States Coast Survey, and to whose skill and training are due the accuracy and comprehensiveness of that work which has challenged so much admiration.

In 1833, when an attempt was made to introduce gaslighting in Philadelphia, many of the principal citizens, amounting in all to several hundred, remonstrated and petitioned the city councils not to adopt it. This action has often been cited as showing the slow and unprogressive spirit of Philadelphians. But a careful examination of the circumstances reveals an altogether different meaning.

The remonstrance was largely inspired by gentlemen connected with the Franklin Institute, who knew as mechanical experts that the proposed method of introducing gas was incomplete and dangerous. In fact, it would now be considered as an intolerable nuisance. The result of the remonstrance was that Mr. Samuel V. Merrick, a prominent member of the Franklin, was sent to Europe to collect information and plans of all the best improvements. He obtained access to all the gas-works in England and on the continent, and was allowed to inspect and draw plans on condition that he would not reveal any of their secrets to rivals in the same community. He returned with a complete and practical knowledge of the best methods then known, and they were combined for the first time in America in the Philadelphia Gas-Works.

Many of the former opponents of gas-lighting united in recommending the new plan, which was copied all over the Union, and works previously in operation were remodelled. Not only did the rest of the country come to Philadelphia for instruction, but her combination of the best methods was returned to Europe, and had an important influence in improving the mechanism of the establishments from which it had been originally obtained.

Another instance of early success in mechanical applications may also be mentioned. The pumping-works at Fairmount, by which the water of the Schuylkill is raised to the reservoirs, were erected in 1819, were unsurpassed at that time in their class of mechanism, and remained without a rival until almost up to the time of the Civil War.

In 1824, when the Franklin Institute started, manufacturing was well under way in Philadelphia, and the city had already become remarkable for its industries. There had previously been a manufacturing society which gave premiums as early as 1789, and the Philadelphia Premium Society had been established in 1801. There was also a periodical called "The American Museum," issued by Mathew Carey, and devoted to the encouragement of mechanics. Manufacturing is now the most characteristic feature and the controlling element in all Pennsylvanian civilization; and this assertion may be regarded as the fundamental proposition, without which it is impossible to understand the modern condition of the State, and especially the modern condition of Philadelphia.

If we look further into the history of the matter, we find that in colonial times manufacturing was positively prohibited by the British government in all her colonies, but that in spite of this command Pennsylvania always had a strong tendency towards such industries, and leaned against the barriers as much as she dared. The colonial governors were required to act as spies in this respect, and there are a number of their letters extant reporting to England that very few attempts were made at manufacturing, and those few hardly worth the trouble of suppressing.

Investigation, however, shows that there was probably more manufacturing than the governors had any idea of, or else they were willing to wink at it. The vicious tendency of the colony in this direction usually showed itself in the making of hats, carpets, glass-ware, linen goods, also in ship-building, and in utilizing the great natural wealth of the mountains to produce pig iron. Nearly all these industries are still in existence, and have had a steady development and success.

It is needless to say that iron-making is still one of the great sources of our wealth. Hat-making is also still a large industry, having had a continuous existence in the State for nearly two hundred years.

Another industry which was firmly established in colonial times, and still flourishes, is paper-making. Some of the early Germans who settled on the banks of the Wissahickon, now within the limits of Fairmount Park, established the first American paper-mills. Wagons loaded with rags can still be seen, as they have been seen for a hundred and fifty years, following the roads which wind through those romantic ravines.

Some of these same Pennsylvania Dutch who settled Germantown established the knitting-mills of that place, which have become famous for their product the world over. The industry has now spread to the city, and become of still greater importance. Like the industries of iron, paper, and hats, it seems to be rooted in the soil.

The British government appears to have had no objection to the ship-building, nor to the manufacture of pig iron, provided it stopped at that stage, and was not turned into steel or into articles or implements. An act of Parliament expressly forbade any rolling- or slitting-mills, or any establishment for the production of steel. But it was in vain for any government to try to keep Pennsylvanians from their natural vocations. At the time of the Revolution, Philadelphia seems to have been full of mechanics, who made steel, nails, screws, gimlets, firearms, saws, and all kinds of machinery.

The natural instinct for manufacturing was still more clearly shown when the Revolution removed the barriers, and all these industries, and others in addition, sprang at once into a flourishing condition. The Pennsyl- vanians became manufacturers and protectionists at one bound. The National Constitution had hardly been passed when, in 1789, they petitioned Congress to lay such duties on imported goods as would give a preference to the mechanics of Pennsylvania.

John Mellish, an English writer, the author of " Travels in the United States of America in the Years 1806–7 and 1809–11," seems to have been very much impressed with his discovery that Philadelphia was a great manufacturing centre. He gives the credit to the steady habits of the Quakers.

Dr. Mease's " Picture of Philadelphia in 1811" is also of some interest. He describes the city as at that time the largest on the continent, with a population of one hundred and eleven thousand two hundred, as against ninety-two thousand three hundred, the population of Manhattan Island. He describes large establishments for edge-tools, tin-ware, silver-plate, oil-cloths, earthenware, brewing, drugs, ship-building, shot, paints, spinning machinery, hosiery, leather, especially morocco, carriages, hats, type-founding, firearms, all kinds of iron-ware, fifteen rope-walks, and ten sugar refineries. Nearly all of these will be recognized at once as industries which still continue, some of them having reached great importance.

But, without going into further details, a glance at the statistics shows that in 1850 the value of Philadelphia's annual manufacturing product was sixty-three million dollars. Following down the column, we see it rolling up every year until it now reaches the enormous figure of over five hundred million dollars, of which two hundred million dollars represents textile fabrics alone.

The remarkable part of this industry is that it is very

much diversified. The coal and iron industries of the State are natural products of the soil, and it would be expected in the ordinary course of things that they should be great. But the other industries are all what might be called artificial. They are not the natural products of the soil, but the products of energy, enterprise, scientific skill, and sound judgment in affairs.

When we come to look into their diversification we find that in Philadelphia alone the industries are divided into over five hundred different classes, conducted in over twelve thousand different establishments. The number of people directly employed is two hundred and fifty thousand, about one-fifth of the whole population.

When we add to all this the manufacturing done throughout the State, the petroleum, glass, iron, and steel, we begin to realize the controlling characteristic before which everything else, except the railroads, must bend, and before which everything else, except the railroads, is insignificant.

It would be long to tell of the many and various instances in which Pennsylvania has excelled in the mechanic arts. Nearly all the great and peculiar mechanical structures of the country have been made in our State; the great iron light-houses, the greatest steam-vessels and war-ships; in fact it has been said that there is no mechanic contrivance or device of modern times which cannot be built within the boundaries of Pennsylvania.

The State was among the earliest in railroad enterprise. The Baldwin Locomotive-Works began with the first development of railroads in the United States about 1829, and have kept even pace with that development ever since, inventing, improving, and perfecting, upholding a high standard, and advancing and improving every department of the art. Philadelphia was among the earliest places to experiment with the steam-engine, and the first successful American engines were made there. Beginning at a time when to build a single locomotive that would draw a train in wet weather and on a slippery track was considered a great feat, the Baldwin establishment has now become the greatest locomotive-works in the world, and receives orders from Canada, South America, Austria, Russia, and, indeed, every country where such machines are used.

In building and managing railroads Pennsylvania has again shown the ascendency of her mechanic skill. By the year 1858 she had more than one hundred and thirty million dollars invested in these enterprises, and in 1878 over five hundred and ninety million dollars. The Pennsylvania Railroad has long been regarded as a model for the whole country. The smoothness of its road-bed, the alignment of the tracks, the convenience of its equipment, and the completeness of its organization have given rise to the expression " Pennsylvania Railroad standard," as a test of merit. It has become a school of railroading, and apprenticeships in its departments are eagerly sought.

In ship-building Philadelphia was long pre-eminent, especially in colonial times and for many years after. It was a Philadelphia ship, the " Rebecca Sims," that in 1807 made the passage from the capes of the Delaware to Liverpool in fourteen days, a speed which has never since been equalled by a sailing vessel. When the American navy was formed after the adoption of the Constitution, the first navy-yard was placed at Philadelphia and the first war-ships were built there. In the re-establishment of our navy, which is still in progress, most of the ships have been built in Pennsylvania, either at Roach's yard at Chester, or at Cramp's in Philadelphia, and a large part of the guns and armor-plate have been made at Bethlehem.

In spite of the large manufacturing population in Philadelphia, there is no tenement-house system, no unwholesome crowding, and none of the suffering and misery often seen in towns of one-tenth its size; the large tracts of level land in the city allow of indefinite expansion, and the workmen live in small houses instead of tenement flats.

Our State is undoubtedly overwhelmingly manufacturing, " saturated with industrialism,"—the result of tendencies that have been working for two hundred years. It has led our people to become distinguished as organizers of men and of industries, as the Massachusetts people are distinguished as organizers of thought and its expression. This is very strikingly shown in the long list of remarkable military men that we have produced,—a list unequalled in any other State.

In the Revolution we had Armstrong, Wayne, Muhlenberg, and Mifflin, all of them remarkable in their way. In the Civil War we had the very great names of Meade, McClellan, Hancock, Reynolds, and Heintzelman; the lesser names of Hartranft, Gregg, Humphreys, Gibbon, and Parke; among the admirals, Porter and Dahlgren ; and before the Civil War, Commodore Stewart.

CHAPTER X.

THE Connecticut people were not a very numerous part of the population of Pennsylvania until about the time of the Revolution, but they made up for this lack of numbers by their activity and the largeness of their demands. Like the other divisions, they wanted to live by themselves. They claimed the northern half of the province as their own, and maintained their possession of a part of it by force of arms.

If any one will look at a map of the United States and carry out the northern and southern boundaries of Connecticut to the westward, he will see that they slice off nearly the whole of the upper half of Pennsylvania. The northern line of Connecticut will correspond very closely with the northern line of Pennsylvania, passing, in fact, only about a mile or so to the north of it, and the extreme southern limit of Connecticut, if carried westward, will pass a short distance above the forks of the Susque-hanna.*

The two little colonies of New Haven and Connecticut, the latter being situated at Hartford, were amalgamated into one commonwealth under a charter granted by Charles II. in 1662. At the time of their first settlement they had no definite legal title to the land they occupied,

---

* See map (frontispiece).

and they had no charter giving them the right of civil government. The Connecticut Colony at Hartford was an offshoot from Massachusetts. The New Haven people had come direct from England. They were all Puritans of the sturdiest stock, aggressive, enterprising, and independent. They occupied the land by squatter sovereignty, and with about the same feeling that inspired their fellow-Calvinists, the Scotch-Irish, who planted themselves on the Pennsylvania frontier. It seemed like a pleasant place; they wanted it. They were the saints, and the saints, as we all know, shall inherit the earth.

The Connecticut Colony at Hartford soon purchased a title to their land from Lord Say and Seal, and others, who had received a grant from the Plymouth Council, who were the grantees of the king. But this grant gave the Connecticut Colony merely an ownership of the land, and conferred no powers of civil government. The New Haven Colony remained without title until amalgamated with Connecticut.

The two colonies began their existence almost entirely independent of Great Britain. Their connection with the mother country was nominal. Even after they were chartered in 1662 they were allowed to elect their own governors, and had pretty much all the essentials of independence.

Having originally acquired their land simply by taking it, and having enjoyed so much independence in their civil government, they naturally grew up with rather liberal views as to their right to any additional territory that pleased their fancy. They were never altogether satisfied with their narrow limits in New England. Large families have been fashionable among them, and they have always overflowed their borders. There is no State in the Union that has colonized so many other communities. They have built up a large part of New York, pretty much the whole of Vermont, the famous Western Reserve in Ohio, and innumerable towns in the Great Valley of the Mississippi. We have already discussed their attempts to effect a settlement on the Delaware in the time of the Swedes and Dutch. We must now consider their more serious and determined devotion to that region.

The charter under which New Haven and Connecticut united themselves after the year 1662 gave them for an eastern boundary Narragansett Bay and the same northern and southern boundaries as at present, namely, the Massachusetts line on the north and Long Island Sound on the south. But, like many of the charters of that time, it extended their dominion westward to the Pacific Ocean, or, as it was then called, the South Sea.

There was a proviso in the charter saying that there should be excepted from this grant any portions of territory "then possessed or inhabited by any other Christian prince or state." Such forms of expression were usually inserted in colonial charters. But they were hardly necessary, because they merely stated a general rule of law which prevailed, whether the charter recognized it or not. The New Netherlands, or New York, long occupied by the Dutch, came within this exception, and, when the Connecticut charter was granted, lay directly in the path of its westward course of empire. But having skipped New York, that empire began again, and passed cheerfully westward, cutting out large portions of the present commonwealths of

The Making of Pennsylvania

Pennsylvania, Ohio, Indiana, Illinois, Iowa, Nebraska, Wyoming, Utah, Nevada, and California.

This was all well enough for many years, and Connecticut held an undisputed dominion over millions of acres of forests and prairie, and millions of buffalo and elk. But in 1681, Charles II., who had given Connecticut her charter nineteen years before, gave another charter to William Penn which overlapped Connecticut's western domain where it passed through Pennsylvania. Connecticut maintained that she was first in time, and therefore first in right, and that this second grant, so far as it covered her territory, was void.

The question was submitted in 1761 by the Penn family to Lord Camden, then plain Charles Pratt, a barrister and attorney-general to the Crown. He decided against Connecticut. Soon afterwards four other distinguished barristers—Thurlow, Wedderburn, Jackson, and Dunning—were asked by Connecticut to give their opinion, and they decided against Pennsylvania. The lawyers had in each instance given what their clients wanted, and each side had a learned opinion in its favor.

In America a final decision was reached in 1782, by a committee of Congress which had full power not merely to give an opinion, but to definitely settle the question. This tribunal decided in favor of Pennsylvania. Previously to that decision, Connecticut had always insisted on what she believed to be her rights, and maintained them against Pennsylvania by force.

About the middle of the eighteenth century her people began to cast longing eyes out on their western way beyond New York. Exploring parties were sent; and in the year 1750 some tired Puritans climbed the last summits of the Blue Ridge, and looked down into the Valley of Wyoming. They never forgot that scene. Nor will our race ever look upon such a scene again.

The valley was about twenty-one miles long, and three miles wide. The broad, rippling Susquehanna wound through it, now burying itself in groves of sycamores, and again flashing into the sunlight in wide expanses. There were woodland and meadow, level plains and rolling plains, and the remains of ancient fortifications of a vanished race. Mountain-ranges bounded every side. The river entered the valley from the north, through a gap called the Lackawannock, and went out at the southern end through the Nanticoke Gap. Both of these gaps were just wide enough to admit the waters, and in some places had perpendicular walls on either side covered with laurel and pine. The valley had evidently been a deep lake which had gradually drained itself by erosion at its outlet, leaving a level fertile floor shut in and secluded by the hills; and this floor, as was afterwards discovered, was underlaid by a bed of anthracite coal.

The Delaware Indians held the eastern side and the Shawanese the western side, with the river between them. At the foot of the valley were the Nanticokes. Game was abundant. The quail whistled in the meadows, the grouse drummed in the woods, and the wild ducks nested along the river. The deer and elk wandered at will from the plains to the mountains. The streams that poured down ravines to join the river were full of trout, and in the spring large schools of shad came up the Susquehanna. Wild grapes and plums grew in the woods, and here and there on the plains the Indians had cultivated tracts of corn. It was an ideal spot, the natural home of the hunter and the poet, a combination of peace, beauty, abundance, and wild life such as is seldom found.

The delight with which the men gazed from the mountain-side, while the smoke from the Indian wigwams rose into the still air, was quickened when they descended and explored the plains. Only one white man had been there before them, Count Zinzendorf, the Moravian missionary. They returned to Connecticut, and with kindling eye and excited gesture described this paradise they had found among the western hills. They were laughed at as romancers. But the thrifty ones who laughed were careful to send others to spy out the land. The reports were confirmed, and from that time parties from Connecticut visited the valley every season.

Wyoming entered deep into the Connecticut heart, and the Yankee lovers were ready to measure their devotion with their lives. The solemn men of "the land of steady habits" became unrestrained enthusiasts. Their speech became eloquent and sometimes extravagant. When Eliphalet Dyer was once urging the assembly to more strenuous exertions in behalf of their western settlement, an unsympathetic wit handed about an impromptu verse:

> "Canaan of old, as we are told,
>   Where it did rain down manna,
>   Wa'n't half so good for heavenly food,
>   As Dyer makes Susquehanna."

Either from unusual ability to express their feelings or from some other cause, these Connecticut settlers succeeded in making the beauty of their retreat known to the whole world. It was the great natural wonder, the Yosemite of that day. It aroused the interest and became the talk of every one in England. It was described as " one of the happiest spots of human existence, both for the simplicity of its inhabitants and the beauty and fertility of the land."

As time wore on, and the terrible conflicts with the Indians were added to the charms of nature, imagination became more and more aroused, until Campbell, the English poet, expressed the general feeling of his countrymen in Gertrude of Wyoming. This work of genius, in spite of mistakes in detail, has now become as much a part of the region as the rocks and streams. Gertrude is not quite so well-known a character as Evangeline, but she is as thoroughly identified with Wyoming as Evangeline with Acadia:

> " Then, where of Indian hills the daylight takes
>   His leave, how might you the flamingo see,
> Disporting like a meteor on the lakes—
>   And playful squirrel on his nut-grown tree;
>   And every sound of life was full of glee,
> From merry mock-bird's song, or hum of men;
>   While hearkening, fearing naught their revelry,
>   The wild deer arched his neck from glades, and then
> Unhunted, sought his woods and wilderness again."

The flamingo and the mocking-bird were far from their native haunts. Campbell, like other Englishmen, was rather mixed in his knowledge of America. But the verse is typical of his merits as well as his defects, and undoubtedly expressed the general feeling of the day as to the peace and beauty of Wyoming.

The Making of Pennsylvania

When in another passage he spoke of Gertrude reading Shakspeare in the woods, he again strained the
realities. But most of his descriptions are within the
possibilities :

> " It seemed as if those scenes sweet influence had
>   On Gertrude's soul, and kindness like their own
> Inspired those eyes affectionate and glad,
>   That seemed to love whate'er they looked upon."
> *   *   *   *   *   *   *
> " Nor, guess I, was that Pennsylvania home,
>   With all its picturesque and balmy grace,
> And fields that were a luxury to roam,
>   Lost on the soul that looked from such a face;
>   Enthusiast of the woods: When years apace
> Had bound thy lovely waist with woman's zone,
>   The sunrise path, at morn, I see thee trace
> To hills with high magnolia overgrown,
> And joy to breathe the groves, romantic and alone."

The Indian wars were not forgotten, and their dark
ferocity forms a contrast to the loveliness of Gertrude :

> " But this is not a time, he started up,
>   And smote his breast with woe-denouncing hand—
> This is no time to fill the joyous cup;
>   The mammoth comes, the foe, the Monster Brandt,
> With all his howling, desolating band ;
>   These eyes have seen their blade and burning pine
> Awake at once and silence half your land.
>   Red is the cup they drink, but not with wine;
>   Awake and watch to-night, or see no morning shine."

The poem made its first appearance among the literary
circle at Holland House, and was published in 1809.
Its success was immediate. A second edition was soon
called for. Those were the days of Sir Walter Scott,

The Connecticut Invasion

Chateaubriand, and the romantic school of novelists.
Simple human nature in the wilderness was the favorite
theme. Campbell, anxious for the fate of his Gertrude,
had intrusted her to the care of the generous Sir Walter,
who introduced her to the world of fashion.

Other poets were inspired by Wyoming, and some of
them have declared that Campbell failed to do justice to
the scenery. Drake, an early American poet, wondered
why such beauty had not aroused the native talent:

> "Romantic Wyoming! could none be found,
>   Of all that rove thy Eden groves among,
> To wake a native harp's untutored sound
>   And give thy tale of woe the voice of song?
> Oh, if description's cold and nerveless tongue
>   From stranger harps such hallowed strains could call,
> How doubly sweet the descant wild had rung
>   From one who, lingering round thy ruined wall,
> Had plucked thy mourning flowers and wept thy timeless fall."

Some years after, in 1823, Halleck, a Connecticut poet,
visited Wyoming, and wrote his impressions:

> "I then but dreamed; thou art before me now
>   In life, a vision of the brain no more.
> I've stood upon the wooded mountain's brow
>   That beetles high thy lovely valley o'er,
>   And now, where winds thy river's greenest shore,
> Within a bower of sycamore am laid;
>   And winds, as soft and sweet as ever bore
> The fragrance of wild flowers through sun and shade,
> Are singing in the trees whose low boughs press my head.

> "Nature hath made thee lovelier than the power
>   Even of Campbell's pen hath pictured; he
> Had woven, had he gazed one sunny hour
>   Upon thy smiling vale, its scenery

With more of truth, and made each rock and tree
   Known like old friends, and greeted from afar;
And there are tales of sad reality
   In the dark legends of thy border war,
     With woes of deeper tint than his own Gertrude's are."
*   *   *   *   *   *   *
" There's one in the next field—of sweet sixteen—
   Singing and summoning thoughts of beauty born
In heaven—with her jacket of light green,
   Love-darting eyes and tresses like the morn,
   Without a shoe or stocking—hoeing corn.
Whether, like Gertrude, she oft wanders there,
   With Shakespeare's volume in her bosom borne,
I think is doubtful. Of the poet player
The maiden knows no more than Cobbett or Voltaire."

Native talent has at times been inspired. But these poets to the manner born appear to have been less impressed than strangers with the beauty of the scenery. The only part of Wyoming life that aroused their imaginations was the deep-dyed atrocity of the Indians. They lack the polish, the refinement, and the tenderness of Campbell. But in vigor of expression they are by no means deficient, and one specimen will suffice:

    " Kind heaven, assist the trembling muse,
      While she attempts to tell
    Of poor Wyoming's overthrow
      By savage sons of hell."

For several years after the discovery of Wyoming the Connecticut people visited it in small parties every summer without attempting any settlement. Their object was to get the land from the Indians gradually, and make sure that it was safe for white men. In 1753 they formed an association called the Susquehanna Company, made up of about six hundred persons,—

some from Rhode Island and Massachusetts, but most of them from Connecticut. One of the first acts of this company was to send a deputation to Albany in 1754 to meet a great council of the Six Nations and purchase from them the land of the Wyoming Valley.

Pennsylvania sent to the same council John and Richard Penn, Isaac Norris, and Benjamin Franklin to resist the purchase. They were unsuccessful, however, and for the sum of two thousand pounds of the current money of New York the Susquehanna Company obtained the land.

No regular settlement was effected under this purchase until 1762, when about two hundred farmers with their families entered the valley. The Indians allowed them to sow and reap their first crop, and then suddenly killed and scalped about twenty of the men and scattered the rest with the women and children among the woods and mountains. Some of them returned to New England, and others took refuge in the Moravian towns on the Lehigh.

For six years after this no settlement was attempted. The Indians, anticipating revenge for the massacre, left the valley, which returned to its primeval beauty unpolluted by either race.

Meanwhile, the Penn family, proprietors of Pennsylvania, were anxious about the purchase at Albany. There was a feeling at that time that the title to land which a charter gave was not complete until the land had been purchased from the Indians. As a matter of strict law this was not so, for the only Indian title ever recognized was a mere title of occupancy,—that is to say, the right of the Indian to hunt game upon the land

and build encampments. This sort of title was not considered inconsistent with the ownership of the fee simple by a white man. The so-called title of the Indian was not really a title at all, but a mere lien or incumbrance, which could be discharged or not as the white man and the Indian might agree.

The Albany purchase was, therefore, not of any great importance, and did not affect the real merits of the question. The final decision of title as between Connecticut and Pennsylvania was to be determined by the grants or charters from the British crown and not by any grants from Indians. Nevertheless, the Penn family felt bound to protect their title at every point, important or unimportant, Indian or British.

They had always taken care to secure themselves within their charter limits so far as possible. Some of the land they had purchased outright from the Indians, and on the rest they had bought what were then called pre-emptions and nowadays options. In these pre-emptions they had made a contract with the Indians that the Indians would never sell the lands to any one until they had first given the Penn family a chance to buy them. In 1736 they had bought from the Indians an option on all the territory in Pennsylvania which remained unpurchased, and this, of course, included the land which the Susquehanna Company bought at Albany in 1754. The Penns maintained that under this contract of pre-emption the Indians had no right to sell to the Susquehanna Company, and that the Albany deed and purchase were void.

It was very difficult to make the Indians understand the binding force of an option. They seldom had much hesitation in selling the same piece of property two or three times over to different persons. The vagueness of the authority lodged with different chiefs gave ample opportunity for some of them to say that they had never consented. Moreover, they had little or no conception of the absolute fee-simple title of the white man. Their only idea of title was a tenancy in common, and when they sold land they supposed that they were merely admitting the purchaser to the privilege of hunting on it along with themselves and any others to whom they had previously sold it. It was a common occurrence in colonial ejectment suits for both sides of the disputed title to show a grant from the same Indians.

The Albany purchase, by the Susquehanna Company, had been from the Six Nations of New York, who held the Pennsylvania tribes in vassalage. Connecticut had easily accomplished the purchase against the protests of the Pennsylvania representatives, because the Six Nations were displeased with the Penn family, who, in order to make assurance doubly sure, had been in the habit of taking deeds from the local and conquered tribes of Pennsylvania.

The legal way to have had the Albany purchase declared void was by an appeal to England, long and expensive, subject to the contingencies of court favor and change of kings and administrations. William Penn had had enough of that in his boundary dispute with Lord Baltimore. The shorter way was to persuade the Six Nations to admit their mistake and give a new deed to the Penns.

Some of the chiefs were approached, invited to Philadelphia, feasted, and flattered. The assistance of Sir

The Making of Pennsylvania

William Johnson, who largely controlled the policy of the Six Nations, was obtained, and four of the chiefs went to Hartford and openly disclaimed the sale to the Susquehanna Company. Finally, as a result of all negotiations, the Six Nations, assembled in council at Fort Stanwix in 1768, gave a deed of the disputed land to the Penns.

Having fortified their Indian title, the Penn family now turned their attention to the much more serious question,—namely, the charter right of Connecticut to the land on her western way beyond New York. Every advantage was taken and every point attacked. For many years, until the final decision of Congress in 1782, the controversy raged, and no theory, argument, or fine-spun inference that the ingenuity of learned lawyers on either side could invent, was left untried. It is impossible in this chapter to go into all these details. The reader who is curious about them must be referred to the voluminous pages of Miner, to Governor Hoyt's able and learned " Brief of a Title in the Seventeen Townships," or to the arguments of Provost Smith and Benjamin Trumbull.

Most of the books and essays which have been written on this subject uphold the Connecticut title. It is another instance of the way in which Pennsylvania has allowed her history to be written by her opponents. Of all the volumes and pamphlets which constitute the material for a history of Wyoming, there is only the single essay by Provost Smith devoted to maintaining the Pennsylvania title.

The writers are usually either natives of Connecticut or natives of Wyoming, whose right to their homes and property is in some way related to the Connecticut claim. Miner, the author of the most important book, was a native of Connecticut, who moved to Wyoming and became a member of Congress. Although he was not a trained lawyer, his argument is the most astute and shrewd that has come down to us; and is so intermingled with romance and misfortune that the ordinary reader is easily captured. Hoyt's work was written when its author was Governor of Pennsylvania; and he frankly gives his reasons for maintaining the Connecticut side. His home was in Wilkesbarre on a lot "certified" from the Connecticut title; and for his final resting-place he had another lot in the green cemetery at Forty Fort. "You will," he said, "be the more indulgent in my taking such views of the case as will enable me to believe these claims to be founded as well on strict law as on sound equity and in good morals."

Some of the points made on the Pennsylvania side are dismissed by the intelligent mind at a glance. These we must dispose of, so as to bring the question to its last analysis, and see the real strength of Pennsylvania's position.

For example, when it was said that the Connecticut charter ought not to be so construed as to extend to the Pacific, or to include the land in question, because of the immensity of the territory that would be embraced, it does not require a legal mind to detect the absurdity. The question at issue was what a formal legal document actually was, and what title its words imported; not what it might have been or ought to have been.

So also as to the argument that the grant all the way to the Pacific was the result of ignorance and a mistake;

geography at that time being little understood, and Charles II. not aware that the distance from Hartford to the Pacific was three thousand miles.

It is true that in the early stages of American exploration, the distance was not known, and there is a curious argument in an old book to the effect that as the distance from the Atlantic to the Alleghanies was about three hundred miles, so the distance from these mountains to the Pacific was probably about the same. But after Sir Francis Drake had circumnavigated the globe in 1589 and explored the coast of California, there were no more mistakes. When the Plymouth council resigned their grant in 1635, they describe what was then called New England as extending " from sea to sea, being near about three thousand miles in length." This was long before the time of Charles II. He knew perfectly well what he was doing so far as the Pacific Ocean was concerned. Others had done the same. The Massachusetts charter and several others extended " from sea to sea ;" and this was done for the express purpose of laying claim to as much land as possible, so as to strengthen the position of England in her contests with Spain and France.

There is also another of the Pennsylvania arguments which deserves some consideration, not because of its merit, but because it was often quoted, and a great lawyer, afterwards Lord Camden, partly relied on it in the opinion he wrote for the Penn family.

There was always a boundary line dispute between the Connecticut colonies and the Dutch in New York, and for a long time no permanent decision could be reached. Soon after 1662, when New Haven and Connecticut were consolidated, and the exact size of their territory was fixed by their charter, the Dutch were conquered by the English and driven out of New York. Immediately after this, on the 12th day of March, 1664, Charles II. gave all the Dutch territory to his brother, the Duke of York, afterwards James II. With characteristic prodigality and recklessness, he included in the gift to his brother all the territory between the Connecticut and Delaware Rivers, which of course covered a large part of the land he had given to Connecticut only two years before.

The exact boundary line between Connecticut and New York was thus made still more difficult to settle. Charles, however, sent over royal commissioners with full power to adjust the absurdity he had deliberately created. They met the agents of Connecticut, transacted their business rapidly, and decided that Long Island should belong to New York, and that the Connecticut line should begin at the mouth of Mamaroneck Creek where it falls into the Sound, and extend northwestward to the line of Massachusetts. This restored the lost territory to Connecticut, and was very near to the boundary as it now stands. But the important words of the decision in the eyes of the Penn family were those that said that this line should be "the western bounds of the said colony of Connecticut."

Soon after, New York again fell into the hands of the Dutch, and remained with them until 1674, when a treaty of peace restored it to the British Crown. A new charter was issued to the Duke of York, containing precisely the same boundaries as before, and taking away precisely the same amount of territory from Connecticut.

The old dispute was renewed, and was finally settled by agreement, without the aid of royal commissioners, between Connecticut and New York. This agreement fixed the line where it now is, not far from the royal commissioners' line, which started from the mouth of the Mamaroneck.

The Penns argued that Connecticut having agreed to both of these boundary settlements, and both boundaries being described as the western bounds of the colony of Connecticut, she was ever afterwards precluded from laying claim to any land to the westward, for she had expressly, and by her own words and admissions, relinquished all such rights. Lord Camden supported them in this, and said "the settlement of the new boundary under the king's commission in 1664, and, what is still stronger, the new line marked out by agreement between the province and New York, has now conclusively precluded Connecticut from advancing one foot beyond those limits." And he goes on to argue that these admissions on the part of Connecticut took place before Penn's charter was given, and therefore released the land west of New York from the Connecticut claim, and laid it open to be included in the Penn charter.

But so far as technical law is concerned, his lordship is now generally believed to have been wrong. The royal commission boundary and the agreement boundary were adjustments of a dispute between Connecticut and New York, not between Connecticut and Pennsylvania. The land west of New York was not mentioned, and at the time of the royal commission was not supposed to be in dispute. The question of the western lands was not raised in either case. The royal commissioners were not given authority to decide that question, nor were the representatives of Connecticut who arranged the agreement boundary given authority to decide it.   In fact, neither the commissioners nor the representatives knew of such a question.   It did not exist at that time, and had never been thought of or mentioned.   There is no principle of law more firmly settled than that a tribunal is strictly bound by the authority given to it, and can decide only the cases that are brought before it. Another principle is also equally well settled, that an agent cannot exceed his authority, and that all acts in excess of his authority are void, and the agents of Connecticut certainly had no authority to agree to anything about the western lands which were within the charter limits beyond New York.

The argument on the Connecticut side is a very simple one, and consists principally of the statement that the king, having given the land in question to Connecticut, could not, eighteen years afterwards, take it away from her and give it to Pennsylvania.   This brings us to the important point of the controversy.   What was the rule of law governing grants of the Crown in the time of Charles II., and were such grants governed by the same law which applies to grants and conveyances between private individuals?

If the grant by the king to Connecticut is to be treated as if it were an ordinary conveyance of land between individuals, then unquestionably the Connecticut title to the upper half of Pennsylvania was perfect.   A man who has sold and conveyed a piece of land to a certain person cannot afterwards sell the same land and the same title to another.   This was the position Connecticut always assumed. She relied on the ordinary rules of law, which were familiar to every one who had ever bought or sold real estate.

But did these rules apply to grants by the British Crown in the time of Charles II.? And would they apply even now to similar grants by the British Parliament, which has succeeded to the power once held by the king? We are in this country so accustomed to a government of limited powers, whose acts are controlled by technical rules like the acts of a private individual, that we are apt to forget that the English Constitution is, and always has been, a very different one from ours. In England the whole power of the nation is lodged in Parliament, which is omnipotent, does what it pleases, guided only by certain customs changing from time to time, and called the English Constitution.

In the time of Charles II. the Crown had many rights which have now been given over to Parliament, among others the right to create corporations and grant away the public domain. This right the king exercised absolutely, just as Parliament now exercises it absolutely. Parliament could now grant away a tract of the public domain to an individual or corporation, and some years after take back part of it and grant it to some other individual or corporation. Such action might be unjust or unfair or bad policy; but Parliament, being omnipotent and representing the whole authority of the English people, would have the right to do it. The act, so far as law is concerned, would be perfectly legal, and the courts would have to uphold it.

Charles II., in his time, had this absolute legal right, and he constantly exercised it and abused it. We have already seen him giving a large tract of land to his brother, the Duke of York, only two years after he had solemnly given it to Connecticut. He did very much the same thing in Virginia, making large grants to favorites, and causing the insurrection in that colony known as Bacon's Rebellion. In fact, so far as concerned selling the same piece of land twice to different persons, Charles II. was no better than an Indian.

But no matter what we may think of his wisdom or foolishness in such things, there is no question about the legality of his acts. They were regarded as legal by the people of that time; and those who were injured by them, instead of appealing to a court to have them declared void, appealed to the king himself to change his action and correct the mischief by a fresh grant.

The Virginians did not complain of the granting away of their land by Charles II. as illegal, but as cruel and unjust. They did not appeal to courts to have the grants declared void, but they sent commissioners to England to buy off the noblemen to whom the grants had been given, or to persuade the king to revoke the grants. We have already seen how Charles II. corrected the injury done to Connecticut by his grant to the Duke of York. He appointed commissioners to meet the agents of Connecticut and settle the question. To those commissioners he delegated a part of his sovereign authority to correct or affirm what he had done; and they restored to Connecticut the land which the king had unfairly and unjustly, but not illegally, given to the duke.

The Susquehanna Company, when it found that Pennsylvania resisted its encroachments in the Wyoming Valley, acted on the same principle, and petitioned the

Connecticut legislature for leave to apply to the Crown for a fresh grant of Wyoming, which would erect it into a separate colony, and wipe out the title of Pennsylvania.

The case of North Carolina is another instance. Charles I. had given it in 1629 to his attorney-general, Sir Robert Heath. Thirty-four years afterwards, in 1663, his son, Charles II., gave it to the Earl of Clarendon, the Duke of Albemarle, and others. Claimants under the old Heath grant started up; the matter was brought, not before the courts, but before the king in council, who simply declared the Heath grant void, reaffirmed his last grant, and the question was settled.

The right of the king in granting land was just the reverse of the right of a private individual. In the case of a private individual, it is the first grant which is valid and all the subsequent grants are void. The first grant exhausts the whole title of the giver. But with the king it was the last grant which was valid, and all the preceding grants void. The title of the king, as sovereign of the land, was never exhausted.

This accounts for the great confusion and overlapping of nearly all the colonial grants and charters. The last grant was always the valid one, and in the race for new territory by individuals and colonies this last grant was eagerly sought. The grants were used to correct the situation and give the best advantage up to date. Every future difficulty or want was to be remedied by a new grant. If we consider the history of the American colonies as a whole up to the time of the Revolution, we shall find that the grants to individuals and communities were rearranged and reapportioned over and over again to meet new emergencies. If we are guided by the principle that all of these grants were invalid except the first, the situation will be ridiculous, and there will be scarcely a single valid title to land east of the Alleghanies.

The system of having the last grant valid was the lesser evil, but it was bad enough. It gave the colonists endless trouble and formed the basis of one of their complaints in the Declaration of Independence. They wanted something more orderly and regular. But bad as this system was, it was perfectly legal, and troubled the colonists all the more because it was legal. It was the abuse of a legal power.

That it was the rule acted upon in preparing the charter for Pennsylvania is very evident. It has sometimes been supposed that the overlapping on Connecticut was an accidental mistake, the result of defective maps and ignorance of geography. But this supposition is quickly disposed of by a glance at the maps that Penn and the officers of the Crown must have used.

The great authorities for American geography were the two maps of Captain John Smith, one of New England and the other of Virginia. Vessels were sailed by them, and all other maps of America were either copies or compilations of them. Considering that Smith made them by his own unaided observations with inferior instruments and without a trained corps of assistants, they are remarkably accurate. The degrees of latitude are in some instances very close to their present locations, and the worst cases of error are only a few miles out of the way. Any one looking at these two maps with the charters of Pennsylvania and Connecticut before him would see at once that the two colonies

The Making of Pennsylvania

overlapped; so the Crown and the Crown officers must have known that Pennsylvania would cut off the westward course of Connecticut.

But there was another authority in existence which shows this still more clearly. Ogilby's "America" was published in 1671. It was a complete description of the whole continent, and was so well and carefully written that it can still be read with the greatest interest and its accuracy recognized. It is full of maps and fine old engravings. One of the maps includes the territory now covered by New England, New York, Pennsylvania, and Maryland, and is evidently made up from Smith's two maps of New England and Virginia, with new places added. Any one who will take the trouble to get down this old volume and look at this map will see at once that no one at that time could possibly have been unaware that Pennsylvania would overlap Connecticut. For here is one of the maps which, in all probability, the eyes of Penn and Charles II. and their legal advisers gazed upon, and there is the end of the forty-second degree, the northern boundary of Pennsylvania, as they had fixed it, passing through New England above the colonies of New Haven and Connecticut.

But there is still better evidence than this. Royal charters passed through the hands of several Crown officers, who criticised them before they were signed, and the Pennsylvania charter was very carefully considered, to see whether it conflicted with the Duke of York, the Maryland, and other grants. The attorney-general at that time was Sir William Jones, and he reported that " The tract of land desired by Mr. Penn seems to be undisposed of by his majesty, except the imaginary lines of New

England patents, which are bounded westerly by the main ocean, should give them a real though impractical right to all those vast territories."

The attorney-general rightly used the words New England patents in the plural. For looking at the maps of that time, it would seem as if the Pennsylvania grant would cut into Massachusetts as well as into Connecticut. As a matter of fact, when measured by the most accurate instruments of modern times, the northern boundary of Pennsylvania fell short by only two or three miles of cutting into Massachusetts.

This statement by the attorney-general, the highest law officer of the Crown, may be fairly taken as showing the general opinion as to these royal grants. He describes the westward lines of the New England colonies as imaginary and impractical. What does he mean by that? Evidently that those lines were extended westward for a purpose proper enough at the time. That purpose was to claim as much land as possible for the king of England as against his rivals, France and Spain. But, clearly, the attorney-general thinks that there can be no objection to cutting off those lines for the practical purpose of settling a new colony. Connecticut or Massachusetts may have a " real right" westward, he says, but it is an " impractical" one. The king can again grant away that part of the land.

If he had thought that those westward lines gave an absolute right, and that the king could not grant away for the second time the land covered by them, he would have said so and stopped the grant. But he did not stop it. He merely called the attention of the privy council to the situation, and the grant was freely passed with the consent of the king, the lords commissioners of trade, who were a sort of committee of the privy council, and all the Crown officers.

The meetings which the lords commissioners of trade held to consider the question are described in full at the beginning of the first volume of the " Votes of the Pennsylvania Assembly." No one can read that account without being struck by two things. First, the care that was taken, the numerous adjournments, considerations, and reconsiderations. Secondly, that in all their discussions the lords commissioners do not seem to have the slightest doubt as to the legal right of the king to make the grant without regard to whose territory it would overlap. That question is not even raised. The sole question seems to be a mere matter of policy as to the wisdom of making the grant, and for that purpose they consulted with the neighboring owners, the Duke of York and Lord Baltimore. As to the wisdom of overlapping Connecticut, the attorney-general disposed of that by saying that her claim westward was " imaginary and impractical."

Among the lords commissioners of trade were some of the greatest lawyers of the age. To Lord Chief Justice North was assigned the duty of drawing the boundaries of Pennsylvania and reporting on them. He saw nothing improper in them, nor did any one else for the next seventy years. Connecticut herself did not object in that time. Not a word was heard from her until the middle of the next century, when she had taken a fancy to the fertile and romantic Wyoming.

The common-sense view of the situation was the same as the law. Connecticut should have abandoned her claim which she supposed was her right. There was no need and no convenience in jumping over New York and New Jersey and exercising jurisdiction on an isolated patch of another colony. If she wanted to settle some of her superabundant population on that spot, they could have lived as happily and prosperously under the laws of Pennsylvania as under the laws, of Connecticut. It was wrong that, for the mere glory of acquisition and ownership, and in the teeth of the law, she should force upon a sister colony a civil war of thirty years, and cause loss of life, loss of property, and untold suffering. She knew that her western lines were what Sir William Jones aptly called them, imaginary and impractical, and she should have acquiesced in the lawful grant to William Penn of land which she could not conveniently govern.

But it suited her to take a different view of the situation, and as soon as she saw that the Penns had succeeded in getting the Indians to disclaim the Albany deed and give a new one in its place, she knew that Wyoming must be taken by force, and she prepared to do it.

In February, 1769, the Susquehanna Company sent forty men into the valley, to be followed shortly by two hundred more. They were given land and two hundred pounds, Connecticut currency, to provide themselves with farming tools and weapons, on condition that they would stay in the valley and defend it against Pennsylvania. They built a block-house called, from their numbers, Forty Fort, and the site of it is still preserved. Their leader was Colonel Zebulon Butler, who had served in the French and Indian wars, and at the taking of Havana in 1762.   He was a brave, skilful, partisan commander, accustomed to the wilderness, and of a manner and address that won the instant devotion of frontiersmen.

When the forty reached the valley, clothed in the stillness of death and its shroud of winter snow, they were surprised to find that the proprietors of Pennsylvania had forestalled them.   In fact, the Penns had adopted very much the same tactics as Connecticut. They had leased a hundred acres of the valley for seven years to Charles Stuart, Amos Ogden, and John Jennings, on condition that they would establish an Indian trading house there and defend against all intruders. This was the beginning of what are known as the Pennamite Wars.

Of the three men entrusted by the Penns with the defence of Wyoming, Amos Ogden was chief and captain. He was an Indian trader from New Jersey, and proved himself a most accomplished warrior of the woods. Miner, one of the historians of Wyoming, assures us that he was also a valiant trencherman, who, after each one of his various triumphs, retired to Philadelphia, where he enjoyed the banquets and festivities awarded him by the followers of the Penns.   Charles Stuart was a surveyor, and John Jennings was the sheriff of Northampton County, within which district Wyoming lay, if it was a part of Pennsylvania.

All the military proceedings were conducted in the name of the sheriff.   All the attempts to drive the Connecticut people out of Wyoming were put forth as the action of a sheriff's posse to keep the peace, and eject intruders and trespassers from private land.   As time passed on and new sheriffs succeeded to the office held by Jennings, the Pennamite Wars were put under the charge of each successive sheriff.

It must be borne in mind, in order to understand the Wyoming situation, that this charming valley was not the property of Pennsylvania, or of the people of Pennsylvania, or of the civil authority of the province as represented in the general assembly, but of the sons of William Penn, who owned all the land of the province, and of whom the inhabitants were merely the tenants paying quit-rents. The dispute was really between Connecticut and the Penn heirs. The people of Pennsylvania had little interest in it, and took no part except as they were hired or persuaded to assist the proprietary family. The governor of the province was the deputy and appointee of the Penns, and directed the movements of the sheriff and his military agent, Captain Ogden.

Ogden had with him only ten men that could bear arms. He fortified himself as best he could in the block-house and huts which had survived the Indian attack of 1763, and stood about a mile above the present town of Wilkesbarre. When the forty Connecticut people arrived they besieged him and prevented his men from shooting deer for food and cutting wood for their fires. Being outnumbered and surrounded, Ogden suggested a discussion, and the invaders, thinking they could easily convince him of the justice of their claim, sent three of their principal men to the block-house to argue. They were instantly arrested by Sheriff Jennings, and carried to jail at Easton, quietly followed by the remaining thirty-seven of the forty. On arriving at Easton, the three who had been arrested were almost immediately released on bail, joined the thirty-seven, and the forty all returned to Wyoming.

Jennings immediately summoned the posse of Northampton County, marched after them, surrounded their quarters in the valley, and this time captured and arrested them all. They were all taken to the jail at Easton, whereupon, as before, they were immediately released on bail, and, with true Yankee persistence, returned to their paradise. Within three months they had been twice taken all the way to Easton on the Delaware, a distance of sixty miles. Going and returning they had walked through the snow in those two excursions about two hundred and forty miles. And yet they still thought Wyoming the loveliest spot on earth, and had a quiet intention of remaining there.

As spring opened, additional settlers from Connecticut arrived, and by the middle of May their numbers were increased to two hundred and seventy. They secured themselves in a new block-house, which they called Fort Durkee. In this position they were found by Ogden and Jennings, who, with a fresh posse, entered the valley during the last days of May. The Connecticut position was too strong to be attacked. Jennings marched his forces back again, and reported to the governor that it was impossible to raise a sufficient posse in Northampton County to oust the enemy.

This difficulty of raising a sufficient force and the ease with which bail was obtained seem to show that the Pennsylvania people were not much interested in assisting the proprietors to recover the valley.

Meanwhile, settlers were pouring into Wyoming, and the Susquehanna Company, to gain time, sent Eliphalet

The Connecticut Invasion

Dyer and Jedediah Elderkin, goodly Puritan names, to negotiate with the Penns. They were received with much courtesy by Benjamin Chew, who promptly rejected all their suggestions, and Ogden was ordered to prepare a force to protect the valley.

By September he had collected two hundred armed men. They took with them an iron four-pound cannon, which figured conspicuously in the subsequent history of Wyoming, becoming a sort of heirloom, and passing with the valley to its different possessors. Jennings took command of the main body. Ogden preceded him with fifty men, arrived suddenly in the valley, and by a skilful movement captured Captain Durkee, at that time in charge of the Connecticut force. He was sent in irons to Philadelphia, and as soon as Jennings arrived the enemy surrendered. Three or four of the leaders were detained as prisoners ; seventeen of the people were allowed to remain to harvest the crops, and the rest were started on their way back to Connecticut.

As soon as they had gone all property was destroyed and the cattle driven off to the Delaware. The seventeen who had been allowed to remain, having nothing to eat, were obliged to follow their companions. Not a life was lost, not a drop of blood was shed. Ogden and Jennings were victorious, and the valley belonged to the Penns.

Ogden, leaving behind him a garrison of ten men, returned to Philadelphia, and all difficulties were supposed to be ended. But he had scarcely entered upon that course of festivity of which Miner accuses him, when he was told that his garrison had been surprised and expelled. This time the trouble was caused by Pennsylvanians. About forty settlers from Lancaster

The Making of Pennsylvania

County, under the lead of Captain Lazarus Stewart, having associated with themselves ten Connecticut people, had been given a township by the Susquehanna Company, and inspired by this they had marched to the valley and compelled Ogden's garrison to surrender. Fort Durkee was theirs and also the little four-pounder. Captain Durkee himself, though sent to Philadelphia in irons, was at large and back among his people.

Ogden again undertook to restore Wyoming. He could usually outwit the enemy, but he never equalled them in numbers, and he lacked their persistence and steadiness. Perhaps it would be more correct to say that the influences behind him, being merely the efforts of a private family, lacked the strength of purpose which marked the movements of Connecticut. On this occasion he led his men to the old fort he had formerly occupied a mile above the present site of Wilkesbarre, and kept very quiet, affecting timidity and caution.

He was soon rewarded, for after Stewart and his party had restored Wyoming to the Susquehanna Company, the Connecticut settlers again poured into their beloved land. A party of them marched straight up to Ogden's fort, believing it to be their own, were received with the most profuse affection, and then arrested.

Meanwhile, Durkee and the others had decided to attack Ogden while he seemed to be weak and waiting for reinforcements. They marched out with the Connecticut flag flying, stepping to the time of fife and drum, and evidently intended to enjoy themselves with a glorious victory. They were performing a movement to which Ogden appeared to have no great objection, for no sooner were they drawn up in martial array before his fort than he rushed out with all his men and seized them. A short struggle followed, in which the Connecticut people lost one man killed and several wounded.

The enemy now decided to surround Ogden's fort, keeping at a respectful distance, and starve him out. They had no desire for any more close encounters. They had the little four-pounder, which they mounted so that the river was between it and Ogden. Day after day it woke the echoes of the forest with its tiny roar. But Ogden seemed to be unaware that they were firing at him, and the little piece of ordnance was removed to the other side of the river, so as to be nearer, and Durkee's forces gradually approached the fort by throwing up breastworks. They got so near that they set fire to Ogden's store-house and burnt all his supplies.

Matters were, indeed, becoming serious for him. He sent a runner to Philadelphia to urge on the governor the importance of sending reinforcements. The governor at that time was one of the Penn family, and it has been suggested that his failure to send troops was caused by the first movements of the Revolution, which had then begun, and his desire to avoid taking any decided and prominent action in favor of his family. But it is more probable that the old cause was at work. He found it difficult to persuade or hire men for an expedition which they knew was to enforce nothing but a private land claim. He, however, wrote to General Gage, who commanded the British forces then in the country, asking him to put down the lawless invasion from Connecticut.

Gage's reply shows how a disinterested person regarded the situation. He declined to interfere, saying,

" The affair in question seems to be a dispute concerning property, in which I cannot but think it would be highly improper for the king's troops to interfere." He probably meant that it was a dispute between the Penn family and the Susquehanna Company about the private ownership of land,—a matter to be settled by the king in council, and not a fit subject for the action of an army.

Ogden had to surrender. He retired from the valley, and as soon as he was gone the Connecticut commander destroyed all property left behind and levelled the fort to the ground. Wyoming was at peace for five months. New settlers came in; Zebulon Butler returned; the surveyors were busy assigning lots and farms; and we are assured that the people that spring enjoyed with a quickened zest the shad which swarmed up the Susquehanna.

But at least one more effort must be made, and again Captain Ogden was sent. With his usual skill he took a path on which he would be least expected, and on the night of the 21st of September, 1770, encamped within the valley, kindling no fire and giving no alarm. The next morning, the settlers being scattered on their farms and meadows, Ogden divided his one hundred and forty men into parties of ten, and directed them to go to each farmhouse and capture all the men. Within a few hours he had in his possession a large part of the population, which he sent to the jail at Easton. The rest fled to Fort Durkee, and Ogden himself returned to his camp of the preceding evening.

The people in Fort Durkee, not knowing either the numbers or the position of Ogden, decided to send four men to a small Connecticut settlement on the Delaware, called Coshutank, for assistance. They directed them to go by the road least likely to be watched. But this, of course, was the very road on which Ogden was bivouacked. The four men walked straight into his camp, and before they could recover from their surprise they had confessed the demoralized condition of their people in Fort Durkee.

Ogden instantly summoned his men, started for the fort, and so sudden was his onset that the first intimation the garrison had of his coming was when the leader of the advance leaped in among them. The struggle was fierce but short. Several of the Connecticut men were killed and several wounded. The rest were taken prisoners and sent to jail. As usual, all property was destroyed, and for the fourth time the Connecticut settlement was wiped off the map of Pennsylvania.

Ogden and Governor Penn drew long breaths and felt persuaded that there was no race of men on the continent who would again return into a snowy wilderness after such defeats. But they made the mistake of leaving a garrison of only twenty men. Within three months, in the middle of December, the garrison was awakened one morning to find Captain Lazarus Stewart at the door with his followers. The usual eviction followed.

A warrant was now out for that troublesome Pennsylvanian, the abettor of Connecticut trespassers, Captain Stewart, and a large bounty was offered for his capture. Need we add that the dismal round began again, and that Ogden again left the pleasures of the city for the warfare of the woods?

Within a month after the expulsion of his garrison he was in the valley with a hundred men. He went to work openly and built a fort within less than four hundred yards of Fort Durkee, calling it Wyoming. After several times demanding the surrender of the Connecticut people, he attacked them on the 20th of January, 1771, but was repulsed with the loss of his brother killed and three men wounded. Stewart, however, was unwilling to risk another attack, and during the night escaped with most of his followers to the mountains. The few that remained were captured next morning and sent to jail as usual. This made the fifth destruction of the Connecticut settlement.

Ogden had now apparently decided to remain in Wyoming, and he spent the next two months in strengthening his position. But in April the Connecticut people came upon him, one hundred and fifty strong, and began a regular siege, throwing up approaches and redoubts. Heretofore their leaders had been men of rather inferior military skill, but now they were again under the command of Zebulon Butler, a soldier of experience, and in every way a match for Ogden.

So closely did Butler draw his lines, that not a single runner could escape to Philadelphia to call for aid. Ogden decided to attempt it himself. Taking off his clothes, and tying them in a bundle, with his hat on top, he stepped into the river at midnight, and, towing the bundle by a string, swam on his back, with only his face exposed. The current, and his own efforts, carried him rapidly down stream. If he had been dealing with less skilful riflemen he might have been in danger of receiving a random shot in the head. But he was perfectly safe. Every ball from the Connecticut sentinels passed into his hat or clothes. When beyond danger he landed, put on his drenched and riddled garments, walked rapidly to dry them, and accomplished the distance of one hundred and twenty miles to Philadelphia in three days.

Great efforts were made in the city to send assistance. A certain Captain Dick was started forward, with men and provisions. Other reinforcements were to follow. Whether Ogden or Dick was in the chief command does not clearly appear. But as the party fell into an ambuscade as soon as they had entered the valley, losing nine of their men and nearly all their provisions, they were evidently not led by Ogden.

Butler, knowing that reinforcements were coming from Philadelphia, pressed his siege closer than ever. Fighting began, a life was lost, and several men were wounded. About the middle of August, Ogden and Dick surrendered, and were allowed to march out of Wyoming with the honors of war. As Dick signed the articles of capitulation, Ogden had apparently been superseded.

Thus the first Pennamite War came to an end in 1771. The Penns were defeated and driven out, and for four years they made no attempt to retake their property.

About a month or two after the surrender of Dick and Ogden, a correspondence was opened with Governor Trumbull, of Connecticut. He denied that the government of Connecticut had taken any part in the violent proceedings at Wyoming, and he declared that the General Assembly would never countenance any hostile measures. The question, he seemed to say, was altogether an affair of the Susquehanna Company.

This was the shrewd position Connecticut had assumed

from the beginning. Governor Trumbull, in the course of the correspondence, admitted, however, that the land in Wyoming which the company was attempting to occupy was in his opinion within the limits of the Connecticut charter. His government had assented to the formation of the company, and to the purchase from the Indians of the land, and yet that government refused to restrain and refused to be responsible for the acts of a company which it had created, and which was acting upon land claimed to be within the charter limits.

In their official capacity, the members of the Connecticut government professed to be entirely innocent of everything connected with the Susquehanna Company, yet it was well known that as private individuals they were interested in the company as shareholders, and were pushing its fortunes to the utmost. When they were accused as a company, they threw the responsibility on the government, and when they were accused as a government, they threw the responsibility on the company.

But when a year or so had elapsed without any attempt on the part of the Penns to regain their property, the Connecticut government took deliberate and formal possession. The Pennsylvania Valley became a New England town. It was called Westmoreland, and constituted part of Litchfield County, Connecticut, and the Susquehanna Company drew up a form of government for it, very republican and liberal in its principles. Representatives to the Connecticut Legislature were elected, and attended its sessions at Hartford, and the inhabitants of the valley felt so secure that they instructed their representatives to demand forty thousand dollars damages from Pennsylvania.

The Connecticut Invasion

It may be asked why did the Penns give up so easily? Pennsylvania was a more populous and richer colony than Connecticut, and in any real contest between the two the result could not have been doubtful. A permanent garrison of five hundred men in the valley would have put its ownership beyond question. The answer is that, if the contest had been with the people of Pennsylvania, Connecticut and the Susquehanna Company would have had to seek other pastures for the excess of their population. But the people of Pennsylvania felt that they were in no sense the owners of Wyoming. It belonged to the Penns, who were holding it, like their other lands, for speculation, intending, finally, to sell part of it, and retain the rest for a rise in value from the improvements on the parts sold.

The Penns could never raise a sufficient force to hold the valley. Even if they had raised such a force they could not have afforded to maintain it. They would have had to pay for it out of their own pockets or draw the money from the public treasury. The pay of five hundred men for a single year would have been a serious drain on their private exchequer, and they would have found it difficult to persuade the Quaker assembly to vote any considerable sum of money from the public treasury for such a purpose.

It was sometimes a little difficult to get the Quakers to vote money even for the defence of the frontier against the Indians. Many of them fancied themselves to be opposed to all war, fighting, and force, and, though they managed to strain their consciences when the Indian massacres became numerous, they would not be likely to strain them merely to assist the proprietors in growing rich.

Ogden, after his successes, always retired from the valley, leaving only a small garrison, which shows very clearly that the Penns felt the necessity of economy, and that they could use only a small portion of the public money for their private ends. They were seldom able to raise for Ogden more than one hundred and fifty men, and it sometimes required three or four months to collect that number.

They were fully convinced of their inability to maintain the contest. They dared not make it a party question in Pennsylvania, for it would have been overwhelmingly voted down and defeated. A large number of the people sympathized with Connecticut, and stood ready to assist her, and some, like those who went with Captain Stewart, actually did assist her.

The Penns being entirely excluded from the valley, the Yankee settlers poured in, and soon began to overflow the mountain bounds. Some of them established a settlement at Muncy, outside of the natural stronghold, and outside the town of Westmoreland, as laid out by the Connecticut government. This gave the Penns an opportunity, and we are compelled to describe the Second Pennamite War.

An Irishman named Plunkett, of doubtful reputation, led the expedition, which in September, 1775, destroyed and scattered the outlying post at Muncy, killing one man and wounding several. Plunkett marched his prisoners into Sunbury with much pomp, and believed himself to be the man of destiny who should restore Wyoming to the Penns.

His spirit was infectious and caught the Pennsylvania government. They furnished him with seven hundred

men, a train of boats, and a field-piece.   Previous to his
setting out, rumors of his expedition reached Connecticut and also the Continental Congress.   The congress
passed resolutions requesting Pennsylvania to refrain,
urging the importance in such trying times of a perfect
union of all the colonies.   But the remonstrance was
useless, and the expedition started.

It is somewhat surprising to find Plunkett setting out
on this campaign with seven hundred men, when the
utmost efforts in former times could scarcely raise a
hundred and fifty.   But the condition of things had
changed.   In 1771, just before the close of the first
Pennamite War, the Penns began to sell the land in the
valley which they had divided up into two manors called
Stoke and Sunbury.   Lists of the purchasers have been
preserved, and there appear to have been fifty-three of
them, twenty-seven for Sunbury and twenty-six for
Stoke, receiving tracts varying from seventy-nine to two
hundred and fifty acres each.   By the time of Plunkett's
expedition, in 1775, many of these purchasers had divided
up their land and sold it to others, so that there was a
considerable body of persons who were financially interested in the Pennsylvania title of Wyoming.   These
people increased in numbers as time went on, and under
the name of Pennsylvania claimants caused the compli-
cations which followed the decree at Trenton in 1782.
They doubtless made a strong interest for Plunkett, and
partially account for the number of his men.

A subscription list has also been found signed by such
people as Francis, Shippen, Tilghman, Allen, Haines,
Morris, Meredith, Biddle, all prominent Pennsylvania
names.   The amount of money given in this list to the

The Making of Pennsylvania

Plunkett expedition is about five hundred pounds, and there may have been other subscription papers. From the one preserved, it appears that there was a committee and treasurer appointed to receive funds.

All this indicates a new interest in Wyoming. The date of the subscription paper is October 9, 1775, several months after the battles of Lexington and Bunker Hill. Pennsylvania had been trying for some time to get rid of the Penn family and put herself under the king; and now it seemed to all hopeful hearts that she might escape from proprietors, king, parliament, and all. In that event, Wyoming would belong to the people and not to a private family. There was good reason for being interested in her fortunes, and Plunkett's enlistments were increased.

If such a force could have been raised six years earlier the possession of the Penns would have been secure. But now even this large force was not enough to insure success. The population of Wyoming had increased; Zebulon Butler was in command, and Plunkett was not Ogden. The seven hundred of the invading force were, it is true, about double the number of fighting men in the valley. But Butler selected a strong position on the side of a steep bluff where Harvey's Creek joins the Susquehanna. He threw out a small force as an ambuscade, and Plunkett, of course, marched straight to the place where he was wanted.

Two fruitless attacks on two successive days were made on Butler's position, and lives were lost on both sides. After the second attack, Plunkett ingloriously retired; and this was the last fighting for the possession of Wyoming by Pennsylvania. Connecticut had won

The Connecticut Invasion

by conquest what she considered her right, and her people now settled down to reap the benefit.

At this time the population of Wyoming was about six thousand. In spite of the excitements of the Revolution and the absence of many of the able-bodied men in the Continental army, the valley for three years enjoyed considerable prosperity and repose. The Gertrudes, Alberts, and Waldegraves increased and luxuriated in the seclusion of their retreat, and they might have continued in this enjoyment had it not been for a new terror from the north.

The State of New York was at that time occupied by the Six Nations of Indians. They held all the land beginning at the head-waters of the Mohawk, passing round by the head-waters of the Delaware and Susquehanna, through the lesser lakes Cayuga and Seneca and westward to the Genesee River. It was a beautiful fertile region, and a natural empire of wealth and power. Within this territory they were rapidly building up a civilization, and advancing in all the arts of life. They had numerous towns, many of them consisting of from twenty to sixty wooden houses, and one of them, Genesee, had one hundred and twenty-eight houses. They painted their dwellings after the manner of white men, and had graveyards with monuments made of planks. They had numerous orchards of peach-trees and other fruit, and cultivated the land, raising large crops of corn.

They had formerly dominated all the other tribes southward to the Carolinas and westward to Lake Superior. The Indians of Pennsylvania were at one time their vassals, and obeyed their slightest command.

Their position at the head-waters of the Delaware and Susquehanna gave them a great advantage. They could launch their canoes on the swift currents of those rivers, and descend with great rapidity into Pennsylvania and the South. At the time of the Revolution, they were believed to be able to muster about five thousand fighting men.

Their politics were controlled by the famous Sir William Johnson, who was an Irishman of birth and education. The refusal of his family to allow a marriage with the woman of his choice brought him to New York to take charge of the landed estates of a relative. From this experience he acquired an intimate knowledge of the Six Nations, and gradually assumed an influence over them. He was soon appointed the official agent of the British government for Indian affairs, a position which for many years he filled with the greatest ability, and prevented the Six Nations from joining Pontiac's conspiracy.

He lived in the style of an English baron, in a large mansion house, which was conducted with profuse hospitality. After the death of his wife he had several women for companions at different times, the last of whom was a very pretty Indian girl, Molly Brant, the sister of the famous Joseph Brant. Several respectable families in Upper Canada are supposed to boast of their descent from this union, and remind us, except for the illegitimacy, of the Virginia families that claim descent from Pocahontas. At the time of the Revolution, Sir William's power had passed to his nephew, Guy Johnson, who had married one of his daughters.

Whether the Americans or the English should have

the alliance of the Six Nations was simply a question of price. If the savages had had the wisdom to remain neutral, as some of their chiefs counselled, they might still be living by their lakes and rivers, an interesting and instructive example of the advancement of a race. The work of Sir William Johnson and the progress they had made in civilization would not have been lost, and the solution of our present Indian problem would, perhaps, be easier. But England was rich and unscrupulous. She bid high in presents, and the Indians were doomed.

The Americans, be it said to their honor, made no attempt to buy these Indians. They tried to keep them neutral, but they would not and could not accept them as allies. The whole feeling and tone in all the colonies were against such an alliance. They had suffered too much from the Indian. They knew him too well, and they would not accept the assistance of his murderous and cruel skill.

During the first three years of the Revolution, the Six Nations were assisting the British to hold the region in the neighborhood of Lake Champlain. But after the defeat of Burgoyne at Saratoga, they were no longer needed for that duty. They had all along regarded Wyoming and the other settlements to the south of them as ripe plums which they could take at any time, and they now prepared for it. They were accompanied by a large body of Tories under the command of Colonel John Butler, commonly called Indian Butler, to distinguish him from his cousin, Zebulon Butler. The Indian contingent was led by Brant, the Mohawk sachem.

Brant probably had some white blood in his veins, although this slight on his purity is earnestly denied by

The Making of Pennsylvania

one of his biographers. He had been educated at the
Rev. Dr. Wheelock's school, in New Hampshire, which
afterwards became Dartmouth College, and could write
a letter in passable English. After the Revolution he
became very popular in Canada, where there is a monument to his memory, and towards the end of his life he
became religious, translated some of the Scriptures into
Mohawk, and visited England to raise money for a
church. His admirers have given him the high honor
of never killing women and children with his own hands,
and taking but little pleasure in the torture of prisoners.

The place selected for the first onset was Cherry
Valley, New York, and so sweeping, fierce, and cruel
was this attack that, for some days after, the cocks
could be heard crowing from the tops of trees and the
dogs howling in the distant woods. Men, women, and
children were indiscriminately slaughtered, and the settlement wiped out of existence.

Mrs. Writer, as she was dragged away by her captors,
saw an Indian draw his knife across the throat of a girl,
and while she was in her death agony cut off her nose,
ears, and breasts, and gash her cheeks. When the party
encamped for the evening, a large belt of scalps was
brought to Mrs. Writer, and an Indian, with uplifted
tomahawk, compelled her to dress them. She had to
open them out with her hands and spread them to dry.
Many of them, she could see, were those of her friends,
and presently she recognized the scalp of her mother.

Brant and Butler could have descended upon Wyoming with great rapidity by putting their forces in canoes.
The rushing waters of the Susquehanna would have
swept them into the valley in a few hours. But they

were in no hurry.   They used their boats only part of the way.   They started from Tioga Point and landed at the mouth of Bowman's Creek, about twenty miles above the valley.   From there they marched down with a deliberation which was intended to show confidence and contempt.

The men able to bear arms at that time in Wyoming are described on the monument erected to their memory as " the undisciplined, the youthful, and the aged."   The rest were in the ranks of the Continental army.   Every effort had been made to bring them home.   The contemplated attack of the Indians was well known, and both officers and men earnestly pleaded to be allowed to return and protect their families.   They had been enlisted on the understanding that they should serve on the frontier, near the valley, and they had been taken away to the sea-board in the dark hours of the contest when Washington was defeated and compelled to retreat through the Jerseys.   As message after message reached them of the preparations of the savages, and the murders north of the valley, they broke through all restraint. The officers resigned, and about twenty-five of the men deserted.   Those who remained were finally allowed to march to Wyoming, but too late.

The enemy quietly entered the upper end of the valley, and took their time in destroying the few forts and people they found there.   It never seems to have occurred to these poor scattered settlers to escape.   They went about their usual vocations, and when the overwhelming force of the enemy came upon them, fought with fury and desperation.   In one instance seven men and a boy were suddenly surprised.   The boy threw himself into the river, where he lay with his face just above the surface, and listened to the fierce struggle of his companions and their dying groans.

Zebulon Butler had returned from the Continental army and found himself in command of about three hundred men, among whom were grandfathers with their grandsons. The opposing force of the enemy numbered between four and five hundred of British troops and Tories, together with about seven hundred Indians.

It would probably have been better policy for the three hundred Americans to have remained in Forty Fort and waited developments. The Wyoming men remaining in the Continental army were known to be coming, and other reinforcements were on the way. Everybody that could send assistance was sending it. The situation could not be worse and might grow better, and the chances within the fort were better than outside of it. Such was the counsel of Zebulon Butler and some of the older officers, but they were overruled by the majority. The Indians, the majority said, had been in the valley three days, were acting leisurely and gradually destroying it piecemeal. By the time they had decided to take Forty Fort, the garrison in it, unable to endure the strain of the danger, would have disbanded, each man intent upon carrying off his own wife and children.

The British and Indians, with sarcastic politeness, had sent a message inviting the fort to surrender, and the fort had replied after the manner of frontiersmen. Its inmates had actually decided that the only possible hope of saving the valley was for the three hundred old men and boys to march out at once, meet the twelve hundred British and Indians, and fight them. So forth they went at noon on the third day of July, 1778, passing out from the friendly shadow of the fort, with the odds more than three to one against them, and knowing it.

Such reckless, desperate courage is seldom seen, and, like the charge of the Light Brigade at Balaklava, is not soon forgotten. The old men and boys arranged themselves by companies with military precision. Officers went ahead and marked off the ground for them, between a high bank and a swamp. It was a mistake to select the ground so far beyond all chance of retreat to the fort, and it was a mistake to rest the left wing on a swamp, the favorite fighting-ground of the Indian. There was but little of the skill of Zebulon Butler shown in the preparations. He had been overruled.

Still he did his best for the people. He told them that if they would only stand the first shock, the Indians would give way. Under his inspiring instruction they advanced a step every time they fired, and they actually forced back part of the British line, and more than held their own for half an hour. But it was useless. Their advance brought them in among the enemy who slipped round on their flank and occupied the swamp. The Indians and Tories kept close under cover, knowing their prey was secure. When the flanking movement was complete, Butler attempted to turn some of his men so as to face it, but they mistook the order for permission to retreat. Instantly the Indians rushed in with the war-whoop, and all was over.

The massacre began. Every captain that led a company had been shot at the head of his men. Some of the Indian marksmen had singled out officers and broken the thigh-bone so as to reserve the victim for torture.

The Making of Pennsylvania

The rest of the three hundred were pursued, toma-
hawked, speared, and butchered as they ran. Some
took to the water,—that last resort of hunted deer and
hunted ranger. They were shot while swimming, or
brought to the shore by promises of quarter and instantly killed. A prisoner was thrown on the burning
logs of a fort and held down with pitchforks. Sixteen
more of the others were arranged round a stone, and
Queen Esther, a squaw of political prominence, passed
around the circle singing a war-song and dashing
out their brains. When night came on the savages
built fires, and, stripping the remaining prisoners naked,
chased them back and forth through the flames with
their spears until they fell exhausted and were consumed. Only two of all the prisoners taken escaped
torture and death.

All that night and the next day there was a general
rush to get out of the valley. Most of those who
fled were women and children. Every road and trail
was crowded. In one company there were a hundred
women and children and only one man. They were
flying in terror and with no provisions. Children were
prematurely born, and when they died had to be left to
the wolves, or their dead bodies carried in exhausted
arms. The aged soon sank by the roadside, and many
of the strongest were overcome. Many perished in
a great swamp lying to the eastward of Wyoming, and
still known as the Shades of Death.

The remnant of the three hundred, together with
thirty or forty soldiers who had returned from the Continental army, remained in the valley, determined to
hold it to the last. They assembled at Forty Fort

and tried to rally the fast-dispersing population. The Indians and British were still picking up fort after fort. Troops of squaws followed them, smeared with blood and brains, and carrying strings of scalps, which they would smell and cry " Yankee blood."

Negotiations were begun for a surrender. In the course of this Indian Butler insisted that the Continental soldiers should be given up as prisoners. Knowing what they might expect from the Indians, their friends gave them the hint, and they all left the valley. The articles of capitulation, in other respects, were fair and honorable. The fort and its stores were to be surrendered; the inhabitants allowed to occupy their farms in peace, and Indian Butler promised that the savages should be restrained from bloodshed and pillage. But he had little control over them.

As soon as the formalities were finished they started on their usual course, breaking open houses and taking everything they wanted. He finally persuaded most of them to withdraw, and his army returned northward. The squaws brought up the rear riding on stolen horses, with scalps stretched on hoops bound round their waists; their bodies covered with dresses worn one over the other, and their heads adorned in the same way with bonnets.

The Indians who remained went through the valley from one end to the other, burnt every house and barn, and shot and scalped every human being that did not escape to the woods. For the sixth time within a period of fifteen years Wyoming was completely annihilated.

And yet within two months the settlers began to return. They hoped to harvest what was left of their grain, and build anew their fortunes. They obtained the protection of some troops, and built forts. But the Indians, though no longer an army, were still prowling in scattered bands through the woods, and for months and even years continued to pick off stragglers and make sudden descents upon the farms. They would lie for weeks in the bushes, living on berries and roots, creeping and watching for their victims. They would imitate the call of wild turkeys to entice the hunter to his death. The horrors and atrocities that continued for years are almost beyond belief, and in their sum total equal all that was done in the massacre and fight of July 3.

That event, now known in history as the Battle of Wyoming, has been given here in its subdued coloring, the result of the careful researches of Miner. Even then it is bad enough. But at the time of its occurrence newspaper accounts were circulated in Europe which greatly exaggerated the worst details. Zebulon Butler and his men were said to have been invited out to a parley, enticed on and on by a white flag, which always moved as they approached, until they were surrounded and destroyed. The terms of the surrender were falsified. Indian Butler, when asked what terms he would grant, was said to have replied "the hatchet." He is charged with dressing and painting his white men like Indians, shutting up the garrison in the fort and burning them alive; also with shutting the women and children in their houses and burning them alive, cutting out the tongues of cattle and leaving them to perish, together with other enormities.

All this was taken from an account sent from Poughkeepsie to various newspapers a short time after the massacre, made up from the statements of frightened women and excited men. It was accepted as the truth for many years, copied into the histories of the Revolution by Ramsay, Gordon, and Botta, and used by Chief-Justice Marshall in his " Life of Washington." But the investigations of Miner during the first half of the present century, his thorough examination of every eye-witness that could be found, revealed the true situation, and reduced the tale to its proper proportions.

Campbell, in his poem of Gertrude, so far as he confined himself to actualities at all, seems to have been influenced by the Poughkeepsie story. He represents the women, children, and men retreating to a fort, or tower, as he calls it, which is attacked, and Gertrude and her father fall bleeding on each other's bodies before the eyes of the lover, Waldegrave.

The story of the battle was valuable in its day, but not because of its exaggeration, for the true story would have been equally valuable. It drew the sympathy of all Europe to the side of the Americans. It weakened the Tory party in England, and encouraged those who, like Burke and Lord Chatham, sympathized with the colonies. It gave an impulse to eloquence and a sting to sarcasm. There was but little moral support for that administration which, as one of those orators expressed it, " had associated with the arms of England the tomahawk and scalping-knife of the savage."

It was the most disastrous victory the British ever won in America. It can be truthfully said that of all the Americans who fell in the Revolution, none died more effectively for their country than the " undisciplined, the youthful, and the aged" who perished in the Battle of Wyoming.

But whatever moral support may have been gained, it was not enough to satisfy Washington and other public men. The Six Nations would come again. They were the worst part of the British army. It was decided to tear out, root and branch, the whole system of Indian alliance in New York, and destroy forever that budding civilization which a great nation was turning from its purpose. The man selected for the task was General Sullivan, who had been born in Maine of Irish parentage, and afterwards became a citizen of New Hampshire. He was of the dashing type, well adapted for a cutting-out expedition, with the faults, that often go with that character, of a hasty temper and a reckless tongue.

His army assembled at Wyoming, and on the 31st day of July, 1779, set out for the north, over three thousand strong. From the time of his arrival at Wyoming the Indians and British played all round him, cutting off stragglers and killing isolated settlers and hunters. Brant attacked the Minisink settlement in Orange County, New York, and also the Connecticut settlement at Lackawaxen. The rangers who went to relieve these places were led on and on, by the apparent retreat of the Indians, until they were ambuscaded, and more than a hundred of them killed. Brant boasted that he returned from these expeditions with double as many scalps and prisoners as he had warriors.

All this was to distract the attention of Sullivan and turn him aside from his main object. But he gave no heed to such attempts, and sent out no side expeditions, either for relief or revenge. He marched straight up the

Susquehanna, aiming for the very heart of the Indian empire. The savages and Tories mustered about two thousand men under the command of Butler, Brant, and the Johnsons, and made a final stand on the Tioga River below Newtown.

The battle was short and decisive, and Sullivan passed on among the beautiful lakes Seneca, Cayuga, and Canandaigua, and reached the Genesee River, in the northwestern part of the State, where the level valley, extending for twenty miles, with scarcely a tree, and all under Indian cultivation, astonished the eyes of his soldiers. We can form some idea of the extent of this Indian civilization when we find that Sullivan reported that he had destroyed forty towns, and that his army of nearly four thousand men had been occupied for a month in this work of destruction. Some towns were left untouched for lack of time. Apple and peach orchards were girdled, and corn and vegetables were burnt. An entry in the Journal of Colonel Adam Hubley shows the method.

"*Wednesday, September 15th.*—This morning the whole army, excepting a covering party, were engaged in destroying the corn, beans, potatoes, and other vegetables, which were in quantity immense, and in goodness unequalled by any I ever yet saw. Agreeable to a moderate calculation, there was not less than two hundred acres, the whole of which was pulled and piled up in large heaps, mixed with dry wood, taken from the houses, and consumed to ashes."

Eleven years afterwards, Big Tree, a Seneca Indian, and member of a delegation to the United States Government, was in Philadelphia. "Father," he said, addressing Washington, "when your army entered the country of the Six Nations, we called you the town-destroyer. To this day, when your name is heard, our women look behind and turn pale, and our children cling closer to the necks of their mothers."

Such was the end of the Six Nations and their alliance with the British. Individual depredations still continued, and for many years scalping parties crept through the woods about Wyoming. But their organization as a nation was destroyed, their empire gone. The following winter most of them were quartered on the Niagara River near Buffalo, where they had to subsist on salt meat, furnished by the British, and were decimated by the scurvy. They soon dwindled to that remnant which we now see, in summer time, selling baskets at Saratoga and Richfield Springs.

No sooner was the Revolution ended than Pennsylvania appealed to the Continental Congress to settle her dispute with Connecticut. The question was growing in importance. The land was no longer the private property of a family to be held for speculation. It was part of the State, belonged to the people, and the rapidly growing population were anxious to enter it and reap the advantage of its fertility.

During the contest with England, Pennsylvania had refrained from pushing the matter, and in fact had been specially requested by Congress to refrain, as there were already contests enough. But within fifteen days after Lord Cornwallis's surrender at Yorktown, a petition was presented to Congress asking that the case be heard under that clause of the Articles of Confederation which provided for the settlement of disputed boundaries. By August of the following year, 1782, the two States had mutually agreed on the persons who should constitute a court, and this Court of Commissioners opened its sessions November 12, at Trenton, New Jersey. William Bradford, Joseph Reed, James Wilson, and Jonathan D. Sergeant appeared as counsel for Pennsylvania, and Eliphalet Dyer, William S. Johnson, and Jesse Root appeared for Connecticut.

The trial and argument lasted forty-one days, and must have completely exhausted the subject. But unfortunately only short notes of the arguments of counsel have come down to us, and the court abstained from giving the reasons for their decision, which was short and carefully worded.

> " The Cause has been well argued by the learned Counsel on both sides.
>
> " The Court are now to pronounce their sentence or judgment.
>
> " We are unanimously of opinion that Connecticut has no right to the lands in controversy.
>
> " We are also unanimously of opinion that the jurisdiction and pre-emption of all the territory lying within the Charter of Pennsylvania, and now claimed by the State of Connecticut, do of right belong to the State of Pennsylvania.
>
> " Wm. Whipple.
" Welcome Arnold.
" Dan'l Brearly.
" Cyrus Griffin.
" Wm. C. Houston.
>
> " Trenton, 30th Dec., 1782."

The decree of the commissioners was quietly acquiesced in by Connecticut. It was the first instance in which a serious conflict between two States had been settled by the powers given to the Union under the Articles of Confederation. The Union had dealt successfully with outside enemies in the Revolution; but it was a question whether it would be strong enough to settle internal disputes. The Trenton decision was an important step in nationality.

Why the reasons for such an important decision should be withheld the commissioners never vouchsafed to explain. When they first met they adopted a resolution that, no matter what their decision should be, they would never disclose its reasons; and neither the prying curiosity of that generation nor the subsequent investigations of learned antiquarians have been able to unveil the mystery.

Probably they were influenced by the thought that this was the first decision under the Continental Union of a serious dispute between two independent States. If their decision should be accepted and quietly acquiesced in, a great step in uniting the country would have been gained. But if the decision should be attacked, criticised, or resisted, any substantial Union of the States might forever after be impossible. It was a case that would test the real intentions of the people. It was an American question, more than a question of either Pennsylvania or Connecticut. It was important, therefore, that whatever was done should be done thoroughly, surely, and with as little chance as possible for attack. They may have heard of Lord Mansfield's advice to the unlearned men who were going out to be judges in India. " Decide the cases," said his Lordship, " by your common sense, and if you never give your reasons it will be hard to prove that you have made a mistake."

If we had full reports of the arguments of counsel it might be possible to supply some of these reasons which the court declined to give. But we have only the short headings which some of the lawyers made in preparing for their speeches, and a letter or two describing in a general way what was said. The headings are very inadequate material from which to reconstruct arguments. Wilson's speech occupied four days; but his headings are all contained in a little over a page of print.

Judging by the material we have, it would seem that the Connecticut counsel treated the question as one of mere title to land as between private individuals, and took advantage of every small technicality and every cause of delay. They professed to have lost their great Indian deed. They declared they had looked everywhere for it in vain, and were chaffed by the Pennsylvania counsel, who asked them if they had looked in their breeches' pockets.

They produced it quickly enough, however, when ordered to produce it by the court. They acted all through the case after the manner of men who knew that the decision would be against them, and were determined to make a good appearance by fighting every point.

The Pennsylvania counsel took broader ground. Some of Wilson's notes point to the argument already made, which had formerly been urged by Provost Smith, that the king as sovereign of all the land had the legal right to alter old grants, and his last grant was binding. One of the notes says, " What was the intention of the parties when the sale or jurisdiction was granted?" Another says, " The power of explaining the old charters in America according to equity and intention was vested in the Crown, now in the United States." Many of his notes refer to the subject of "intention," and he apparently dwelt long on that point.

The Making of Pennsylvania

Some of Sergeant's notes are to the same effect. He reminds the court that the Susquehanna Company, at the suggestion of the Connecticut Assembly, had applied to the Crown for a new grant of Wyoming. This showed that they believed the Pennsylvania title valid, and wanted to correct it by a fresh grant. He also calls attention to the point that, although the king had made the famous Plymouth grant, he afterwards granted to others some of the lands comprised in it.

Wilson and Sergeant were both well-known men. Wilson a few years after took a prominent part in the convention which framed the National Constitution. Sergeant had been a member of the Continental Congress, attorney-general of the State, and was the father of John Sergeant, one of the famous leaders of the Philadelphia bar.

Hoyt, in his "Brief of a Title," suggests that one of the arguments made by the Pennsylvania counsel must have carried great weight. It was in evidence that from the time of her charter in 1662 up to the middle of the next century, a period of almost a hundred years, Connecticut had made no attempt to take possession of or settle her western land. It, therefore, became derelict, abandoned, and opened to the next actual settlers who should enter it under any authority from the Crown. As a matter of fact, the Penns had built some huts at Wyoming a short time before Connecticut effected any actual settlement, and thus made their right secure.

Several of Wilson's notes refer to the argument from policy and convenience, and doubtless this point was fully elaborated. It was evidently for the best interests of the country at large that the Pennsylvania title should prevail. There was nothing to be gained by having a State split up into fragments, with other States intervening between the fragments. There was no advantage in Connecticut having a piece of jurisdiction in New England, another piece in Pennsylvania, and perhaps a third in Ohio. Why should there be a Connecticut No. 1, and a Connecticut No. 2?

If Connecticut were allowed to do this, other States must be allowed to do it. Massachusetts claimed seven millions of acres in the western part of New York, because her charter, like that of Connecticut, reached from sea to sea. Virginia also had similar western possessions. It would be better for the peace and stability of the new Union for each State to be centralized and compact. Connecticut in New England was large enough. But if she attempted to enlarge herself by taking half of Pennsylvania, she would cut down Pennsylvania to an insignificant commonwealth, and not materially benefit herself, for the branch would be too far from the parent stem to be a source of power. These western claims of New England States were a continuous cause of civil war. The Massachusetts claim in New York had already, like the claim of Connecticut in Pennsylvania, brought about a great loss of property, and led to cruelty and bloodshed. If all these claims were cut off, New England would lose no real advantage, and trouble would cease.

These were the views of the political leaders of the time, and all the disputes about outlying western lands were settled on that basis. The lands outlying within the bounds claimed by another State were given to the

State within which they lay. The far western lands, beyond the bounds claimed by any State, were surrendered to the United States as a common fund for the benefit of all. Massachusetts, Connecticut, New York, Virginia, North Carolina, and Georgia accepted this rule, and in the end gave up their outlying territory to the general government. It was the obviously wise policy.

So wise was it, and so thoroughly in accord were the public men of the time, that it has been supposed that there was a secret understanding between Congress and the members of the Trenton Court that the Pennsylvania title should be quietly allowed to prevail, and that Connecticut should receive a grant farther west to quiet her people. Connecticut did receive from Congress such a grant, and held for a time that part of Ohio still known as the Western Reserve. But that there was a conspiracy or agreement of this kind is a mere supposition, unsupported by a single fact.

The fair Wyoming was turned over to her Pennsylvania lovers, and everybody felt that the new union was valuable for other things than war. It might have been supposed that troubles would cease. But, unfortunately, the Trenton decision settled only the question of political jurisdiction. That was the only question before the court, and the only point on which they were willing to hear testimony and argument. The right of the Connecticut settlers to retain their lots and farms, after the question of political jurisdiction had been passed upon, was left undecided.

The Articles of Confederation provided a method for settling this private right of soil by a tribunal separate from that which decided the political boundaries. After they had entered their decree at Trenton the commissioners had addressed a letter to the chief executive of Pennsylvania, urging that, for the sake of peace and order, the Connecticut settlers be left undisturbed on their lands until their title could be tried in the way provided. This letter was kept secret by the Pennsylvania government for many years, and for reasons which will become clearer as we advance.

As to the right of these settlers to continue to own their farms, there has never been but one opinion among the honest and intelligent. They had entered under color of title. They had been led by all the circumstances of the situation to believe their title good. It had been given to them by a recognized and orderly government. They had cultivated the land, improved it, and, with a heroism almost unequalled in history, defended the northern border of Pennsylvania against the British and the Indians. The transfer of the valley from Connecticut to Pennsylvania should have been merely a change of political government, allowing private titles to stand as they were found. The Pennsylvania claimants, who had been induced to buy paper titles from the Penns, but who had never occupied or improved the land, should have been reimbursed for their loss from the public treasury.

The precedents governing the case were numerous. There had already been boundary disputes between Rhode Island and Connecticut, between Massachusetts and Connecticut, between Massachusetts and New Hampshire, and between New York and Connecticut. In all of these the private right to the soil had remained unaltered by the change of political jurisdiction. Pennsylvania herself had already had two famous boundary disputes, one with Maryland and another with Virginia, and in both of these the same rule had been followed.

The only instance in which an attempt had been made to disregard the rule was in the contest between New York and New Hampshire. The land in dispute was that known as the " New Hampshire Grants," afterwards the State of Vermont. This territory had been settled under New Hampshire titles, which New York attempted to abrogate in favor of the titles she had subsequently granted to her own citizens. The consequence was a long, petty civil war in which the gallant Vermonters were successful, expelled the invaders, and New York finally acquiesced in the rule which she found herself unable to break. All this was perfectly familiar to the men of that time. It was an age of boundary disputes, and it is scarcely too much to say that every man in the country capable of doing a day's work was well informed as to what was right and just in such matters.

But, as already shown, a class of people had grown up in Pennsylvania who loved Wyoming, but not for her beauty and romance. These were the persons who had obtained title to the land through the sales made by the Penn family in 1771. As time went on, and the original tracts were divided and subdivided by sales and inheritance, these people became more and more numerous until they were a power in the community, and acquired the doubtful honor of forming our first legislative lobby. Upon their heads rests a large part of the responsibility for the subsequent vacillating and disgraceful conduct of the government. How easily wrong begets wrong, and misfortune breeds misfortune! Every new tribulation of Wyoming is more complicated than the last, and now we have a Third Pennamite War.

The full details of the struggle would fill the remaining pages of this volume, and the legal problems involved are more intricate than those of the charters. Pennsylvania never offered to submit the question of private ownership to the tribunal provided in the Articles of Confederation. Such a tribunal would have, in all probability, decided in favor of the Connecticut settlers. The settlers made repeated efforts to have it appointed, and in 1784 the Continental Congress actually passed a bill to that effect. But the strong remonstrance of the Pennsylvania Legislature and the efforts of the Pennsylvania members in Congress compelled its repeal. Pennsylvania was determined to work out the problem in her own way, through her own courts and legislature.

The first action taken by the assembly was to appoint commissioners to inquire of the matter, and, meantime, all legal proceedings against the settlers were stayed. The commissioners set out for Wyoming, and were under the control of the land-jobbers. They coolly informed the settlers that they could remain on half their land under a lease for one year. At the end of that time they must surrender all. The widows of the men slain by the savages were to have a further indulgence of an additional year, but only on half their land.

That these proposals should be refused, and refused with indignation, was to be expected. But when the commissioners returned, the land-jobbing legislature justified all their doings and sent them back with two companies of soldiers to carry out their plans.

The Making of Pennsylvania

The commissioners had previously remodelled the government of Wyoming, dividing it into two Pennsylvania townships, and electing justices of the peace. Under the lead of a certain Alexander Patterson, a Scotch-Irishman, who was now in charge of proceedings, the name of Wilkesbarre was changed to Londonderry. Zebulon Butler was arrested and imprisoned on the charge of high treason. He had protested against the disorders of Patterson's soldiery. Old and respectable citizens were seized, thrown into loathsome jails, starved, and insulted. Land-owners were ejected, their cattle driven off, their barns burnt, and the Pennsylvania claimants put in possession.

A slight show of resistance gave Patterson the opportunity he wanted, and with a little bloodshed he annihilated the settlement. The plundered and homeless Yankees once more sought the paths to the eastward,— those paths so often trod by the faint and failing. They passed again through the Shades of Death, and the scenes of the Indian massacre were repeated. The women and children hunted through the swamps and mountains had but little to choose between their former and their present pursuers, the Indian Brant and the white man Patterson.

This Patterson had been in the employ of the proprietors all through the Pennamite wars, a service of which he was very proud. Some of the men under him were also veterans of the same campaigns. They had cultivated a fierce hatred for the Connecticut settlers, which they expressed in violent language. Patterson's official communications to the government denounce the settlers as banditti, perjurers, ruffians, and a despicable herd.

He gave prominence to the story that at the time of the massacre the three hundred defenders of the valley were drunk.

A flood which swept down the Susquehanna and obliterated landmarks greatly assisted his designs. He resurveyed the country on Pennsylvania lines and boasted that he had restored to what he called his " constituents" the " chief part of all the lands." Again Wyoming was wiped off the map, and for the seventh time.

The indignation of the better element in Pennsylvania was aroused. The troops were recalled and a sheriff sent to restore order. Messengers were sent after the dispersed settlers. They needed only a slight excuse, and many of them began to return. Under the pretence of a flag of truce and permission to revisit their property in Wilkesbarre, Patterson captured several of them, whom he tied up and whipped with iron ramrods. But the others kept returning in still greater numbers, and under the leadership of John Franklin swept up and down both sides of the river, dispossessing every Pennsylvanian. They drove them with Patterson into a fort, where a sharp fight took place, with loss on both sides.

Some magistrates were sent in obedience to the better feeling in the State to open negotiations and quiet both parties. An attempt was made to persuade both sides to surrender. The Connecticut party were willing, but as Patterson and his men refused, the Yankees were allowed to keep their arms. Meanwhile, Colonel Armstrong, another Scotch-Irishman, was marching to the assistance of the situation with four hundred militia.

He was supposed to be sent for the purpose of disarming everybody and compelling peace, but in reality he was in the service of the jobbers. He was that same Armstrong who in the Revolution wrote the "Newburg Letters," which almost brought on a mutiny in Washington's army on the Hudson. He was undoubtedly a man of talents, very skilful with his pen, and afterwards achieved political prominence as a senator, Secretary of War, and Minister to France. He was the son of a much better man, General Armstrong, famous in the Revolution and in the Indian fight at Kittanning in the French Wars.

An irregular company, under a mulatto named Logan, also appears to have marched at this time, taking the "rebel route" by way of Easton, that route over which prisoners had passed and repassed so many times. A popular ditty of the day throws some light on the affair, and doubtless represented the feeling of many people.

> " The twentieth of September,
>   We marched the rebel route,
> From Easton to Wyoming,
>   To drive the Yankees out.
> The wary dogs and savage beasts
> Would rather steal than show their face.\

> " We halted all at Romig's,
>   Our forces to review ;
> Our chief commander Logan
>   Encouraged thus his crew,—
> ' Brave lads,' he cried, · who steals the most,
> He shall obtain the highest post.' "

Armstrong pledged to the settlers his faith as a soldier, and his honor as a gentleman, that if they would surrender, the Patterson party should also be disarmed, but as soon as their weapons were stacked he had them all seized as prisoners. Not a gun was taken from Patterson. The jobbers were again in power, with their feet on the settler's neck. The prisoners were coupled, two and two, in irons, and marched, some to Sunbury and the rest to Easton.

This disgraceful business was denounced by a large part of the people of the State, as well as by the Council of Censors, a body existing at that time for the purpose of keeping inviolate the Constitution. John Dickinson, President of the State, opposed it with all his power, but he was unsupported by the Supreme Executive Council, of which he was the head, and by the majority of the legislature. Armstrong and Patterson still went on with their work, and were upheld and encouraged in it by the government.

But they could raise no militia. Armstrong himself confessed that he was everywhere met with the objection "that it was a quarrel of a set of land-jobbers." With less than a hundred men he attempted to attack the fast-rallying Yankees. His prisoners had nearly all escaped. Some were released on bail, and the rest had knocked down their keepers and fled. Desultory fighting, siege and counter-siege, and the sharp-shooting of hunters followed for several months. Seven or eight lives were lost, wounds given, and prisoners taken. Each party seemed to hold its own. But in the end Patterson and Armstrong were recalled.

A new difficulty was rapidly appearing. As there seemed to be no hope of justice from Pennsylvania, New England and a large part of New York began to take sides with Wyoming. The idea, so often suggested, of making the valley a new State of the Union, began to take definite shape. John Franklin urged it with vehemence upon Connecticut, Massachusetts, and the Susquehanna Company. Some of the ablest men in Pennsylvania believed that he would succeed. They feared that, unless the insane course of Pennsylvania was checked, there would either be a new State, or a civil war, involving the New England with the Middle States, which would wreck the Confederation, and destroy every hope of a permanent union.

Fortunately, Pennsylvania saw her folly, and began to retract. She passed acts to restore the settlers to possession, to pardon all past offences, and she repealed the acts remodelling the government of Wyoming. Other acts were passed organizing the country, and giving the settlers representation in council and assembly.

It was none too soon, for all the time the Susquehanna Company was working at its project of a new State. Some of the most prominent men in New England had been engaged as commissioners with power to determine when an independent government should be established. The services of Ethan Allen were obtained. He was fresh from his creation of the new State of Vermont and his triumph over New York, and he was stimulated by a gift from the Susquehanna Company of a few thousand acres of land. He appeared at Wyoming in his regimentals, followed by " Green Mountain boys," and " half-share men," as the new subscribers to the Susquehanna Company were called.

Luckily the old settlers did not altogether sympathize with this project. They were perfectly willing to live under the Pennsylvania constitution, provided their land was secure. Still the pressure to join the new State movement was strong, and it might have succeeded had it not been for the exertions of Timothy Pickering, seconded by that brave and judicious soul, Zebulon Butler.

Pickering appeared representing Pennsylvania and the sober, second thought of her decent people. He had at one time been quartermaster-general of the Continental army. He was a native of Massachusetts, and had been selected for that reason, as likely to have influence with men of New England origin. In after years he became very prominent in national politics as an extreme Federalist, was Secretary of War, Secretary of State, and a member of the Senate.

He was an altogether different man from Patterson. With patience and discretion, and no ulterior purpose, he labored for the just settlement of the unfortunate problem. He bought land on the Connecticut title, identified himself with the people, went up and down among them for a month, and by the most strenuous exertions turned the tide, but only on the express condition that the possession of their land should be confirmed.

And now began the legal war. The legislature passed an act which became familiar to a whole generation as " The Confirming Act of 1787." On its face it appeared somewhat fair and likely to succeed. Every Connecticut claimant, who was an actual settler and owner of land before the Trenton Decree, had his title confirmed. The Pennsylvania claimants were disposed of by giving each of them other lands of equal value in the unseated territory of the State.

The chief defect in this act was that it was largely unconstitutional. It provided for taking away the property of the Pennsylvania claimants and indemnifying them with other land. But when private property is taken by the government the indemnification must be in money. Again, the act provided that the amount of other land to be given as indemnification should be determined by the board of property. That was unconstitutional, because the amount of indemnification in such cases can be determined in only one of three ways,—by agreement of the parties, by agreement of persons specially appointed by them for the purpose, or by the verdict of a jury.

In one respect, however, the act was perfectly valid. A large part of the land in dispute was now owned by the State. This had happened in two ways. The part of the land which the Penns had not sold had, of course, after the Revolution, become the property of the State. Some of the land sold by the Penns had not been paid for, and this also had come into the possession of the State.

As to the surrender of this State land to the Connecticut claimants, the act was, of course, perfectly constitutional. No Pennsylvania citizen was being deprived of his property. The State had a right to do what she pleased with her own, and the act was a contract which could not afterwards be rescinded without violating that clause of the Constitution of the United States which says that no State shall pass an act impairing the obligation of a contract. As regards this State land, the opinion of the best lawyers has always been that the confirming act of 1787 gave it out and out to the claimants beyond any power of revocation.

That the land-jobbing section of the legislature knew that they were passing an act largely unconstitutional, and did so purposely, is not at all unlikely. Other diffi-

The Connecticut Invasion

culties which interfered with its execution crept out from time to time, disclosing the secret purpose of its framers.

The act required the Connecticut people to present their claims within eight months, and required the commissioners who were to examine those claims to meet within two months. Of course, these provisions were not complied with, and could not in the nature of things be accurately complied with. In the confusion of the last ten years, title papers had been scattered or lost, and the means of communication were slow. The commissioners who were appointed kept resigning, and the two months soon passed. The land-jobbers took advantage of this, and said the act had not been complied with. It was a failure, as a large part of the legislature intended that it should be, and they now had a good excuse for repealing it.

But, nevertheless, the actual effect of this insincere legislation was valuable. It had on its face so much appearance of justice that it stopped the new State movement at the time of its most rapid growth. Just before its passage, Oliver Wolcott, one of the New England commissioners, had drawn up a constitution for the new State. William Judd, of Connecticut, was to be governor, and John Franklin lieutenant-governor. Preparations had been made, so soon as the decisive moment should arrive, to pour an enormous New England population into the valley, and every new settler was to be given two hundred acres of land.

The passage of the act brought on a crisis. The Wyoming settlers met in a mass meeting. Should they accept or reject the act? Franklin still clung to the new State movement and was pitted against Pickering. The speeches were earnest, but the intense feeling was restrained, until one of the majority aimed a blow at Franklin while he was speaking. Instantly the wild passions of the frontiersmen broke forth. Each party rushed to the nearest wood, cut sticks, and turned on each other with savage blows.

The contest deserves mention for other reasons than the mere fact of its occurrence. It is another instance of the honorable way in which the rough type of colonial Americans fought among themselves. They all possessed firearms, were trained to their daily use, and had no hesitation in using them on enemies in lawful warfare. But in their private quarrels they invariably laid aside both the rifle and the knife, and took the Saxon method of fists and sticks. They had no love for murder, and they had none of that modern instinct of shooting and killing for every petty difficulty which for the last sixty years has disgraced our American civilization.

On this particular occasion, when their fight was over, they settled down to business and passed a vote. They were warned that Pennsylvania had always dealt treacherously and would repeal the act. The prophecy was true. But, nevertheless, these sturdy men voted for acceptance. Of all their remarkable qualities, their courage, their persistence, their fairness, and their intelligence, nothing is more remarkable than their patient, abiding faith that justice would be done them in the end, and that that justice would come from Pennsylvania.

Most of the settlers having voted against the new State movement, John Franklin was arrested on the charge of high treason, and his project troubled the people no more. A step had been gained, and an important one. In spite of the repeal of the act, the better element of the State argued that it had had effects which could not be done away.

Perhaps this feeling was nowhere so well expressed as in the dissenting votes of William Rawle and William Lewis, members of the legislature from Philadelphia. They were then comparatively young men. Rawle was thirty-one and Lewis forty. But they were both rapidly rising to that position in which, with Sergeant, Ingersoll, Binney, and others, they made the name of the Philadelphia bar a synonyme for ability and integrity throughout the whole Union. Their dissenting votes are strong with the flavor of the old school; that unmistakable touch of the gentleman and the scholar which so long distinguished the Philadelphia lawyers.

Lewis's statement is longer than Rawle's, and forms almost a complete history of the subject. He rather delicately insinuates the suspicion that the former legislature passed the confirming law merely to stop the new State movement, and with the full intention, when that object was accomplished, of repealing the law and proceeding with the land-jobbing projects. Both he and Rawle argue that the confirming law while in force conveyed to the Connecticut settlers vested rights which could not be revoked. But beyond all matters of mere technicality the confirming law was an act of justice, a solemn pledge of the public faith and honor, to be regarded in the light of a covenant, and a treaty which could never be broken without disgrace.

Nevertheless, on the 1st of April, 1790, the repeal was passed by the overwhelming vote of forty-two to four-

teen. The preamble declared the confirming law to
have been unjust and oppressive, because it deprived
Pennsylvania citizens of their land without their consent,
which deprivation was unconstitutional, and that it had
been passed hastily and without proper information.
The repealers then proceeded to reverse all judgments
which had been obtained by default against Connecticut
claimants, and provided that new suits might be begun.
This seemed to recognize to a certain extent the justness
of the Connecticut position. It cleared the ground and
left everything to be begun again anew.

The effect of the repeal was to turn the whole matter
over to the civil courts to be settled by ordinary law-
suits. But the Connecticut settlers continued to occupy
the land and were undisturbed. Within the next eight
years, although many suits of ejectment were begun,
only one was tried: so true was the argument of Rawle
and Lewis that the confirming act had done its work in
spite of the repeal.

The case which was tried was the famous one of Van
Horn *vs*. Dorrance, brought in the United States Circuit
Court. On one side or the other were nearly all the
leaders of the Philadelphia bar. Jared Ingersoll, Sergeant, and Tilghman were for the plaintiff, who was
a Pennsylvania claimant. Rawle, Lewis, and Thomas
were for the Connecticut defendant. Charters, Indian
deeds, and everything relating to the subject were put
in evidence, and witnesses described every step in the
sad history of Wyoming. When these failed the works
of historians were added. Such a case, involving history, romance, adventure, and constitutional law, had
seldom, if ever, been tried.

The Connecticut Invasion

The Connecticut defendant attempted to protect his title first by the Connecticut charter, and second by the confirming act. As to the Connecticut charter, the judge decided that it did not cover Wyoming. Unfortunately, he followed the example of the court at Trenton and refrained from giving his reasons. He was justified in silently following the higher authority of the Trenton commissioners, but it would have been more interesting if he had given us an argument. As to the confirming act, he held it to be unconstitutional and void, and on this point he gave his reasons in a very clear and convincing manner. The title of the Connecticut defendant failing on both points, a verdict was rendered against him, and apparently he had lost his land.

But the learned judge might have spared his breath. The case was appealed to the Supreme Court of the United States, where it slept the sleep of the dead, and was never heard from again. The decision had no more effect than if it had never been rendered. The justice of Wyoming's cause had been so wrought into the sense of the community that her rights were beyond the reach of legislatures, courts, and land-jobbers. The settlers continued on that land, which was theirs by devotion, courage, blood, and right, and in 1799 that astute and remarkable body, which called itself the General Assembly of the Commonwealth of Pennsylvania, passed what became known as the "Compromise Act."

This act was rendered necessary by the position of the Pennsylvania claimants. They were entirely out in the cold. They were not getting the land they wanted by suits at law, and all legislation giving them compensation had been repealed. By the new compromise act all claimants, both of Pennsylvania and of Connecticut, were required to give up their titles to the commonwealth ; that being done, the Pennsylvanians were to be paid for theirs in money, and the Connecticut claimants, who were actual settlers and owners before the decree at Trenton, were to have their land given back to them by the State, but they were required to make a small payment, ranging from two dollars an acre for the best land down to eight and a third cents for the worst.

The Connecticut settlers, with the events of the last ten years fresh in their minds, were at first a little slow about giving up their titles to the State ; but finally, with that confidence they always showed, they came forward in large numbers and released. The Pennsylvania speculators would not release at all, and another act had to be passed in 1802, which allowed the commissioners to give title to the releasing Yankees without regard to whether there was a release from the land-jobbers or not. The jobbers were told that they might go before a jury and prove their right to compensation against the State, but that their right to sue the Connecticut claimant was gone. After ten years of dishonor a gleam of justice had at last penetrated the legislative mind.

The impulse once given, that mind moved on. In 1807 an act was passed by which Connecticut claimants were not obliged to have been occupiers before the decree of Trenton, and Pennsylvania claimants could release and be paid in money if they had acquired title any time before the confirming act of 1787. Thus, after a shameful waste of life, property, and money, the legislature was compelled to do what it could have done just as well fifteen years before.

The Connecticut Invasion

Seventeen hundred and forty-five certificates were issued to the Connecticut settlers. The land included was about three hundred thousand acres, pretty much the whole of the seventeen townships, and the troubles of Wyoming were ended forever.

What shall be said of such a history? If ever there was a quarrel unnecessary, wasteful, and foolish, it was this dispute about Wyoming. Yet no part of Pennsylvania history has attracted more attention. No part of Pennsylvania history has been so thoroughly investigated and so carefully written. Besides the elaborate and learned works of Miner and Hoyt, there are histories by Chapman, Peck, Stone, Hollister, and others, together with pamphlets and documents innumerable. Many of these histories have passed through several editions, and some of the most inferior have had large sales. During the first half of the present century there was great interest in the subject both here and in England, but since the Civil War, and the more rapid development of recent years, other topics have occupied the public mind, and Wyoming has been forgotten.

This interest of the outside world was purely an interest in romance and heroism, for there was nothing else in the story. For fifty years, so far as material development was concerned, Wyoming was a failure. It was the paradise of the hunter, the adventurer, and the poet, but the despair of the thrifty colonist.

If Wyoming had been peaceful from the beginning, if the strong, keen, enthusiastic New Englanders had been willing to settle it under Pennsylvania laws, and had not fought for what did not belong to them, they could have developed the valley at their ease, and we might have something very different to record. We might have had remarkable men appearing from the valley,—statesmen, men of literature, more vigorous, striking, and original than even the Scotch-Irish.

But between the successive annihilations of their settlements these unfortunate people were scarcely given time to draw their breath, still less to become great. They were not firmly established until about the year 1810. Soon after that began the influx of foreign emigrants from every nation of Europe, and the original elements of the population were overwhelmed.

The discovery of the enormous coal deposits of the valley, bringing wealth at last to the struggling settler, made the inpouring of the foreigner more mixed and numerous than ever. Irish, Germans, Swedes, Poles, Hungarians, and Italians now fill and have for years filled the haunts of Gertrude and Waldegrave, and made them the seat of the most mixed and various population in mixed and various Pennsylvania. All chance of a homogeneous development was destroyed, and destroyed for hundreds of years to come. The lonely hills are stripped naked of their forests, the ravines and cascades are dry, the trout, the deer, the elk are gone, and the diligent miner has transformed the earth beyond all recognition of the heroes of old.

One characteristic, however, those heroes succeeded in impressing on the land. That was the New England school system. One of their first acts, amid their poverty and misfortunes, was to make provision for public schools. All through their ancient records we find entries to maintain this institution, without which the New-Englander is not of New England. When, in the second quarter of the present century, the State adopted that system, it was simply extending to the whole commonwealth what had been in force in the valley for nearly a hundred years.

But, after all, there may be something in this record of misfortune which cannot be weighed in the scales of science and exactness. There is a moral grandeur about the men of Wyoming, a fearless directness of purpose, a sublime confidence in justice, which is perhaps more valuable to humanity than any material development. Let us hope so. Let us hope that something besides cruelty, devastation, and wrong resulted from that mistaken persistence of Connecticut,—a persistence which attempted to grasp a western empire which the lawful decrees of the British Crown had given to another commonwealth.

CHAPTER XI.

THERE were three points of boundary dispute with
Maryland: one in relation to the lines between Maryland
and the present State of Delaware, which had been given
to Penn by the Duke of York, and was a part of Pennsylvania, sometimes known as The Territories or The
Three Lower Counties ; another in relation to the northern boundary of Delaware on Pennsylvania, that curious
half-circle as now marked on the map ; and a third about
the line which this circle was supposed to cut, and which
would start westward from the circle, and form the
boundary between Maryland and Pennsylvania, now long
known in history as Mason and Dixon's line.

The dispute with Virginia followed immediately after
the settlement of the difficulties with Maryland, and
concerned the extension of Mason and Dixon's line
beyond Maryland. Virginia claimed about fifty-four
miles of the western end of Pennsylvania, which included the present site of Pittsburg.

The controversies with Maryland clung to Pennsylvania all through the colonial period. They began at
the founding of the colony in 1682, and were not finally
settled until 1774, just before the Revolution. The contentions on either side were far reaching and vital, and
the claim of each colony threatened the existence of the

other. If Lord Baltimore's line had been accepted, it would have passed just north of Philadelphia, and brought that city within the limits of Maryland. On the other hand, if Penn had been allowed the boundary given in his charter, the southern line of Pennsylvania would have passed just north of Washington; Baltimore would have been a Pennsylvania town, and Maryland would have been reduced to a few insignificant counties on the Chesapeake.

Our boundaries have now long since been settled, and we have long been accustomed to think of our State as an empire in extent. But few of us know of the difficulties that were encountered and the persistence that was required to create this broad domain. There was a time when it seemed as if our limits would be very narrow ones, and that other provinces would succeed in dismembering us. All through the colonial period we were troubled with boundary disputes on the north, west, and south, which, if they had not been successfully resisted, would have left us a very small patch of territory.

Connecticut claimed the northern half of the State, Maryland a long tract on the south as high up as Philadelphia, and Virginia the western end almost to the Alleghanies, and what was left was merely a narrow strip in the middle of our present State, about seventy miles wide and two hundred and forty long, containing neither Philadelphia nor Pittsburg.*

Maryland was a much older colony than Pennsylvania. Cecil Calvert, the second Lord Baltimore, received his grant of it in 1632, thirty-nine years before the date of

---

* See map.

The Making of Pennsylvania

Penn's charter of 1681. At the time of Baltimore's grant, Virginia had been settled and also Massachusetts, and the geography in the neighborhood of those two places was tolerably well known and marked out on Captain John Smith's two maps, the authorities alike for navigators and kings. But the coast and country between New England and Virginia was unexplored. Smith had known of Delaware Bay only by hearsay from the Indians, and it does not appear on either of his maps. His map of New England gives only the coast line of Maine and Massachusetts, and stops at Cape Cod, and his map of Virginia is really only a map of Chesapeake Bay and its tributaries.

It is true the Dutch had been going to the Delaware ever since 1623, and at the time of Baltimore's grant, in 1632, the existence of the Delaware was well known. But there were no surveys or maps of the part of it where Pennsylvania now is, no one in England seems to have been familiar with any of its prominent landmarks, and there were no reliable observations of latitude to supply their place.

We must be careful to bear in mind the exact meaning of latitude. Degrees of latitude are the measures of distance north and south of the equator. A single degree is a band about sixty-nine and a half miles wide, extending around the earth parallel to the equator; and when provinces are bounded by these degrees it is important to know whether the beginning or the end of the degree is meant. The figures marking the degrees on maps are always placed at the end of the degree, and a degree always begins immediately after these figures where the preceding one ends. Thus, if it should be said that Maryland's northern boundary was the fortieth degree of north latitude the description would be very vague, for the beginning of that degree is near Washington, and the end of it passes through the northern part of Philadelphia.

Lord Baltimore intended to have his colony just north of Virginia, and its boundary on Virginia was easy to determine, for that part of the country had been surveyed by the valiant and boastful little Captain Smith, who, when he entered on his map the places he had actually visited, was often fairly accurate.

Lord Baltimore took for his principal landmark a place called Watkin's Point, which was a cape on the east side of Chesapeake Bay, directly opposite the mouth of the Potomac. Thence his line went eastward across the peninsula to the ocean; and so far he was safe enough and knew what he was doing. But having reached the ocean, he turned his line northward along the coast and began to enter the unknown. He had heard there was a bay called Delaware Bay somewhere up there, and he had Smith's map before him, which showed the end of the fortieth degree crossing the country about seven miles north of the head of Chesapeake Bay, while to the northward and eastward were the pretty pictures and flourishes with which the old geographers always decorated their ignorance.

He thought that the southern boundary of New England was the end of this fortieth degree as marked on Smith's map; and he had some reason for this belief, for the New England charter described the territory it granted as "All that part of America lying in breadth from forty degrees to forty-eight degrees north latitude." It was not altogether unreasonable to suppose that this meant from the end of the fortieth degree to the beginning of the forty-eighth, although the words do not expressly say so.

The Penn family always contended that it meant from the beginning of the fortieth, because New Jersey was at that time included in New England, and the southern extremity of New Jersey was close to the beginning of the fortieth. The words of the New England charter were vague, and either meaning could be plausibly drawn from them.

Baltimore took them as meaning from the end of the fortieth, and we can hardly blame him. He accordingly said in his charter that his province should run northward along the ocean " unto that part of Delaware Bay on the north which lieth under the fortieth degree of northern latitude from the equinoctial where New England ends."

But although he doubtless intended his province to reach to the end of the fortieth degree, he did not succeed very well in expressing that intention, and it has been much disputed what the words " under the fortieth degree" mean. Do they mean all the way to the completion of the fortieth degree, or only to the beginning of it at the end of the thirty-ninth? The description in the charter says " unto that part of Delaware Bay which lieth under the fortieth degree," and the natural meaning of this is that the bounds were to extend north until they subjoined that part of Delaware Bay which lay under—that is, was within, or was covered by—the fortieth degree, and this would make the end of the thirty-ninth degree the boundary.

The land within the fortieth degree was not granted ; the grant extended only up to the land which lay within the fortieth. If the grant had extended to the completion of the fortieth it would have been coterminous with the fortieth, and not up to that part which lay under it.

This construction harmonizes with the other contention of the Penns, that New England extended to the beginning of the fortieth, and gave them a very strong argument for their position that Maryland's northern boundary was the beginning of the fortieth degree, now just a little north of the present District of Columbia.

But, although the language of Baltimore's own charter supports this view, it is difficult to suppose that he really intended his northern line to be so far south. He used very inaccurate and careless language in his charter, and in point of law was bound by his mistakes, but no one can look at Smith's map without being convinced that Baltimore intended his northern boundary to be the end of the fortieth degree, which, on that map, passed about seven miles north of the head of the Chesapeake.

On Smith's map the end of the thirty-eighth degree passes close by Watkin's Point and along the Maryland southern boundary. If, therefore, Baltimore gave himself two degrees northward, to the end of the fortieth, he would have a province of reasonable size. But if he only went north one degree, to the end of the thirty-ninth, he would have, as any one can see by looking at Smith's map, or any other map, a mere patch about sixty miles wide.

Moreover, the end of the thirty-ninth would be inconsistent with his other boundaries ; for after saying that he is to go north to the part of Delaware Bay lying under the fortieth, his charter goes on and describes the northern boundary as extending westward "in a right line by the degree aforesaid unto the true meridian of the first fountains of the Potomac," the farther bank of which was to be followed down to its mouth, and thence a straight line drawn across the Chesapeake to Watkin's Point, the place of beginning. Now, on Smith's map the end of the fortieth degree reaches westward to the head-waters, or first fountains, of the Potomac, but the end of the thirty-ninth does not touch the first fountains at all, and crosses the river about half-way between its mouth and its source before reaching the meridian of the fountains.

Lord Baltimore intended to define his boundaries so as to include within his province the present State of Delaware as well as Maryland. He used the limited knowledge at his command, not as carefully as he might, but was doubtless well satisfied with his ocean shore and bay, and never dreamed that he was creating a serious controversy. He died in•April, 1632, before his charter had passed the seals, and it was given to his son, Cecil Calvert, the second Lord Baltimore, in the following June.

Year after year passed away while the settlers enjoyed the canvas-backs and terrapin of the Chesapeake. Cecil Calvert never visited the colony, and governed it entirely by deputies. The settlements were confined to the neighborhood of Baltimore and the shores of the bay, and there was little occasion to test the northern and eastern boundaries. The Dutch and Swedes, however, were known to be settling in that direction, but more than twenty-five years passed before any attempt was made to dispute their possession. Finally, in 1659, the governor of Maryland sent Colonel Utie to New Amstel, on the Delaware, to demand that the Dutch leave the country or submit themselves to Lord Baltimore. The colonel not only made demands, but went from house to house to induce the people to revolt.

The Dutch seem to have been very little disturbed by this demonstration, but they sent a delegation to Maryland to see if the difficulty could be settled. Their delegates declared that they could not understand why Baltimore, who had not colonists enough to settle the shores of the Chesapeake, should want to encroach on Holland's possession of the Delaware, and they asked to see the Maryland charter.

They had scarcely read ten lines of it before they saw one of its weakest points, for the opening paragraph declared it to be the intention of the Crown to give Lord Baltimore such lands as had not yet been cultivated and planted. Similar phrases were in nearly all the English colonial charters, the more usual one being, such lands as "are not actually possessed by any Christian prince or people," and this was done in recognition of the law universally accepted at that time by all the colonizing nations of Europe. The Dutch had been in possession of the shores of Delaware Bay for ten years before Lord Baltimore's charter was issued, and his boundaries in that direction were evidently defective. The sensible Dutchmen proposed a compromise, and offered to help survey a line which would divide the peninsula between Chesapeake and Delaware Bays equally between the two parties, and, curiously enough, this was the arrangement which, after eighty years of wrangling, was finally agreed upon.

The Making of Pennsylvania

Four or five more years passed, and in 1664 the Dutch were conquered by the English, and the Delaware region passed into the hands of the Duke of York, who, though without legal title to it, governed it as an appendage to New York. Now was the time for Baltimore to protest and say that he owned all the way to Delaware Bay. But he said nothing and allowed the duke to maintain against him an adverse possession of seventeen years. Moreover, this Delaware country, having been conquered from an enemy, belonged in strictness to the king, which still further weakened the Maryland title.

And now came the year 1681, and the charter to William Penn, which soon disclosed both of the weak points of Maryland, the careless description of her northern boundary as under the fortieth degree, and her unfounded claim to what is now the State of Delaware.

Penn wanted Delaware, as we now call it, because it stretched all the way along the west side of the river and bay, down to Cape Henlopen, and gave him a long water frontage and complete control of navigation to his colony. As it was outside of the limits of the Pennsylvania charter, he took a conveyance of it from the Duke of York to cover any claims that nobleman might have by reason of his possession, and the duke warranted his title, and agreed to obtain and convey to Penn a more perfect title within seven years. Afterwards, when the king had conveyed to the duke a good title, the duke gave the letters patent of it to Penn as security, and some years later, when he became James II., was about to make a final and perfect conveyance to Penn, when he was driven from the throne. His acts, however, as was afterwards decided by Lord

Hardwicke, had given Penn a complete equitable title; and so Penn, having both Delaware and Pennsylvania, obtained with them all of their boundary disputes with Maryland.

When the privy council were debating the boundaries that should be given to the grant in Penn's charter, formal notice was sent to all persons likely to be affected by the grant, and among others to Lord Baltimore. His agent replied to the notice by requesting that Penn's southern boundary be limited by lines drawn east and west through the Susquehanna Fort.

This fort was somewhere on the river of the same name, but no one has ever been able to fix the exact place. The Indians often built small stockaded forts, and there may have been several of them called Susquehanna. Baltimore doubtless thought that the one he intended was at the end of the fortieth degree; and in after years the Penns maintained that the true Susquehanna Fort was at the mouth of the Octorara, some miles within the present limits of Maryland. In 1681, William Penn seems to have had some knowledge about the position of this fort, and readily agreed with Lord Baltimore that it should mark his southern boundary.

But Lord Chief-Justice North, who had special charge of the boundary questions involved in the charter, ignored this agreement, and gave Pennsylvania's southern boundary as the beginning of the fortieth degree. He evidently understood the words, "unto that part of Delaware Bay which lieth under the fortieth degree," in the Maryland charter, to mean the beginning of that degree and not its end. He could see no reason why the boundaries in the two charters should

not be coincident. He said it was not necessary to
follow the agreement which Penn and Baltimore had
made, because the notice to Baltimore to appear had
been merely formal, which was another way of saying
that the privy council and the Crown could make
the grant as they pleased without regard to anybody's
wishes or agreements.

When we look at the maps which Lord Chief-Justice
North must have used, Smith's map, and the other maps
which at that time were collected in Ogilby's " America," it is hard, at first, to see how he could have deliberately carried the southern boundary of Pennsylvania
down to the neighborhood of Washington and deprived
Lord Baltimore of the greater part of his province.

The maps in Ogilby's " America" have the degrees of
latitude marked in the same places as on Smith's map.
The end of the fortieth is about seven miles north of the
head of Chesapeake, and its beginning is far down the
bay, and the end of the thirty-eighth is close to Watkin's Point and the mouth of the Potomac. If his lordship was relying at all on these degrees, he must have
seen at a glance that he was cutting down Maryland to
almost nothing.

But there is every reason to suppose that he was not
relying at all on those degrees, for it seems to have been
the general opinion at that time that all those degrees
were too far south. We have a letter written to the
privy council by John Werden, agent of the Duke
of York, in which he says that he and the duke were of
opinion that the beginning of the fortieth degree was
about twenty or thirty miles north of New Castle, and
also another letter from him in which he says that

he had been talking on the subject to William Penn, who thought that the fortieth began about twelve miles north of New Castle.

Lord North was evidently of the same opinion as Penn, for he described the southern boundary of Pennsylvania as a circle twelve miles distant from New Castle as a centre, and drawn northward and westward until it touched the beginning of the fortieth degree, which it was to follow westward. He never supposed that he was putting Pennsylvania far down in the middle of Baltimore's province; but, on the contrary, he thought he was placing the line very near where Lord Baltimore and Penn wanted it, and probably not very far from the Susquehanna Fort. His confidence that a radius of twelve miles from New Castle would touch the beginning of the fortieth shows that he was not in the least relying on the degrees as marked on Smith's map.

Baltimore was apparently much better informed on these matters than either Penn or the privy council, but he did not see fit at that time to disclose his knowledge. The Maryland government, it seems, had in 1669 ordered an observation to be taken of the latitude of New Castle, and the report made to them showed that town to be in 39° 30′, which would place the end of the fortieth degree many miles to the north and the beginning far beyond the reach of a radius of twelve miles.

There was also in existence at that time a map published about 1670 by Augustine Herman, a Maryland land speculator, and owner of the famous Bohemia Manor, and on this map the end of the fortieth degree is shown not far from its present location, a long distance north of the head of the Chesapeake, with its beginning much more than twelve miles from New Castle, and the end of it crosses the Susquehanna at a place marked as the Susquehanna Fort. This map, however, was more or less of a private one, and neither it, nor the fact that an observation had been taken by the Maryland government, appears to have been known to Penn or the privy council.

North, Werden, Penn, and the others, in the absence of better knowledge, simply assumed that the degrees on the maps they had were all too far south. Instead of dealing with such matters with the accuracy necessary in mathematics, they made a wild guess. But the degrees were much nearer right than they supposed. The end of the fortieth was, it is true, some thirty miles too far south, but the beginning of that degree as marked on Smith's map was very near its present location, and the beginning of the thirty-ninth close to Watkin's Point was wrong by not much more than ten miles.

The explanation of this is, that when Smith made his map he may have fixed the position of the beginning and end of the thirty-ninth by actual observation, but never took an observation for the end of the fortieth, and, when he drew his map, simply guessed at its position.

Penn, having obtained his charter, decided to do what should have been done long before. He sent his deputy, Markham, to the Delaware to take an observation of the latitude, and he was also to meet Lord Baltimore, or his agents, and settle the boundaries.

There was a meeting at Upland, now Chester, on the Delaware, about twenty miles above New Castle; the observation was taken, and the absurd mistake in latitude revealed. Lord Baltimore, finding what he already knew by the observation of his government some years before, that the end of the fortieth degree was many miles north of its position on Smith's map, renewed his old claim that his province extended to the fortieth degree complete.

This claim was, of course, a serious inroad upon Penn's land, for it carried Maryland up above the present position of Philadelphia. Nevertheless, Penn had a very strong case against his opponent, for his charter gave the southern limit of Pennsylvania, in plain words, as on the beginning of the fortieth degree, which would cut out of Baltimore's province even more than Baltimore was attempting to cut out of Penn's, and, in fact, would pretty much destroy it. Penn's grant was a later grant of the Crown's, and, so far as it overlapped Baltimore's, would be taken to have annulled it.

But Penn, though in a stronger position, was willing to compromise, and all he wanted was to have the line placed where it was supposed to be when his charter was granted. An unfortunate mistake in latitude had been made which had thrown everything into confusion. Penn's boundaries on Delaware were rendered ridiculous; for the circle of twelve miles radius from New Castle could not possibly touch the beginning of the fortieth degree, which, instead of being within twelve miles of New Castle, was forty miles to the south of it.

The proper course, in such circumstances, was for neither party to obstruct the peaceful settlement of the country by pushing the extravagant claims which seemed to be justified by the strict letter of their patents. Penn did even better than this. He offered to buy from Baltimore enough land to give Pennsylvania a harbor at the head of Chesapeake, and he also, in an interview with Baltimore, at West River, suggested another compromise, which was still more favorable to the Maryland proprietor, and the fairest compromise that could possibly be made.

It might, Penn said, be supposed that the king, in granting Lord Baltimore's charter, had intended to give him two degrees of latitude from Watkin's Point, and this would be what he would get if he went to the end of the fortieth degree, as marked on Smith's map. Degrees of latitude, at the time of the grant in Baltimore's charter, were supposed to be sixty miles wide, and had only recently been made sixty-nine and one-half. Baltimore, therefore, should have two of the old degrees, or one hundred and twenty miles north of Watkin's Point, and this would place his northern line about seven miles north of the head of Chesapeake, where the first Lord Baltimore evidently intended it should be.

But all compromises were refused by Baltimore. He fancied he saw great acquisitions of territory; he was determined on having Maryland, Delaware, and a large piece of Pennsylvania; he urged the vague and absurd descriptions in his charter to the utmost, and on him is the responsibility for the eighty years of wasted time and money, the enmity and bitterness, and the strife and bloodshed among the settlers near the disputed line.

Agreement being impossible, Baltimore and Penn resorted to the privy council, the usual tribunal for settling disputed land grants in the colonies. It was the privy council that always considered the advisability of a grant in the first instance, and reported to the king whether or not it should be made, and if the grant was afterwards discovered to ¦be inaccurate or in any way wrong, it was supposed that the privy council would advise the king to correct it.

But this privy council was a very unsatisfactory sort of tribunal for settling such questions. It was not obliged to act at all unless it chose, and in matters which came before it, often told the applicants to settle their difficulties among themselves or resort to the ordinary course of law.

The application to the privy council appears to have been made by Baltimore, who wished to stop a further assurance of Penn's title to Delaware, which the Duke of York was preparing to make by getting a more complete and accurate conveyance from the king. The case was argued before the council by Baltimore, Penn, and their lawyers at great length, and on many different occasions for more than two years. The council finally decided that Baltimore's charter did not give him a title to Delaware, because at the time of granting the charter that region had been in the possession of the Dutch, and they ordered the two proprietors to divide Delaware equally between them by a north and south line midway between the Chesapeake and the Delaware. This was the same settlement that had been suggested in the beginning by the Dutch delegates, and it was a very fair way of establishing the western boundary of Delaware.

The deeds of the Duke of York left that boundary uncertain, and simply conveyed in a general way the land from twelve miles north of New Castle on the north, to

333

Cape Henlopen on the south, with the Delaware River and Bay for an eastern boundary, and no mention of any western boundary. It was rather difficult to say what the western boundary was, for the Dutch had never established one, but had simply occupied the western shores of the Delaware, and, therefore, it seemed reasonable to divide the peninsula equally.

The decision of the council was confined to the boundary between Delaware and Maryland, and nothing was said about the disputed boundary of the fortieth degree between Maryland and Pennsylvania. But Delaware was the first and most important subject of controversy, for Penn considered it very essential as controlling the navigation to Pennsylvania, and Baltimore wanted it for the same reason.

It was impossible, of course, to divide Delaware, for the two proprietors would not agree. When William III. came to the throne after the Revolution of 1688, he deprived Penn of both Delaware and Pennsylvania for a few months, for fear they might fall into the hands of France or Spain, and when he restored them he described Penn as proprietor of " New Castle and the territories depending thereon," which was in accordance with the decision of the council, and, of course, favorable to Penn, but could not be regarded as marking out the exact western boundary line, which the council had ordered and which Baltimore refused to accept.

For twenty-three years after the decision of the council, Lord Baltimore allowed Penn to occupy, plant, improve, and settle Delaware, without attempting to interrupt him, and then in 1708 had the temerity to offer a petition to Queen Anne, saying that the previous order in council

had been surreptitiously obtained and should be revoked.

The queen dismissed his petition in a few days; but,
nothing daunted, he offered again the same petition in
the following year. Her majesty, by an order in council,
directed that a day be fixed when all parties should be
heard, and accordingly, on the 23d of June, 1709, Baltimore and Penn again appeared before the privy council,
and the whole question was gone into anew, with the
result that the petition was dismissed, the old order of
council, directing Delaware to be equally divided, ratified
and confirmed, and directed to be put in execution without delay.

The order was never obeyed by Baltimore. He disregarded it as he had disregarded the first order, and
made no effort to mark out the western boundary of
Delaware. But Penn was never again disturbed in his
possession of the country below New Castle, and he
and his heirs always regarded this last decision of the
privy council as, in effect, securing them in the enjoyment
of the full limits of their grant from the Duke of York.

The boundary on the beginning of the fortieth degree
between Pennsylvania and Maryland still remained unsettled. Year after year passed away; the people on the
border, uncertain of their position, refused to pay taxes
to either government; the sheriffs of adjoining counties
carried on a warfare of petty annoyance, and rough, lawless men appeared, who willingly made the disputes
between the provinces an excuse for fighting. One of
the most notable of these was Tom Cresap, a mixture of
Indian trader and hunter, called by the Indians, in return
for his liberal hospitality, the Big Spoon. He was a

most sincere and unselfish supporter of the Baltimores, and was thoroughly convinced that their land went all the way up to the end of the fortieth degree. When arrested for one of his murders and taken to Philadelphia, he coolly called it a pretty Maryland town.

In the midst of these disturbances, in 1718, Penn died, leaving the question as unsettled as it was in 1682. Cecil Calvert, the second Lord Baltimore, who had received the grant of Maryland in 1632, was long since dead, having died, in fact, before the Pennsylvania charter was granted. His son was also dead and also his grandson, who had petitioned Queen Anne in 1708. Charles Calvert, the fifth Lord Baltimore, was now proprietor of Maryland, and the first of the family to show a glimmering of reason.

He went to Penn's widow, now the proprietress of Pennsylvania, and admitted that he had no color or pretence of title to Delaware, and with surprising good sense suggested that no more land should be granted near either of the disputed borders by either government for eighteen months, within which time he hoped all difficulties could be settled. An agreement to abstain from granting land was accordingly signed in February, 1723; the eighteen months wore away, and also several years, and yet the agreement was faithfully observed by Hannah Penn, and after her death by her children. Baltimore seems also to have observed it, although the Penns charged that he made a number of vague, general grants of land without specifying any particular locality, in the hope, as they said, that the persons to whom the grants were made would take up land in the disputed territory.

Boundary Disputes with Maryland and Virginia

The death of Hannah Penn in 1726 and the youth of her children delayed the marking of the boundaries, and Baltimore now assumed the part of a much-injured person, and in 1731 petitioned the Crown to compel the proprietors of Pennsylvania to join with him in settling the boundaries. At the same time he applied to John and Thomas Penn to hold meetings with him and draw up an agreement of settlement. He seemed to be altogether consumed with zeal for agreement, and he proposed the terms of it, all of which were accepted and the articles signed May 10, 1732.

So far as Delaware was concerned, the settlement was the same that the Dutch delegates had suggested to his ancestor seventy years before, and the same that the privy council had twice ordered to be carried into effect. The line for the southern boundary of Pennsylvania was about seven miles north of the head of Chesapeake, and the same which Penn in his interview with Baltimore at West River had offered by way of compromise when he said that he was willing Maryland should have two of the old degrees, or one hundred and twenty miles northward from Watkin's Point. There is no question that by this agreement Baltimore was getting all that ever belonged to him, all that the first Lord Baltimore possessed, and all that impartial judges had decided to be justly due.

His lordship prepared a map to be annexed to the agreement, and on it he marked the boundaries he wished established. The map was entirely his own suggestion. He said he had procured it from his agents in Maryland, and the Penns accepted it as correct.

There was some controversy at the time, and much

more afterwards, about the true position of Cape Henlopen. There were two capes which at different times were known by that name. The cape now called Henlopen, directly at the mouth of Delaware Bay, was in early times called Cornelius, and the name Henlopen, or Hinlopen, was given to a point of land twenty miles to the south, sometimes called the False Cape. It was not a cape at all, but merely a slight rounding of the beach and a boldness of outline on shore, which when seen from the sea became, by a common optical delusion, a long tongue of land stretching out into the ocean.

This phenomenon is quite frequent on that part of the coast, a very small change in the contour of the shore often becoming greatly exaggerated, and these places are usually known among sailors as false capes, or points no-point. There is an instance of them on the coast of Virginia, just below Cape Henry, and it is still called the False Cape.

When the early Dutch navigators approached the mouth of the Delaware, coming, as they usually did, from the south, the lower cape always deceived them, and the name which they gave it, Heenloopeen, or Hinlopen, is said to mean the disappearing cape. Most of their maps, and also the English maps, display it as very much extended into the ocean, making, together with the real cape farther north, a sort of double cape at the southern corner of the bay. The real cape at the entrance of the bay became gradually called by its present name, Henlopen, either by transfer of the name of the false cape, or, as some have contended, from the corruption of another Dutch word, Inloopen, which meant the entering cape.

Penn had always insisted that the title he got from the

Boundary Disputes with Maryland and Virginia

Duke of York placed the southern boundary of Delaware at the false cape now known as Fenwick's Island. Lord Baltimore's agreement and map admitted this claim, and Delaware was divided between the two proprietors by drawing a line directly west from the false cape across the peninsula to the Chesapeake. From the middle of this line another line was drawn directly north, tangent to a circle of twelve miles radius drawn round New Castle. This settled the boundaries of Delaware : on the north the circle ; on the east, Delaware river, bay, and the ocean ; on the south, the line drawn west from the false cape ; and on the west, the line drawn north from the middle of the false cape line.

The boundaries of Pennsylvania and Maryland were settled by continuing the line drawn from the middle of the false cape line until it reached a parallel of latitude which was fifteen miles south of a parallel passing along South Street, which was then the most southerly portion of Philadelphia, and the parallel thus reached, drawn westward, was to be the southern limit of Pennsylvania.

Nothing could have been more fair and satisfactory than this agreement, for it placed the boundaries where common sense and justice demanded, and where the Dutch delegates, the privy council, King James II., William Penn, and everybody, except the Baltimores, had always said they ought to be.

As Baltimore had offered the agreement, and all his suggestions for its provisions had been accepted by the Penns, there was every reason to suppose that he would be the one most ready to fulfil it. Each side appointed commissioners, who were to meet and mark the lines, and they were given eighteen months to complete the work, namely, to December 25, 1733. John Penn sailed for Pennsylvania, and Lord Baltimore for Maryland, to superintend the final settlement.

But Baltimore had proposed the agreement in one of the lucid intervals which had been rare in his family, and the papers were scarcely signed before he repented of it. He soon began to take advantage of every trivial circumstance for delay, and it was said that he was largely influenced in this course by the persuasions of the seven commissioners he had appointed to mark the lines, and by others interested in land grants.

The seven commissioners, and many other people in Maryland, held those general warrants, granting large tracts of land, without specifying exactly where they were to be situated. So long as the boundary lines were unsettled, such people could take up their land in the disputed regions in Delaware and Pennsylvania, and, after the boundaries were settled, hold the land as having been granted to them by a regularly organized government under the British Crown, even if they found themselves within the limits of Pennsylvania. It was a cheap and convenient method of acquiring some of the fertile tracts which lay outside of Maryland.

Certain it is, that those seven Maryland commissioners, who had been appointed by Baltimore to assist in marking the boundaries, were most delinquent in not marking them, and in absolutely preventing their being marked. The history of their ingenious devices for delay would fill many pages; and they had to be very ingenious, for the agreement provided that whichever side should be in default and prevent the execution of the agreement should forfeit five thousand pounds.

Boundary Disputes with Maryland and Virginia

The holders of the land-warrants, it is said, had urged on Baltimore to simply break the agreement, and they would subscribe among themselves the five thousand pounds. But this was unnecessary, for the commissioners were fully equal to the occasion.

They began their meetings with the Pennsylvania commissioners October 6, 1732, and the first thing they did was to object to the validity of the commission held by the Pennsylvanians, because certain legatees of forty thousand acres of land under William Penn's will had not signed it. They refused to have minutes taken of the joint meetings, and refused to have clerks appointed. They suffered a great deal from ill health. They called for the production of original documents which they hoped were in England and would take months to procure. They insisted that they had no power to fix upon the exact spot for the centre of the circle round New Castle, and that the circle of twelve miles round that town meant a circle of twelve miles circumference, and not twelve miles radius. They appointed meetings at a little village called Joppa, seventy miles from New Castle, and without accommodations for men or horses. Sometimes they suggested meetings at Cape Henlopen, and when they had no other excuse they would retire to their lodgings, play at games, or refuse to be seen. In this way they wore out the eighteen months, and the 25th of December, 1733, came without an inch of boundary being marked.

Having thus broken the agreement, as he thought, Lord Baltimore, in the following summer, presented a petition to the Crown, claiming the whole of Delaware, and asking to be put in possession of it, although his name was still signed to an agreement giving the whole of that country to the Penns. He gave no notice of this petition to the Penns, two of whom were in America, and the one in England a mere boy just come of age. Baltimore seems to have had on this occasion the deliberate intention of forcing his petition to a conclusion in the absence of his opponents and without their knowledge.

But the end of his chicane was now in sight. The Penns heard of the petition in time to resist it, and the committee of the privy council, to whom it was referred, ordered the disputants to proceed at law under the articles of agreement, and this revealed Baltimore's mistake.

The lawyers of the Penn family, in the suit which followed, always complained, with much bitterness, of the way in which Baltimore had forced the agreement on the sons of William Penn, then young men lately come of age, and with little or no knowledge of the intricate boundary disputes; how he had insisted on all of his own points, and rejected all of theirs, and how the agreement was, in the end, entirely of his own making, with not a single request of the young men granted, and with a map attached which he had himself prepared.

If, however, Baltimore had intended to overreach the Penns, he succeeded only in overreaching himself, and he had unconsciously made a trap for his own catching. He made a great mistake in signing that agreement, and it is difficult now to see why he signed it. Without that agreement he had to deal only with the privy council, which was not a court of law, not obliged to decide any question definitely, and careless about enforcing the few recommendations it made. But the agreement took the case away from the privy council and brought it before the chancellor in a court of equity. The agreement was simply an ordinary legal contract which belonged to the courts, and with which the privy council had nothing to do. The courts of England at that time could not decide between conflicting royal grants in the colonies, but they could enforce a contract which related to those grants.

The Penns were now in a very strong position. They had their agreement, and the privy council had advised them to enforce it ; and, accordingly, in 1735 they filed a bill in equity to compel specific performance. The bill was a long and complete history of the whole dispute. The answer was equally long, and both were perfect specimens of that skilled equity draughtsmanship which delighted the lawyers of that time. These two documents, with the proofs and exhibits, now fill seven hundred and ninety closely printed pages in the sixteenth volume of the " Pennsylvania Archives," and to any one who is at all familiar with the main points of the controversy are as interesting and exciting as a novel.

The defence which Baltimore's solicitors prepared for him in such rich old legal English was, however, absurdly weak. Beyond the astute attempt to throw doubt and uncertainty on everything said by the Penns, it consisted of only three points.

The Dutch and Swedes, he said, were mere itinerant traders, and so few in numbers that they could hardly be said to have occupied any part of Delaware before the grant of the Maryland charter in 1632. The agreement of 1732, not having been executed by December 25, 1733, had expired and could not be enforced. Even

343

if it had not expired, it should not be enforced against Baltimore, because he had been led into it by a mistake. The young Penns had deceived him, and he had mistaken his rights and foolishly consented to part with his property. The map upon which he had relied and had attached to the agreement was a fraud. It had been imposed on him by the Penns, who had secretly had it prepared and sent to Maryland, so that it would get into the hands of his agents. In this way the false cape had been forced upon him, and he had consented to it as the beginning of the southern line of Delaware, when in truth that line should have been farther north at the real cape. He entirely failed, of course, to establish any of these extraordinary propositions, and the court found no difficulty in deciding against him.

He was, however, very successful in gaining time, and every delay that could be invented to check the progress of the proceedings was used. He saved himself much time by his privilege of Parliament, and by having the bill referred to a master for scandal and impertinence, so that more than two years had passed before he filed his answer. The taking of testimony in America also caused great delay, and while the suit was in progress the troubles among the people on the border grew worse and worse.

In the hope of checking them, a royal order was issued in 1738, commanding the proprietors to mark a temporary line, which should be accepted as the boundary until the question was permanently settled. The order unfortunately had an effect just the reverse of what was expected. The sheriffs of the border counties seemed to think that they had now full authority for acting against intruders, and they raided each other's territory to make arrests. There was also a long squabble with the Maryland commissioners about marking the temporary line, which was at last marked by the Pennsylvania commissioners alone.

The case on the articles of agreement was not finally argued and disposed of until 1750, fifteen years after it had been begun. It was an important occasion, attracting much interest, and the speeches of counsel occupied five days. The decision was rendered by Lord Hardwicke, one of the greatest equity lawyers of England, and the case has become a leading authority for the well-established doctrine that a court of equity deals directly with the individual, although the subject matter of the controversy may be outside of its jurisdiction. His lordship had some severe comments for the conduct of Baltimore, and ordered the agreement to be enforced without further delay or quibbling.

One might suppose that this was the end, but it was not, and a quarter of a century elapsed before the boundary question could be put at rest. Baltimore could still raise difficulties, and he found an excellent point for himself in the circle round New Castle, the radius of which he said must be measured on the ground up and down the hills, instead of in a horizontal air line.

Another application had to be made to the court to convince him of his error. But, true to his family traditions, he soon had another objection. The western side of Delaware was by the agreement to begin at the middle of the line drawn from the false cape to the Chesapeake, and he insisted that the middle of this line was half-way between the false cape and the first creek that was reached flowing into the Chesapeake. This would have reduced Delaware to very narrow limits, and still another application had to be made to the court to convince him that the line crossing the peninsula must reach from the false cape to the shore of the bay. He died about this time, and his successor, Frederick, Lord Baltimore, raised the objection that the suits had abated, and declined to be bound by any of the acts of his predecessor or by any decrees made against him.

In this way ten years were frittered away until 1760, when a new agreement was made with the new Lord Frederick, ratifying with slight changes the old one of 1732. Preparations were immediately made to mark the lines, and the Pennsylvania commissioners appointed were the governor, James Hamilton, Richard Peters, Rev. Dr. Ewing, William Allen, William Coleman, Thomas Willing, Benjamin Chew, and Edward Shippen, Jr., an excellent selection, and an assurance of good faith and skill. Three years were spent by the surveyors employed by the commissioners in marking the lines of Delaware. The circle round New Castle was drawn by Rittenhouse, and added much to his reputation.

But the work seemed too slow to satisfy the proprietors, and in 1763, Mason and Dixon, two well-known English astronomers, were sent out to revise what had already been done and complete it. They resurveyed the circle and the tangent drawn to it for Delaware's western boundary, but were unable to make it vary by a single inch from the lines of Rittenhouse and the others.

They then set about the more difficult task of marking the long line to the west for the boundary between Pennsylvania and Maryland. Four years were spent on it, as they proceeded step by step, cutting a vista twenty-four feet wide among the trees, in the middle of which they marked the exact line. At every fifth mile a stone was set up marked on the side towards Pennsylvania with the arms of the Penns, and on the side towards Maryland with the arms of Baltimore. The intermediate miles were marked with stones having P. on one side and M. on the other.

As they proceeded, the Indians became more and more suspicious. They could not understand the object of an exploring expedition that spent every clear night gazing at the stars through big guns, and they soon stopped its advance. The Penns used their influence with the chiefs of the Six Nations, and the work began again. The western extremity of Maryland was reached and passed, and the astronomers were encamped on the banks of the Monongahela. Here the Indians again interposed, and many of the servants and workmen of the expedition deserted. But the delight of running an astronomical line through primeval forests raised Mason and Dixon above all fears, and they pressed on to the Warrior Branch of the great Catawba Indian trail.

The patience of the Indians was now exhausted, and they were determined that this star-gazing folly should penetrate not another step into the sacred West. Mason and Dixon were obliged to return, and the Warrior trail remained the terminus of their line for many years. On their way back to Philadelphia they often amused themselves by climbing to the summits of the mountains, from which they could see the vista of their line stretching for many miles to the horizon, and they noticed, with great pleasure, that it seemed to have the true curve of a line of latitude encircling the round earth.

It was really a great achievement, and a new thing in the science of that day. The two unpretending and skilful men had made themselves immortal. Their line was what we call an imaginary one. There was no river, or mountain chain, or natural feature to mark it; and to this day the farmer that lives upon it cannot tell, from anything he sees in nature, whether he is ploughing in Maryland or Pennsylvania. But this line, fixed after nearly a hundred years of conflict, is more unalterable than if nature had made it. It grew more and more unalterable with every year after it was made, and it was soon discovered that it was more than the boundary between two States: it was the boundary between the conflicting ideas of the continent, between the North and the South.

A civilization peculiar in itself formed on one side of it, and another civilization peculiar in itself formed on the other. It almost seems, as we look back at its history, as if there must have been some instinctive feelings guiding the long struggle for its position, and inspiring the determined, violent, and sometimes extraordinary contentions which never rested until the exact point of difference was found.

The feelings of the rough border population that lived along its course were, however, slow to be satisfied. Astronomy was not enough to determine the limits of their civic pride. They had grown accustomed to the temporary line, which was a quarter of a mile above the true one, and they became as much excited over that

narrow strip as they had been when they hoped to penetrate miles into Pennsylvania.

The government of Pennsylvania was determined to
push its jurisdiction home. Preparations were made to
assert authority within that quarter of a mile, and quiet
the disturbances, and to this end a proclamation was
issued in 1774, which has generally been considered the
final act which ended the controversy forever. But the
Baltimores had one shot left, and, though a feeble one,
they fired it. Frederick Calvert had died, and his heir
was under age. An application was made to the king
to stop the proclamation, because the guardians could
not assent to it during the minority of the heir. It was
the last hopeless effort of eighty years of opposition.

The boundary on Maryland being settled, another
question arose as to our boundary on the lands claimed
by Virginia, which lay west of Maryland. The charter
of Pennsylvania extended the province westward from
the Delaware through five degrees of longitude, or about
two hundred and sixty-seven miles. The circle round
Delaware, and Mason and Dixon's line on Maryland,
consumed all of this distance, except about fifty-four
miles, which ran through the region which Virginia said
was hers. In fact, she claimed upward into Pennsylvania above the present site of Pittsburg.

By her original charter, Virginia's northern boundary
was supposed to be at the end of the fortieth degree,
which was as far north as Philadelphia. The dissolution
of this charter, in 1624, instead of narrowing, apparently
increased her limits, and in becoming a royal province
without any definite boundaries, she considered herself
as a keeper or trustee for the king of all contiguous ter-

ritory not lawfully granted to any other colony. The Maryland grant was taken out of her domain, and she acquiesced in it. But west of Maryland she insisted that her ownership extended for an indefinite distance northward and westward, and she had made it good by occupation as far as Pittsburg. This was certainly a broad claim of title, and the only remnant of it now is that curious narrow strip of land, called the Pan-Handle, which extends northward between Pennsylvania and Ohio for some distance above the end of the fortieth degree.

The Indian trade at Fort Pitt had always been an object of Virginia's desire. The situation of that place at the point where the Alleghany and the Monongahela unite to form the Ohio was an evident strategic position, and the natural seat of empire. It had the command of three valleys stretching north, south, and west, and the nation or the colony that held it would be given a great advantage. In 1752 the governor of Virginia announced his intention of erecting a fort there, and the governor of Pennsylvania, equally well aware of the place's importance, told him he was willing he should erect a fort to stop the French, their common enemy, but he must remember that the land belonged to Pennsylvania.

The French were also fully alive to the importance of the locality, and before Virginia had well established herself they took possession of it. The expedition against them under command of young Colonel Washington and his surrender at Fort Necessity are familiar history. The French called the place Du Quesne, and held it till 1758. It was abandoned by the English in 1771, and in 1773 Virginia again took possession of it, calling it Fort Dunmore, after her governor.

Boundary Disputes with Maryland and Virginia

Virginia now deliberately formulated her claim, and said that her right to the country was secured by her charter and by exploration and settlement not only, but that when the French conquered that part of the country, and afterwards the British government conquered it from the French, all rights that the Penns may have had under their charter were extinguished. Under this belief many Virginians began to enter and settle the region in 1773, just as the disputes with Maryland were drawing to a close. Both Pennsylvania and Virginia attempted to divide the country into counties and govern it. The conflict of jurisdiction brought on fierce disputes among the frontiersmen, who were nearly all hot-headed Scotch-Irishmen, and the two colonies attempted to negotiate a settlement.

The Penns maintained that, instead of Virginia running up into Pennsylvania at this point, the true boundaries would take Pennsylvania down into Virginia for a distance of about fifty miles. The Pennsylvania charter made the beginning of the fortieth degree the southern boundary of Pennsylvania, and although, in the case of Maryland, this boundary had been changed by compromise and brought farther north until it was nearer to the end of the fortieth degree than to the beginning of it, yet, Maryland being passed in marking the line westward, the line immediately went south again to its charter limit, at the beginning of the degree.

To this Virginia replied that the western extent of Pennsylvania was to be measured from the Delaware five degrees of longitude, not on the southern, but on the northern boundary, which was the end of the forty-second degree, and from the end of this a meridian line was to be drawn south for the western boundary, which, the Pennsylvanians were assured, would pass at least fifty miles east of Pittsburg. The Delaware was at that time supposed to trend so far east at the northern boundary of Pennsylvania that five degrees of longitude measured westward from that point would easily save Pittsburg for Virginia.

The claims of each side were so violent and far-reaching that no settlement could be made. The Penns, however, suggested one of those sensible and moderate compromises at which they were so skilful, and with which, in the end, they usually won. They offered to extend Mason and Dixon's line westward to the Monongahela, and follow that river to the Ohio as a temporary line. But as this cut off Pittsburg from Virginia, it was rejected.

In this condition of affairs the Revolution came on, and nothing could be accomplished for four or five years. Both governments attempted to maintain jurisdiction in the disputed territory, and Virginia offered temporary lines which were always refused.

But in 1779 a joint commission peaceably settled the question and agreed on the boundaries as they now are. Mason and Dixon's line was extended westward from the Delaware through five degrees of longitude, and for the western boundary a meridian was drawn from the western extremity of Mason and Dixon's line to the northern limit of the State. The credit of this very wise and fair settlement of a difficulty, which seems to have given much uneasiness to the public men of that time, is said to have been due to David Rittenhouse, one of the commissioners, whose good sense and moderation in boundary disputes had now succeeded to the skill the Penns had so long exhibited. This agreement was finally ratified in 1780, but, as in the other boundary disputes, the disorders and quarreling among the border population continued for some time, and caused serious difficulties.

In 1784 the lines were surveyed and the western terminus of Mason and Dixon's line, exactly five degrees of longitude from the Delaware, was definitely fixed, a delicate piece of astronomical work, never before attempted in any country, and in which David Rittenhouse distinguished himself.

This was the end of all serious difficulty with our boundaries. The eastern boundary on the Delaware was never questioned. The northern boundary, described in the charter as the beginning of the forty-third degree, was easily agreed upon with New York, and marked out by Rittenhouse in the years 1785–87. The break in the west end of this northern border, which gives us a long frontage on Lake Erie, was accomplished by purchase. Our charter borders just barely enabled us to touch Lake Erie without giving a suitable harbor on it. The Erie triangle, as it is called, belonged to New York and Massachusetts, was ceded by them to the United States, and bought from the United States by Pennsylvania in 1792 for one hundred and fifty-one thousand six hundred and forty dollars.

It should enable us to draw the great traffic of the lakes through Pennsylvania to tide-water at Philadelphia, but unfortunate circumstances have prevented this result. It was a purchase, however, that would have pleased Penn and harmonized with his plan of buying enough

The Making of Pennsylvania

land from Lord Baltimore to give a good harbor on the Chesapeake. With a harbor on Lake Erie and a canal connecting it with the Delaware and the Chesapeake, it would certainly be our own fault if we were not a great commercial as well as a great manufacturing State.

When we consider all these boundary disputes, including the one with Connecticut, the long years through which they extended, the violence and bitterness with which they were maintained against us, the largeness of their demands, cutting us down from greatness to littleness, and depriving us of our two important cities and points of advantage, it is hard to restrain a feeling, not merely of satisfaction at our success in resisting these attacks, but of gratitude for the skill and persistence of the Penns who accomplished this result.

For nearly a century they followed every doubling and turning of the enemy with perfect good temper, perfect fairness, and inexhaustible patience. They never resorted to violence and they never retaliated for injuries. They were always ready to compromise, and yet they were always dignified. They secured the ablest and most astute counsellors, and their arguments were always well prepared and fortified, but always reasonable and never strained the truth or justice. The dignity, the peace, and the honor of the commonwealth, during those eighty years of contest, could hardly have been in better hands.

CHAPTER XII.

IT was fortunate for the interests of peace and quiet that the incongruous elements of population, which have been described in the preceding pages, had plenty of room, and spread themselves out far and wide in the forests of Pennsylvania. If they had been forced to live close together, it would, perhaps, be more to the interest of the historian, for he would have some savage contests to describe. The passive determination of the Quaker and the fiery aggressiveness of the Scotch-Irish, if confined in close quarters, might have been that irresistible force meeting an immovable object from which so much may be expected.

But we need not follow out the speculation, for the fact is that they spread out. The Scotch-Irish got as far away from the others as possible. The Connecticut people, in the fastness of their valley, held aloof from all association and intercourse with the rest of the province. The Germans congregated by themselves in the fertile valleys of the Schuylkill and the Lehigh, and the Welsh were at first isolated on their barony. Only two of the elements were brought in close contact,—the Quakers and Episcopalians who occupied Philadelphia; and the bitterness of their quarrels shows what might have been the result if there had been less room for the others.

While the province was geographically divided in this

The Making of Pennsylvania

manner, with the Quakers and Episcopalians in Philadelphia, and each of the other elements in a little section by itself, the political power came in time to be divided between two of the elements in a most curious way, the like of which has seldom been seen in history. At first the Quakers held all the political power, and ruled the province in their own way. But after the death of William Penn, as his sons gradually left the Quaker faith and became members of the Church of England, these sons gave as much of the political power as they could to the Episcopalians. Under the charter they had a right to appoint the executive officers of the government, the deputy governor, the judges, and other officials, and these positions were all turned over to Episcopalians. But the Quakers had the legislature, and retained control of it down to the time of the Revolution.

Philadelphia, as well as the province, was accordingly ruled by two classes,—the Quakers and the Episcopalians; and it would be difficult to say which was the more important and which did more for the city. The Quakers were, of course, the more numerous, and had a strong social life of their own which held aloof from the equally strong social life of the Episcopalians. As time went on there came to be two sources of respectability, two tests for entrance into good society; in fact, there were two "societies;" or, perhaps, it would be more accurate to say that there was one society with two very distinct branches; and this state of affairs still in a measure exists.

The isolation of the Scotch-Irish led to serious results which are also acting in almost full force. They occupied the western frontier and kept moving westward with it

until the western half of the commonwealth came under
their influence, as it still is. In colonial times they lived
very much to themselves, with customs of their own, and
felt more and more that they were a separate community. When the French and Indian Wars came on in
1755, large numbers of them were massacred, and the
contempt which they had for the Quaker government
at Philadelphia ripened into a bitter hatred, for they believed that the Quakers could have protected them. At
the close of Pontiac's conspiracy, they marched to attack
the Quakers and revolutionize the government, and were
deterred only by the preparations for their reception
which they found had been made at Philadelphia.

At the outbreak of the Revolution they joined with
others of the patriot party in completely overthrowing
the Quaker power, and, together with the other Presbyterians, they may be said to have controlled the State
during the whole of the Revolutionary period. Their
feelings of self-confidence and independence were now
fully developed; and when the National government
was formed under the Constitution, and Congress laid
a tax on whiskey, they broke out in open rebellion,
which was finally suppressed by Washington at the
head of an army. At this time they hoped to separate
from Pennsylvania and form themselves into a new State.

This brief summary of their history reveals the origin
and cause of that strong feeling of jealousy for Philadelphia which has always been shown by the rest of the
State. The city has been regarded by the country not
as a metropolis to be proud of, but as a distinct community to be disliked and suspected, a condition of
things which has often seemed strange and inexplicable

to those who were not familiar with the history of the State.

The only important element in the country districts which in colonial times was inclined to be in sympathy with the city was that part of the German population which was composed of what were called the sects. These sects, as already shown, were of almost the same religious belief as the Quakers, and the Quakers had encouraged them to come to the province. They always voted on the Quaker side, and kept the Quakers in control of the Legislature down to the Revolution. Many of the Lutherans and Reformed—the church people, as they were called—appear to have been more or less inclined to vote with the Quakers, but as a class the Quakers had not the control over them that they had over the sects. As the church people increased more rapidly in numbers than the sects, the Quaker power was slowly undermined.

Although the sharpness of all these old colonial divisions and contests has worn off, the original feelings and the results and habits still exist and seem likely to continue descending from father to son for many generations. The people of the western half of the State, with Pittsburg for their capital, feel that they are a separate division, almost a separate State, and sometimes speak of themselves as Western Pennsylvanians. The people of the northern half of the State, which was permeated by the Connecticut influence, have much the same sort of feeling, and they also had at one time the thought of creating a new State. We are really three States in one. In addition to this, the Germans still retain their feeling of isolation, and believe themselves to be the typical

Pennsylvanians; the Quakers have very much the same feeling; so have the Scotch-Irish, and there is a trace of it among some of the Episcopalians. The only elements that seem to have been completely absorbed are the Swedes and the Welsh.

A State so constituted necessarily lacks the civic pride and united action which have given commonwealths of inferior situation and resources, like Massachusetts, such an ascendency in the Union. Massachusetts, with a population homogeneous from the beginning in race, thought, and religion, and with no feeling for dismemberment, has built up out of her rocks and barrenness a name and fame which communities with greater resources but less unity can only envy.

The results of our lack of unity might be traced in many channels. If we were more united and homogeneous, we might be the first instead of the second State in the Union; and those who are familiar with our vast resources of iron, petroleum, coal and lumber, temperate climate, fertile soil, railroad and water facilities, and the skill of our people in the mechanic arts and manufacturing, often wonder why we are not.

Our State once contained the metropolis of the country; the most important events in the Revolution and in the framing of the Constitution happened within our borders; and these, with our own conflicts, were of the sort that bring into prominence strong characters and high intellect. There has been no lack of good ability among our people. Bright and able men have appeared at all times, and from pretty much all the cliques into which we are dissipated. But almost every one of them has been neglected and forgotten, or his reputation deliberately attacked and ruined. It is really extraordinary the vindictiveness with which the Pennsylvanians have assailed any one of their own people who has shown striking or supreme ability.

Mediocrity they can endure well enough, and the mediocrity that can sink its individuality far out of sight and balance among the divisions is the best of all. But distinct opinions are fatal. The man who holds them may be mildly supported by his own small division, but he is sure to have all the others against him.

The Abbé Correa, who was Portugese Minister to the United States and a well-known wit in Philadelphia at the beginning of the present century, used to say that the Pennsylvanians reminded him of the little boys in the streets. When they saw a comrade getting a ride at the back of a wagon they always called out to the driver, "Cut behind!" Other States were proud when one of their citizens achieved distinction or secured an appointment from the government. They supported his fame as part of their own good name, and when he was dead carefully guarded his reputation.

Our tendency in this respect has been commented on by others. Horace Binney thus described it as affecting Philadelphia:

"She does not take and she never has taken satisfaction in habitually honoring her distinguished men as her men, as men of her own family. It is the city that is referred to as distinguished, perhaps, from the rest of the State. She has never done it in the face of the world as Charleston has done it, as Richmond has done it, as Baltimore has done it, as New York has done it, or did it in former times, and as Boston has done it and would do it forever. She is more indifferent to her own sons than she is to strangers."

Results

In his essay on Chief Justice Gibson, Judge Porter described it for the State:

" For many years a disposition has prevailed in Pennsylvania to overthrow rather than to sustain men of distinguished ability. It has long been the subject of remark at home and abroad, that it seems only necessary for a man of more than ordinary capacity to appear in the politics of that State to be struck at by every other politician, great and small. . . . If the same feeling had prevailed in Virginia and South Carolina, Massachusetts and Kentucky, where then had been the great lights of our firmament ?"

The most effective injury the Pennsylvanians inflict on their distinguished men is neglect after they are dead. While living they fight their own battles, and usually have ability enough to hold their own in some degree. But dead, the cold indifference, though slow, is sure. No biographies of them appear; nothing is said; until as years roll by a generation appears that can sincerely ask, Who was he ?

Sometimes a public man of supreme distinction and importance, like Dickinson, is commented on outside of the State, his character attacked, silly stories invented to his injury, and his reputation torn to shreds. The Pennsylvanians say not a word, make no defence, until the destruction is complete, when they accept it all. " We were mistaken in him," they say; " he was a nobody, after all."

It might be supposed that within the last hundred years, while we were becoming a State of such wealth and power, some Pennsylvanian would have been found with an interest in history extending far enough beyond genealogies to enable him to write a good life of William Penn. But the founder of the State has not been so fortunate. The best life of Penn was written by Samuel Janney, who was a Virginian and never lived in Pennsylvania. The other biographies of value are those by Clarkson, Dixon, and Stoughton, all English. There is also a French life, by Marsillac. The life in Sparks's "American Biographies" was written by Dr. Ellis, of Massachusetts. There are a few essays and pamphlets by Pennsylvanians, like those by Howard Jenkins and J. Francis Fisher, but no regular biography.

The founder has, however, several times narrowly escaped having a complete biography by a Pennsylvanian. Mrs. Mary Hughes began a biography in England, which she finished in 1828 after she had emigrated to Philadelphia. She became famous for an academy she kept for young ladies, and for a work in ten volumes called "Aunt Mary's Library for Boys and Girls." In 1882, Robert Burdette, of the *Burlington Hawkeye*, wrote a comic life of Penn. Burdette was born at Greensborough, Pennsylvania, but migrated when a child to the West and lived in Illinois and Iowa. In 1888, William J. Buck, a thorough Pennsylvanian, wrote an account of Penn, but confined himself to describing minutely the two short visits which the founder paid to the province. At this rate it is possible that in the course of another one hundred and fifty years a complete biography written by a native of the State may appear.

Even if Penn was neglected, it might be supposed that Franklin, most of whose life was spent in Colonial public office, who was connected with every important interest in Pennsylvania, and whose world-wide fame rivals that of Washington, would arouse some interest and pride among our people. But he has fared even worse than Penn. He is admired and studied in other States and everywhere in the world except in Pennsylvania. The two largest and best editions of his works, Sparks's and Bigelow's, come one from Boston and the other from New York. As his writings were translated into Latin, Italian, French, and German, so all nations have written biographies of him; and there are about fifty in existence. The best, those by Parton and Bigelow, are by New Yorkers, and the rest are from every corner of the earth except that which knew him best.

Like Penn, he has had a narrow escape. In 1887, Mr. McMaster, a New Yorker at that time living in Philadelphia, where he was a professor in the University of Pennsylvania, wrote an excellent sketch of the literary side of his career for a serial called "American Men of Letters," undertaken by a Boston publishing house. Boston has, indeed, always treated him as one of her sons, and in her public library has an alcove devoted entirely to the collection of books which relate to him.

Penn had the advantage of belonging to a sect which, although not much given to enthusiasm for any one, was at least bound not to attack him. The main facts and the school-book story of his life are generally known; and, with all his faults, he is unquestionably admired by the people. But Franklin comes in for positive dislike, and there is no place where all the evil and mistakes of his life are so well remembered and so freely spoken of as, in Philadelphia. There is a chapter on him in Scharf and Westcott's "History of Philadelphia," in which, amidst faint praise and abuse, he is called an old granny,

363

a man of no genius, whose most conspicuous excellence was a certain luminous mediocrity.

We raised no monuments to him and had no statue until within a few years, when a statue of him was erected on the Campus of the University of Pennsylvania. But it was a gift from Chicago, and was constructed of such inferior material that it has now been removed and stored away under cover.

We had no statue of Penn until recently, when the one on the tower of the City Hall in Philadelphia was procured; and this is one of the rare instances in which Pennsylvanians have been willing, of their own accord, to erect a statue to one of their great men. They will sometimes have statues of comparatively insignificant persons; they will gladly give their money for statues of foreigners, and will fill a city park with images of Joan of Arc or other irrelevant personages; but about their own they care little and know little.

There is no character that shows the Pennsylvanian feeling so well as Bayard Taylor. He was a thorough son of the soil. His German and Quaker ancestors had been Pennsylvanians for many generations. He always felt that he belonged to the State. He tried to identify himself with it as much as he could and as much as it would let him. He built himself a home in his native valley, and tried his best to live there. He wrote novels and ballads to describe its scenes. But his difficulty was not merely that he was forced to say that there was a "tyranny of public sentiment" there which was against him. His real difficulties were still larger. The whole State rejected him. Its chief city, Philadelphia, would have nothing to do with him. It seemed extraordinary that, after the State had produced its first great poet and its first really gifted man of letters, of whom any commonwealth might be proud, the State and the city should unite in kicking him out of doors.

Fortunately for these children who are so summarily ejected, they are usually of sufficient ability to be valued by other communities. Taylor was of a loyal and honorable nature. He felt that he belonged to his old home, and was always trying to get back. But, undesired and unappreciated by his native State, he sought for sympathy abroad. Germany honored him, and he received more encouragement and regard in a few years on the Rhine than he received in his whole life on the Delaware. New York adopted him as her son. When he was appointed minister to Berlin, Pennsylvania and Philadelphia were silent; but New York gave him a banquet. When his dead body was brought home from Germany, New York received him, and he lay in state, with a guard of honor, in her City Hall. When he was carried to Kennett Square to be buried, his native State was again silent, and seemed to be unaware that she was receiving him into her soil.

Robert Morris and John Dickinson are also notable instances. Morris stood high in national councils during the Revolution, and his services have always been fully appreciated by the country at large. But at the very time he held this exalted position in the Continental Congress he was so unpopular among the mass of the people in his own State that, together with Wilson and Mifflin, he was threatened with mob violence. Since his death his reputation has been utterly neglected by Pennsylvanians, and they scarcely realize that he once lived among them.

Both he and Dickinson were left out of Sparks's "American Biographies," although the series contains such persons as Ezra Stiles, doubtless a very good man and a valuable president of Yale College, but not of national importance. No Pennsylvanian has ever undertaken to investigate Morris's career, collect his letters and writings, and prepare a life of him. The work had to be done finally, within recent years, by Professor William G. Sumner, of Connecticut.

Dickinson not only had a very distinguished career in Pennsylvania politics, but up to the Declaration of Independence he was the chief controller of the Revolutionary movement. Every public document of national importance in that movement down to June, 1776, was draughted by him, and his character shows a devotion to principle and a moral courage unexcelled by any of the great men of that time. But in the furious conflicts of factions in Pennsylvania he was so set upon that he was driven into exile, and had to live in Delaware until the storm had passed by. During this exile he served as a common soldier in the ranks of the Continental army.

He returned to Pennsylvania, was restored to power, and became Governor of the State. But once in his grave, his name and fame were carefully ignored, and soon almost forgotten, until in 1891, almost a century after his death, Dr. Stillé wrote an exhaustive and interesting life of him, to be added to an edition of his works. He is almost the only one of our distinguished men who has had a Pennsylvanian for a biographer.

If the biography had appeared seventy years earlier, Dickinson's name would have remained in the conspicuous place he occupied while living. But after seventy or eighty years of neglect it is almost impossible to restore an historical character and reproduce the position which was once a living force. The people's estimate of him has been formed too long; valuable papers and letters are lost; and the most important material of all, the personal anecdotes, which can be collected only from the lips of the living, are utterly beyond recall.

Massachusetts sets the highest example in this respect. Not even a minor character is allowed to die without being followed within two or three years by biographies so keenly written that every salient point is driven home into the minds of the whole nation. The man's personality is continued while everything is fresh. His picture is drawn for the future before the color has left his face. The encouragement and hero-worship which developed him to greatness in life preserve him, with Egyptian fidelity, in death.

General Wayne, who was certainly one of the remarkable soldiers of the Revolution, slumbered for a century in his grave before any one thought it worth while to write his life. The same hand that had resurrected Dickinson performed the task, and the same Philadelphia publishers issued the book. When the book was read, people were surprised to find that, instead of having appeared at long intervals and in only a few incidents, the dashing Pennsylvania soldier had had a career, a continuous and steady life of public service.

But there is no one to resurrect Mifflin, Armstrong, Clymer, Thomson, and others who were conspicuous before the whole continent in their day and are now utterly forgotten. Mifflin was in some respects more prominent than Wayne. He commanded the best disciplined brigade in the Continental Army, and had a long service in the Continental Congress, as Governor of Pennsylvania, and as a member of the Legislature and of the Constitutional conventions.

Dr. Benjamin Rush, who achieved the remarkable distinction of being the leading physician of his day and one of the leading statesmen, has also suffered from neglect. His life remains unwritten, and his numerous pamphlets and letters, some of them of unusual interest, have never been collected. He was a man of the most vigorous power of expression, and this, combined with the eccentricity and the violent contests of his life, has saved him from complete oblivion. These same qualities would add great interest to a biography, which might be made one of the best that has ever been written of a Pennsylvanian, for it would include the whole Revolutionary struggle, and a rather new aspect of it.

Albert Gallatin chose Pennsylvania as his adopted State, lived there most of his life, and was given his political prominence and importance by the votes of our citizens. There are comparatively few people, however, who even know that he ever had anything to do with Pennsylvania, and of his two biographers one is from Boston and the other from New York.

What is to become of Thaddeus Stevens, so conspicuous as a member of Congress in the times of the Civil War? He has been dead nearly thirty years, and, although his will is said to have provided for a biography, none appears.

James Buchanan made this same provision in his will; for he well knew the fate Pennsylvania prepares for all her distinguished sons. But although the money, and a good round sum too, was provided, many years passed away while vain attempts were being made to persuade some Pennsylvanian to write the book; and in the end it was written in New York.

Was there ever a Commonwealth that produced so many eminent characters and was so indifferent to them? What difference does it make which sect or clique was the principal creator? Why should we still debate the question who is the typical Pennsylvanian? One orator maintains that the true Pennsylvanian is the German. Some object to the east, others to the west. Some are for Philadelphia; others for the State outside Philadelphia; still others point to the State and insist that it is the work of the Scotch-Irish. The Welshman says he is the cause, and that William Penn was a Welshman. The Quaker, as usual, is silent and makes no claims.

INDEX

Index

Index

Index

Index

Inspiration of Scriptures, Quaker doctrine of, 52.

Johnson, Sir William, controls Six Nations of New York, 280.
Jones, Sir William, attorney-general, 260.
    report of, on boundaries of Pennsylvania, 260.

Keith, George, controversy with the Quakers, 50.
Kelpius, learning of, 83.
Kinnersley, Ebenezer, assists Franklin in experiments, 217.

Lafayette at Bethlehem, 153.
Lancaster Turnpike, inns on, 208.]
    through Welsh Barony, 207.
Latitude, degrees of, meaning of, 320.
Laws of Pennsylvania very liberal, 209.
Liberty of conscience, Quaker belief in, 54.
Light, inward, doctrine of, 43.
Locomotive-Works, the Baldwin, importance of, 234.
Log College, the, 185.
Lutherans, the, affinities with the Episcopalians, 114.
    arrival of, in Pennsylvania, 111.
    disorders among, 114.
    in Revolution, 116.
    not opposed to education, 122.
    their belief, 112.

McKean, Chief-Justice, as a Scotch-Irishman, 179.
Manufacturing, history of, in Pennsylvania, 231, 233, 236.
    in Philadelphia, 230.
Markham, takes latitude of New Castle, 330.

Maryland, boundaries of, 321, 337, 339.
    boundaries of, finally marked, 346.
    boundary disputes with, 318, 319.
Mason and Dixon, line of, 347, 348.
Massachusetts attempts to cut off beaver trade on the Delaware, 21.
Medicine, early study of, in Pennsylvania, 223.
    school of, in Pennsylvania, 224.
Mennonites arrive in Pennsylvania, 74, 105.
    doctrines of, 71.
    origin of, 71.
    persecution of, 74.
    protest against slavery, 73.
Mey, Cornelius, conducts expedition to the Delaware, 13.
    gives his name to the capes, 13.
Military men in Pennsylvania, 236.
Mittelberger, description of German voyage to America, 102.
    journey to Pennsylvania, 102.
Molinos, the Quietist, 45.
Molly Maguires in Pennsylvania, 168.
Moravians, the, as missionaries, 142.
    as pietists, 137.
    cast lots, 138.
    ceremonies and liturgies of, 137, 138.
    come to America, 140.
    communion with Church of England, 139.
    communism of, 141.
    emotionalism of, 137, 139.
    history of, 134.
    inns of, 150.
    marriages of, 138.
    objection to war, 154.

375

Index

Index

Pennsylvania claimants, denounced by the people, 305.
    Patterson Acts for, 302.
    send commissioners to Wyoming, 301.
    home of American liberalism, 210.
    not interested in helping Penn family, 266.
    rapid development of, 212.
Perfectionists, Quakers were, 53.
Philadelphia, home of American liberalism, 210.
    meeting-place of the Indians, 30.
    site for a great city, 29.
    Swedes reach present site of, 28.
    Swedish church in, 28.
Philanthropy, Quakers the earliest philanthropists, 54.
Philosophical Society, American, founded at Philadelphia, 225.
Physicians, famous ones in Pennsylvania, 325.
Pickering, Timothy, checks new State movement, 307.
Pietism, looseness of views on, 148.
Pietists come to Germantown, 78.
    Muhlenberg one of them, 113.
Plunkett attempts to restore Wyoming, 276.
    defeat of, 278.
    reasons for support of, 277.
Population of Pennsylvania, 125.
    on Delaware, 25.
Poughkeepsie account of battle of Wyoming, 288, 289.
Presbyterians, the, contrast to the Quakers, 156, 161.
    devotion of, to education, 185.
    Pennsylvania the home of, 156.
    religion of, 157.
    severity of belief, 159, 160.

Priestley, Joseph, his connection with Pennsylvania, 223.
Printz, establishment at Tinnicum, 18, 19.
    Swedish governor, 18.
Privy council orders division of Delaware, 333.
    Penn and Lord Baltimore appeal to, 333.

Quakers, the, aversion of, to dogmas, 40.
    compared with Puritans, 34.
    condemn amusements, 56.
    decline of, 66, 68.
    discipline of, 56.
    disgusted with Presbyterianism, 161.
    doctrines of, 41-69.
    form of government, 58.
    good living of, 34.
    hate the Scotch-Irish, 157.
    human passions of, 42.
    imprisoned, 55.
    likely to control Pennsylvania, 187.
    numbers of, 68.
    object to learning, 60.
    object to oaths and war, 57, 59.
    origin of, 33-40.
    remarkable men among, 61.
    substance of their faith, 52.
    traits of, 41-69.
    wealth of, 43.
    went beyond the Baptists, 40.
Quarry, Colonel, attempts to drive Quakers from office, 195.
    judge of the Admiralty, 194.
    leader of the Churchmen, 194.
Quietism among the Quakers, 44.
    in Italy, 45.

Railroads in Pennsylvania, 235.

Index

Index

Index

Weiss, Rev. George Michael, leads Reformed to Pennsylvania, 113.

Welsh, the, agreement with Penn, 203.

as an element in the population, 206.

at first the most numerous immigrants, 202.

exclusiveness broken up, 205.

most of them Quakers, 202.

names of, 205.

patron saint of, 206.

possessed of means, 204.

their system of government, 204.

tract, a barony, 204.

situation of, 203.

Wilburites, division of the Quakers, 51.

William III. describes Delaware as belonging to Penn, 334.

Wilmington settled by the Swedes, 17.

Wilson, Alexander, first American ornithologist, 221.

Wilson, James, argument of, at Trenton, 295.

Woman of the Wilderness, Society of, 82.

Wounds, litany of, 138.

Wyoming, Valley of, arouses interest in England, 243.

battle of, 284, 288.

discovery of, by Connecticut, 241.

Wyoming, Valley of, discovery of coal in, 316.

first massacre in, 247.

first settlement in, 247.

histories of, 315.

moral grandeur of men of, 317.

movement to make a new State in, 306.

New England school system in, 316.

not the property of people of Pennsylvania, 265.

population of, 279.

settlers of, fight fairly, 310.

vote against new State movement, 316.

York, Duke of, deed to, of New England, 26.

deed did not include Pennsylvania, 27.

laws of, 31.

occupies Pennsylvania, 7, 27, 28.

takes Dutch territory, 253.

Zinzendorf, Count, arrives in Pennsylvania, 143.

as a Lutheran, 144.

character of, 143.

controversies of, 149.

converts Lutherans and Reformed, 147.

resigns his title, 145.

restores the Moravians, 136.

romantic life of, 149.

Zwanendal, settlement of, 14.

THE END.